Poetic Justice

A Restaurantland Romance

Kathleen McFall

Clark Hays

ISBN: 979-8-9882974-1-3

Library of Congress Control Number: 2024917217
Cover design by ebooklaunch.com
Pumpjack Press
Portland, Oregon, USA

Also by Clark Hays and Kathleen McFall

The Cowboy and the Vampire Collection
A Very Unusual Romance
Blood and Whiskey
Rough Trails and Shallow Graves
The Last Sunset

Bonnie and Clyde
Resurrection Road
Dam Nation
Radioactive

The Halo Trilogy
Gates of Mars
Scorched Earth
Mars Adrift

The Restaurantland Romance Series
Kitchen Heat

1

May 1, 1996—May Day protest

Across the street from Fleet Motors, Portland, Oregon

Roz felt the cold bite of metal and heard a dry click before she understood what had happened. Hudson had slipped one end of a pair of handcuffs around Roz's right wrist in a single, fluid motion. She looked at him as the metal ring cut tight against her flesh.

"What are you doing?" Roz asked.

"Sorry," Hudson said. "But trust me, it's for your own good."

The handcuff links were threaded through the top of a wrought-iron railing of a fence protecting a stately old tree at the sidewalk's edge; the other cuff loop was still open. Roz raised her arm and looked at the unexpected bracelet, shook her head angrily, disbelieving, and tried to jerk away, but Hudson was too quick. He clicked the other cuff around his wrist, locking them together through the metal railing.

"Stop fooling around," she said.

Roz was trying to keep her cool, wondering why on earth Hudson would lock them together after everything that happened between them. No matter how stupid or misguided his reason, there had to be one.

He grinned that uneasy, lopsided grin that two weeks

ago would have melted her heart, probably falling into his arms instantly.

"Unlock us."

"I don't have the key," he said. She could hear the nervousness in his voice, but it was steely, too, like he had made an important decision.

"What the hell are you doing, Hudson?" She jerked her right arm again, which pulled him closer, but the handcuff lock didn't budge. "It's not funny. Let me go this instant."

"Can't," he said. "I left the key at the restaurant."

"At the Rose and Thorn? Why? Why on earth would you do that?"

"So I wouldn't be tempted to set you free," he said.

They were cuffed together across from Fleet Motors, a fancy car dealership on Grand Boulevard in close-in east Portland. The irony was not lost on her that Clay's ex-wife shot all those racy commercials for the owner of this very car lot. It wasn't so long ago that Roz had been seriously hot for Clay. But then Hudson walked into the Rose and Thorn kitchen and turned her world upside down.

It had all been so unbelievably great.

Until it wasn't.

Wasn't that the way it always went for her? She had been foolish to expect anything else.

"Get these cuffs off me now," she said, her voice low, almost a growl.

"I can't, I won't. It's my job to protect you."

"Your job is to be a chef at a pretty awesome restaurant. My well-being is no longer your concern. I don't need your help or your pity or whatever misplaced virtuous thing you think you're doing."

Roz glared at Hudson. He held her stare, but she could see something else in his eyes. Maybe it was pleading or wavering, but it only made her angrier at the almostcomical situation she found herself in—handcuffed to her irritatingly handsome ex-boyfriend. He was six feet tall plus some change, had thick, black hair almost down to his collar and dark, beautiful skin. He wore a sleeveless *The Cramps* T-shirt that showed off his wiry frame—ripped from all the climbing and hiking—and muscular arms, the right one decorated with snaking tattoos.

She had a flash of those arms, dark against her pale skin, wrapped tightly around her waist as they spooned together in bed. It wasn't so long ago that they might have done some sexy role-playing with handcuffs, channeling Rob and Meredith. She felt safe with Hudson and trusted him enough to say yes if he had asked.

Roz had been sure he was the one. But what he did to her, to her sister—what he had put her whole family through—was unforgivable.

She looked around, exasperated, as the protest unfolded. They were surrounded by a crowd of thirty or forty people, mostly young activists, with a few aging hippies thrown into the mix. The protestors carried homemade poster-board signs, many wore tie-dyed shirts, and all of them were now moving across the busy street—drawing honks of irritation from commuters—to the dealership. All of them, that is, except for her and Hudson.

"I'm supposed to be with them," she said, looking at the group as they made their way to the lot filled with hundreds of new vehicles angle-parked and gleaming in the sun. A few people sat down to block traffic completely, others formed a line on the sidewalk and still others rushed into the dealership and began handcuffing themselves to the doors of a brand-new shipment of shiny black luxury sport utility vehicles

Roz jerked on the cuffs again, yanking Hudson's hand. He looked at her nervously, but mixed with stubbornness.

It was late Wednesday afternoon, a beautiful sunny day—the first after a long winter of rain—and the protestors aimed to create maximum disruption during rush hour. The May Day protest had been planned for months, and that plan had, so far, come off perfectly. The protestors arrived in unison and organized quickly into their assigned roles.

Everyone except Roz.

A man with a long brown braid and the easy smile of someone happy simply to be in the sunshine was banging out a protest rhythm by hitting his tambourine against his hip with one hand and starting a call-and-response through a bullhorn with his other.

"What do we want?" the ringleader shouted.

"Justice," the crowd called back.

"Who should be free?"

"Eco-warriors everywhere!"

"Eco-warriors," Roz whispered. She would not cry, she told herself. She would not give Hudson the pleasure of thinking she needed his comfort or sympathy. Even after that excruciating conversation yesterday with her mother, she would not cry.

"Roz, I'm begging you," he said. "Hear me out. Please let me explain."

"The only thing you need to explain is how long it will take to get the key here to unlock these," she said.

"I'm not getting the key."

She spun to glare at him. "Fuck you," she said. "I'm here for my sister. You remember her? I'm supposed to be handcuffed to a car to help her. Not chained to a lying asshole across the street from the action. I hate you for this and for everything."

She turned her attention back to the crowd, her long, silky red hair swirling like liquid fire.

"Free eco-warriors everywhere!" she screamed, making a fist with her uncuffed hand and raising it defiantly.

2

Sept. 22, 1995—Seven months before the protest

The Rose and Thorn restaurant, Portland, Oregon

Hudson wasn't exactly nervous, but starting a new job was always a little tense. Starting a new job after three years, ten months and eleven days in prison, even more so.

He needed this job, though. It was part of the release agreement.

Hudson took a deep breath, stepped into the kitchen, and immediately pulled up short at the sight of a woman leaning on the counter, a fork in one hand and a happy smile on her face. She had long red hair, bright, kind eyes set off by light blue makeup that would look just as natural in an old 1975 action flick as it did now in 1995, and the same kind of dangerous movie-star curves. She hadn't noticed him yet, and he hesitated, staring in wonder until it started to feel creepy, and he forced himself to walk toward her heat.

"Kassi, does it bother you that your man can satisfy so many other women?" the woman asked as he got closer before turning to look at him curiously.

"Hi, I'm Hudson. The new guy," he said.

He couldn't stop staring at her, and she seemed to be checking him out, maybe? He couldn't be sure he even remembered what it was like to be checked out.

"I'm Clay, head chef, and that's LuRon, Rob and Gilroy, line cooks," someone said, stepping up next to him. The voice sounded distant and tinny. "Dave-one is on the salad bar, and Jon is back in the dishwashing bay."

Hudson was having a hard time focusing, wholly distracted by this woman. She smiled back at him as if they shared a secret joke. He hoped he wasn't the joke.

"There are two Daves," someone else said. "You'll meet Dave-two tomorrow."

"Thanks for helping me piece that together," Hudson stammered.

"On the server side of the house, we've got Roz …" The person next to him, who Hudson assumed was the head chef and his new boss, nodded in the direction of the red-haired woman. The man kept talking, saying more words and names, but all meaning was lost.

Her name was Roz. Fitting. A rose. A wild, beautiful rose. At the Rose and Thorn.

"Ahem," she said, smiling and cocking her head in the direction of the rest of the kitchen crew.

Right, he thought, snap out of it. This is your job now. He turned around finally, smiling and nodding. "Nice to meet you all. Thanks for taking a chance on me. I appreciate it."

"It's just a job, bro," one of the cooks said. "Not a life choice." He stroked his scraggly mustache like an absent-minded professor. "You'll probably regret ever setting foot in the Rose and Thorn."

That seems highly unlikely, Hudson thought, watching Roz leave the kitchen along with the other two women. She was as perfect from behind. She looked back over her shoulder and caught him looking at her. He ducked his head, embarrassed. But not before catching a sparkle of …

was that satisfaction? Curiosity?

"Probably be gone in two weeks if you're like most of the new guys," another one of the cooks said, a white guy with weird energy.

"Great pep talk, gang," the head chef said.

Clay. He said earlier his name was Clay. Or maybe Ray? Crap, Hudson thought. My first job since prison, and I can't even pay attention long enough to remember my boss's name. One thing about prison cooking—there weren't too many distractions of the female variety in the kitchen. Zero, to be precise.

"Welcome to the team. I think we threw one too many names at you," the probably-Clay man said. "So, in case it got muddled, I'm Clay. Head chef. And that's Gilroy, who predicted you'll be gone. You can ignore him. He's fighting with his girlfriend."

"We're not fighting," Gilroy said. "It's worse than that. Angel isn't talking to me. I'm getting the silent treatment."

Hudson pretended to listen. One of the many things he learned in prison was how to look interested—or disinterested when the situation called for it—no matter the circumstances.

Roz came back into the kitchen, and he was suddenly very interested again. He bent slightly to see her through the window, watching her lips moving as she read the order, listening to the melody of her voice, and then watching her pale, delicate hand snake behind the window to hang the ticket.

"Hudson, are you involved?" Clay asked.

Hudson swallowed, his mouth suddenly dry as he watched Roz through the window. She paused and lingered. Did she want to hear his answer?

"No," Hudson said with a forced smile. "I've been, uh, out of the game for a little while."

Roz seemed to relax at that, and she went back into the dining room.

"Whatever you do, don't listen to anything we have to say about relationships," Clay said.

"Guys," one of the waitresses said, poking her head through the door. "I think we're about to get slammed." It was the blonde, Kassi, the one who kept staring at Clay. His girlfriend? Another thing prison taught him was how to gauge alliances quickly.

Clay peeked through the window. The dining room was nearly full. He turned to Hudson. "You ready to jump into the deep end?"

"I'm happy to start now."

"Rob, get Hudson a knife and turn him loose on some prep. We're going to need more mashed potatoes and half a case of broccoli florets, pronto," his new boss said.

Rob, the one with the weird energy, waved for Hudson to follow him.

Less than thirty minutes later, Hudson had trimmed a half case of broccoli, made mashed potatoes and sliced a quarter tray of tomatoes for LuRon to use on his sandwich special. The dining room orders were piling up, and Clay waved him over to the line.

After watching Clay once, Hudson took over the specials, turning out chicken piccatas at a blistering pace. Hudson was in his element now, fast and unflappable, calmly plating orders and joking good-naturedly with the others. But whenever Roz came in, he made a point to face the order window.

As the night wound down, Roz stayed out front to handle closing duties. At ten o'clock, Clay pulled off his apron. "Hudson, if this shift didn't scare you off, you'll fit in well here."

"Compared to my last cooking job, this was fun, and

you all seem pretty cool."

"Where was your last job?" Rob asked. "Hell?"

"Kind of. I assumed Molly told you. I was a cook at EOCI."

"Not familiar with that restaurant," Clay said.

"It's not a restaurant. It's the Eastern Oregon Correctional Institute."

Everyone looked at him blankly.

"Prison. I was in prison."

There was a long, awkward silence.

"Probably less shanking here," Rob said.

"Rob, for fuck's sake, stop it," Clay said.

Hudson smiled. "I certainly hope so."

"We're going to finish cleaning up and get things ready for tomorrow," Clay said. "Takes about twenty minutes. You get a shift meal and drink for helping today, plus I'll see that these extra hours make it into your first paycheck. If you can hang around, I'll join you for a beer and we can talk through a few things."

"That's kind of you," Hudson said. "But I'm in recovery so I'll pass on the beer." He wasn't really in recovery; he just found that ever since his release from prison, alcohol hit him way too hard. Restaurants were full of booze, and he figured it would be less complicated to say he had a drinking problem than to try and explain why he *could* drink but didn't want to over and over again.

Roz, who was back in the kitchen with a bus tub of dishes, stopped what she was doing to listen.

"What's your stance on club soda and bitters?" Clay asked.

Hudson smiled. "That sounds pretty good."

"Roz, why don't you show Hudson where he can wait and maybe fix him one of your non-alcoholic specials?"

Roz nodded and motioned for Hudson to follow.

He trailed behind her into the front of the house.

"So, how'd your first night go?" she asked.

"Not bad," Hudson said.

"You must be pretty good. Clay doesn't like to work with many people."

She pointed at the bar, and he took a stool and watched her walk behind the counter.

"He seems like a decent guy," Hudson said. "What's your take?"

"On him or the restaurant?"

"Either."

"Damaged," she said. "But grows on you."

"Are you talking about Clay or the Rose and Thorn?" he asked.

"Yes," Roz said, a mischievous sparkle in her eye.

He laughed. "I'll take your word for it about the chef, but I do kind of like it here."

"You'll fit right in if you have a broken heart or some other kind of emotional dysfunction," Roz said. She used the soda gun to fill two glasses with club soda, then shook in a few drops of Angostura bitters, followed by lime wedges. "One's for me," she said, sliding them in front of him.

"What's your dysfunction?" he asked.

Roz smiled at him. "I don't know you well enough to tell you about my problems. Not yet, anyway."

Hudson took a sip of his drink. "That's okay," he said. "I'm patient."

3

April 13, 1991—Five years before the protest

Coos Bay, Oregon

The manager stood at the door to his office, holding the phone in one hand, covering the receiver with the other. "Roz, it's for you."

The manager's name was Roy, but everyone called him Ropey for reasons Roz could never figure out. Ropey was not smiling. "You know I don't like personal calls during work," he said, waggling the phone in her direction.

"I'm sorry," Roz said. It was only her third week waiting tables at the popular diner and she didn't want to get on his bad side, especially after the unfortunate incident with the tray of glasses on day two. Things were tight at home since her dad was laid off, and every dollar helped.

She took the phone hesitantly. "Hello?"

It was her mom.

"Honey, Dad is down at Dinkingers. He's had a few too many."

Roz slumped her shoulders. "Again? It's not even five yet."

"You know it's hard for him right now," her mom said. "Can you please pick him up on your way home?"

Roz sighed. This was becoming a bad habit. He'd been laid off from the sawmill a month back and hadn't gotten past it. It was starting to seem like he didn't want to get past it.

"Sure, Mom," she said. She handed the phone back to Ropey. "Sorry about that. My mom needs me to run an errand for her after work."

He nodded. "Well, family first. Just don't make a habit of the phone calls."

She nodded and got back to work. Only two patrons were in the diner, both eating apple pie and drinking coffee.

Roz worked the late morning shift through lunch, serving eggs, hash browns, bacon, pancakes and French toast to late breakfast eaters, then switching mostly to burgers and fries, hot turkey sandwiches, and soup and grilled cheese sandwich combos to the lunch crowd. The tips weren't great because most people in this rural coastal town in Oregon were barely scraping by, but it was a job, and the money was better than she could make anywhere else.

It was almost 4:30 in the afternoon now, and the folks from the nearby senior center would start coming in soon for the blue-plate specials and human connection, counting out their pennies to pay. She needed to be gone by then, mostly because it was too easy to get drawn into conversations, and then she'd be here all night.

Roz finished her side work, wrapping silverware sets and filling ketchups and mustards, as Patty, the night-shift waitress, clocked in.

"Hi, honey, how's your dad these days?" Patty asked.

"Truthfully, not great," Roz said, taking off her apron. She didn't bother correcting Patty. Stan was her stepdad, but he'd been on the scene since she was a little. Roz didn't have many memories of her biological dad. Very rarely, her mom would tell her a story about him. Roz kept a picture of him in her diary but didn't look at it too often. Stan, her stepfather, was a decent enough guy. At least, he was until he got laid off.

"Something will come around soon, I'm sure of it," Patty said, reaching for the coffee pot. "Those goddam tree-huggers." As if an afterthought, she paused. "And how's your sister?"

"Camille is … still passionate about her beliefs," Roz said, choosing her words carefully.

Her half-sister Camille was a senior in high school. Camille was part of a small but vocal group of student environmentalists. Tree-huggers to the locals. An easy target for misplaced anger as the timber dollars dried up due to a combination of federal regulations and uninspired local management of the millions of dollars flowing to timber country from the government to mitigate the economic effect of those new regulations.

"That girl," Patty said, clucking her tongue. "I hope she doesn't fall in with the wrong crowd."

Roz wanted to say that people trying to save the planet probably weren't the wrong crowd, but she didn't have the energy for that conversation.

"Me too. I have to run," she said, giving Patty a quick hug. Roz glanced in the mirror by the front door. She had recently cut her hair into a super short pixie style on a dare from Camille and was still getting used to looking like a forest elf. All she needed were pointy Spock ears, and the look would be complete.

Outside, she hopped in her battered Honda Accord, one front fender a different color than the rest, and drove to Dinkingers. It was a dark and uninviting clapboard building, the wood stained by perpetual rain. The neon sign in the window blinkered unsteadily *Drink at Dinks*.

She pushed her way in and looked around the smoky bar. There were only a handful of patrons at this hour. Her stepdad, Stan, was one of them. He was leaning back in his stool, talking animatedly with an old man she recognized from the now-shuttered auto parts store.

"I'm just saying, fucking trees are sustainable," he said, slurring. "They grow back. We ain't gonna run out. We ain't never gonna run out."

His companion was nodding in agreement. "It's what you call a renewable resource."

"Dad," Roz said, walking up quietly. "Mom wants you to come home."

"Oh, my little baby," Stan said. "My Rosalyn." He hugged her. "I'm not ready to leave yet."

"I'm going home. Please ride with me. I don't want to have to come back."

He shook his head. The beer and whiskey were making him stubborn. Borderline belligerent.

"Please," she said, tugging his sleeve.

"Listen to your daughter," the bartender said. His name was Billy, a burly man with a tangled beard and three fingers missing on his left hand from a mill accident years ago.

"Tell you what, darling, you have one drink with me, and I'll get in your car after. Not another peep."

"You know I can't serve her," Billy said. "She's not old enough. Your twenty-first isn't for a few more months, right, Roz?"

Roz nodded, but it made no difference to her father.

"You will fucking serve her," Stan said. "If my girl is old enough to work a 40-hour job, she's old enough to do a fucking shot with her old man. Now put two shots of whiskey on the bar, or I'll go to my truck and get my pistol."

"Dad, I don't want to drink," Roz said.

He swiveled angrily. "If you want me to come home

tonight, or ever again, you will drink a shot with me. Right now."

She looked at Billy, worry in her eyes, then nodded. She'd drunk before, everyone in high school did, and now she did when she was hanging out with the few friends who stayed in town after graduation and were lucky enough to find jobs like she did. Mostly, it was just drinking beers and wine coolers around a fire on the beach or in the woods by the quarry. But drinking in a bar was still out of reach, at least until this moment.

Billy poured two shot glasses with well whiskey and slid them forward. "You're a real asshole. Don't ever come back. You're 86'd."

"Like I want to drink in your shitty little rinky-dink bar," Stan said. He picked up his shot and nodded for her to do the same. "To better days for lumbermen," he said, clinking his glass against hers and then downing the whiskey.

"To better days," she said. It burned at first, but then a glow spread pleasantly in her stomach and brain. "Okay, you promised," she said. "Let's go home."

She helped him into her car and drove home, the windshield wipers scraping but largely failing to do their job against the rain. She pulled up in front of their house, a small two-story a few miles outside of town at the end of a dirt road with a roof that needed repairs, an overgrown lawn and a broken, rusted-out refrigerator in the backyard. Her mom, Susan, was watching worried through the kitchen window and came out to help bring Stan inside.

"Stop fussing over me, woman," he said, staggering up the porch stairs.

Camille was sitting on the couch reading *The Monkey Wrench Gang.* She had light brown hair with natural curls and a slender frame. She and Roz barely resembled each other, at least from a distance, and no one ever mistook them for sisters.

Camille wore a baggy T-shirt with a print of the Earth that said, *Save your mother.*

"Get that hippie shit out of my house," Stan said, snatching her book.

"Give that back," Camille said, leaping up.

"You want to read this communist shit, you go live somewhere else," he said. "Under this roof, which was paid for by timber dollars, you will respect my beliefs."

He threw the book through the open door out into the rain.

Camille looked at him, stunned. "How dare you."

"How dare you," he slurred. "People like you are why I got laid off."

"I hope the mill shuts down for good," she said, and then he backhanded her.

Camille stumbled backward, holding her hand to her cheek. Her eyes brimmed with tears and pain and disbelief.

"Stan," Susan screamed. "Don't you dare strike our child."

"Oh god, oh god, I'm so sorry," he said, sinking to his knees.

Roz held her breath and pressed herself against the gray wall, willing herself to be as small as possible.

Camille held her palm over her cheek, now a livid red, her eyes cold. She snatched her backpack and jacket off the sofa and walked out without a look back. The screen door that long ago lost its spring slammed again and again in the wind behind her like a smoker's cough. Susan called after her, and Roz too, but she was moving fast and disappeared into the shadows of the heavy woods, the dense trees—branches dripping with rain—closing behind her.

By midnight, she hadn't returned, and—after calling all

her friends to no avail—Susan called the police.

As her tearful parents answered questions in the living room, the red and blue emergency lights strobing inside the house, Roz scribbled furiously in her journal, trying to make sense of it all. She couldn't. She stole a bottle of whiskey from Stan's liquor cabinet and sat in her darkened bedroom, trying to block out the pain with the warm glow.

4

June 7, 1991—Five years before the protest

Old-growth forest near Veneta, Oregon

Hudson crouched in the shadows of the tree line and looked across the parking lot—a square of packed earth and stubborn clots of grass ringed by idled heavy equipment. His target was just across the open area. She was waiting for him, graceful and glowing in the moonlight.

She was a tree—an enormous Douglas fir. She was slated to come down the next day, and when that happened, it would open the rest of the steep-sided valley for the slow advance of the skidders.

Thinning, they called it. Necessary for forest health and preventing forest fires, they said.

But he knew the truth. Her demise was necessary to make a few lousy bucks.

He adjusted the heavy pack slung over his shoulder.

They'd been watching for weeks, taking shifts and hiding, studying their patterns through binoculars and making notes. There was a guard, but on Friday nights he generally stayed in the cab of his truck with a fifth of Jack and listened to the game on the radio.

Hudson checked his watch, the numbers and hands glowing faintly in the darkness. Timing was critical. He stood and peered over the pile of logs, his palms resting on the rough bark. He could almost feel the silent pain. When will people start treating this planet like our home instead of a some kind of going-out-of-business sale at a candy store, he wondered?

He took a deep breath to steady himself, hitched his pack one last time and then broke into a run that gradually accelerated into a sprint. He was almost across the lot when headlights flared on in the truck.

"Hey, dipshit," a voice called. "Hold it right there."

Dammit, the guard spotted him too soon.

Hudson heard the truck door open, followed by now-panicked yelling and thudding footsteps, but Hudson had a good lead on him and was fast, even with the heavy pack. He'd been training on the campus track for weeks, even gave up smoking weed to make sure he was in top shape.

The tree was almost in reach, but he could hear the guard gaining.

"No, no, no," the man was yelling.

Hudson planted and leaped as high as he could, catching one of the lowest shards of an old branch jutting out from the trunk almost eight feet above the ground. He was strong and agile from years of rock climbing and hoisted himself up easily. There was a quick fumbling tug on his heel as a heavy hand tried to grab him, but Hudson was already too far up.

"Aw, kid, come on, don't do this. They're gonna fire my ass."

"Sorry, man," Hudson said, pulling himself higher, grunting from the exertion. "Nothing personal. Just trying to save the planet." He had a light mounted to a headband and turned it on, casting surreal shadows into the darkened forest as he climbed higher into the canopy.

"You know the sheriff is gonna drag you down in the

morning," the guard called up after him. He had a heavy flashlight in one hand, shining the beam up at Hudson's retreating form.

"No way he's coming up this high," Hudson called.

"They'll cut it down with you in it."

"My friends already called the press. You kill a kid, an innocent, idealistic college kid like me, and they'll shut the whole thing down. And I'm not leaving until every one of *you* leaves this valley."

"Jesus wept," the man muttered. "Fucking tree-huggers." He stomped back toward the truck. "I'm calling this in," he yelled. "You can bet your ass I'm calling this in."

Hudson relaxed a little as he saw the man leave. He checked his watch. If all had gone to plan, his friends had by now sent a missive to the local press, the college paper and the local police with details. He was committed.

He climbed higher, using the headlamp to guide his way. Judging from the lights on the truck below, he was a good 150 feet above the ground.

"This will do nicely," he whispered, and used a rope around his waist to secure himself to the trunk and then hung his pack. Opening it, he pulled out a hinged section of thin panels of plyboard—scavenged from a construction site—that unfolded into a platform about the size of two bathtubs, then used ropes and tie-downs to secure it to the thickest branches.

He tested it by jumping up and down lightly a few times, and when he was satisfied it would hold, he unrolled his sleeping bag and stretched out on it, looking up through the swaying gaps in the branches to the starry night sky beyond.

They would get him down eventually, but not without a fight. And possibly not without killing him. The thought made him sad, but there was no future without a living Earth, so why worry about his insignificant life? Better to sacrifice it for necessary change.

Standing, he hung his supplies—water and food—on nearby branches. His crew would bring him more soon. In the meantime, all he had to do was sink into the rhythm of the forest.

Now that his training was over, he rewarded himself by rolling a joint and getting fully, profoundly and blissfully stoned. As the sweet smoke did its work, he relaxed into the moment and smiled at the sense of peace and contentment. A shooting star blazed overhead, and the wind passed gently through the branches, a simple melody as old as existence and as nurturing as a drink of cool spring water.

Above it and inside it, he felt connected to everything and mostly happy.

Still, even in this moment of bliss, there was a space in Hudson's heart, long ready for love, but that was okay too because in that quiet, magic time, the tree whispered to him how grateful she was for his sacrifice. She told him her name, Chrysopeleia, but that Hudson could call her Sophie, which meant wisdom.

That night, in what would be the first of many nights to come, he fell asleep in Sophie's arms.

5

May 1, 1996—May Day protest

Across the street from Fleet Motors

Three car salesmen, all in baggy double-breasted suits with their shirts open at the neck, walked out of the dealership to survey the protest. Two lit cigarettes. The third flipped off the protesters and grabbed his crotch with a sneer. More employees came out, half-mystified and half-curious about why so many people were making a ruckus in their parking lot.

"The cops are coming," the manager yelled. He held a wireless phone to his ear, with the antenna extended. And sure enough, sirens could be heard in the distance.

"Roz, please, let me explain," Hudson said again, touching her shoulder.

She looked at him, eyes narrowed and lips pressed together.

"Don't touch me," she said. "I can't believe I slept with you, can't believe I let you read my poetry." She stamped her foot in frustration. "Or wrote poetry about you. You've ruined everything, Hudson. This protest, my life, my family. I'll never forgive you. Never. When the cops come, they'll cut me loose and send you back to prison where you belong."

Reporters were arriving with camera crews in tow.

Roz looked at her wrist and then at the video cameras. If Camille saw her cuffed to Hudson, she would be crushed. She wouldn't understand. How could she possibly be expected to understand? Roz hadn't found the time or courage to tell her sister about the Hudson catastrophe.

She spotted Trey, a friend from the PDX Eco Artists Collective, and waved him over.

"Roz, why are you handcuffed here?" He was genuinely puzzled. And stoned. "We're taking action on Fleet Motors for poisoning the environment with their gas guzzlers."

"I *know* that," Roz said. "That's why I'm here."

"You need to get your people out of there," Hudson said. "It's not safe."

"Nah, man, everyone is welcome, this is a peaceful protest," Trey said. "We got it all planned out. Once the cops get here and hopefully arrest a few people, the press will film it, and we'll make the news. We got a banner and everything. Then we go home. Already got a pot-luck planned with some killer brownies."

"Please hear me on this, man. It's dangerous," Hudson repeated.

"Saving the planet is only dangerous because our government is in the pocket of the big polluters."

"I'm on your side. But you have to trust me—"

Roz shook her head. "No way, don't trust him, Trey. He betrayed me, betrayed the movement and betrayed the Earth. Don't say another word."

The police began to arrive, driving their squad cars up on the sidewalk to get past the blocked traffic.

"I gotta go," Trey said. "The action is starting. All these cops make me nervous. Good luck or whatever."

"Remember where you saw us!" Hudson yelled. "Far from the dealership lot."

"Wait, Trey!" Roz called after him. "I need bolt-cutters.

Find Harvest. She'll have some in her truck." But it was too late. Trey disappeared behind a protestor holding a sign that read *Be kind to your mother, or else,* with a child-like painting of the Earth.

"If you fuck things up for my sister, again, I swear I'm going to ruin your life. At some point, she'll be up for parole or get a chance to get out on good behavior or whatever, and your little stunt could mess it all up for her. Again."

"I asked LuRon to bring the key by in three hours, and then I'll take the cuffs off," Hudson said. "I've got water and sugar-free banana carob chip muffins. I've got a lot I want to tell you. After that, if you never want to see me again, that's fine. Deal?"

"I never want to see you again this second," she said. "And I don't want any of your muffins." Roz did want a muffin, he was such a good baker, and she was starving, but she wouldn't give in to that urge under any circumstance. Never.

A policeman walked by with his own megaphone. He looked at them curiously. "You know the protest is over there, right? Get a little too excited? Premature cuffing among lovebirds?"

He laughed at his joke.

"Officer, this man is holding me against my will," Roz said. "Can you release me and arrest him?"

"That's a new one," the cop said. "Kind of busy with the whole protest thing right now. Let me get back to you a little later."

"Remember where you saw us," Hudson said.

The cop turned his megaphone toward the edge of the dealership lot. "Time to pack up your patchouli and bongos and go home. If you leave now, we'll call it a day. If you stay, it's gonna get real serious, real quick."

"We're not going anywhere," the protest leader with the braid yelled back. "This is a peaceful protest. I repeat, a peaceful protest, and we have a right to assemble. We're striking a peaceful and lawful blow for Mother Earth. And we want a fair trial for our imprisoned comrades!" He raised his arms like he was directing a symphony.

"What do we want?" he shouted.

"Justice," the protesters called back.

"Who should be free?"

"Eco-warriors everywhere!"

"It bugs me that the chanting doesn't rhyme. Does it bug you, Roz, being a poet and all?" Hudson asked.

"Shut up," she said.

The cop talked into his crackling radio. "Better inform the mayor. Tell her it could get messy." He walked back to the patrol cars parked at an angle to block the main exit to the dealership.

"Please hear me out," Hudson said to Roz. "Three hours, and after that, you'll never have to see me again."

"We work together. I'll have to see you."

"I'll quit. Seriously. You stay at Rose and Thorn, and I'll disappear."

"It's not like I have a lot of choice in the matter," Roz said, looking at her handcuffed wrist. "You can talk, but that doesn't mean I'll listen. Also, you're an asshole. Now give me one of those stupid muffins."

6

Oct. 12, 1995—Six and a half months before the protest

The Rose and Thorn restaurant

Hudson held a five-pound tub of sour cream in one hand while looking at the recipe in a binder open on the counter.

"This calls for so much sour cream," he said. "Like an obscene amount."

He'd been at the Rose and Thorn for a month and was already lead lunch cook. They were in the lull between breakfast and lunch, and he was working to cross items off the prep list.

"People love it," Rob said. "It's one of those things that can't be explained, like ghosts or why Hootie and Blowfish sell records."

"Hey, come on," Roz said. "It's a good song." She was making espressos, fiddling with the knob to get the steam pressure just right.

"It's a terrible song," Rob said. "And probably commissioned by the wedding industrial complex to convince hapless brides there's only one person out there for them."

"You have a dark view of the world," Hudson said, turning his attention back to the recipe. "I wonder if people realize how bad this soup is for them."

He dropped a pound of butter into the huge steam kettle and, when it started sizzling, pushed in a mound of diced onions from his cutting board.

"Better than a steak," Dave-two said. He was passing by with the salad cart.

Hudson had both hands around a long wooden spoon to stir the onions, looking like a witch at a cauldron. When they started to brown, he added minced garlic.

"Is it, though?" Hudson asked. "I mean, it's better for the planet than a steak, but probably not better for your health. This is basically liquid cholesterol."

"Hold up," Rob said. "You're not some kind of freaky vegetarian, are you?"

"You're asking *him* if he's a freak?" LuRon asked. "You, the guy who dresses up in leather on his days off and wears a hood with a blindfold and sometimes a ball gag, and you're judging him."

"It's even worse than that," Rob said, grinning. "It's not just my days off. My appetites are bigger than that."

"Enough!" LuRon said, holding up his hand.

Hudson laughed, adding thyme, oregano and paprika. "It's even worse than that for me, too. I don't eat dairy or eggs either." The fragrant smell of the simmering spices filled the air.

"Wait, what?" LuRon asked. "No cheese? Okay, I take it back, that is freakier than Rob's thing."

"I think it's cool," Roz said. "I'm glad someone is sticking up for the planet, even though I'm pretty irritated I just had to make three soymilk lattes. I cannot get that stuff to foam for the life of me."

"How do you get your, you know, protein and whatnot if you don't eat meat?" Rob asked.

"Nuts, beans, broccoli," Hudson said, regretting his decision to say anything. "It's not that hard." He added a bucket of sliced mushrooms to the steam kettle, watching as they cooked down and the nascent soup turned darker.

In his experience, when people found out he was vegan, they usually had one of two reactions: anger, as if his choices posed some kind of threat to their choices, or an almost apologetic listing of the many ways they were almost-vegetarian and didn't really like meat. Both reactions were unnecessary. He knew it was a personal choice and didn't fault anyone for what they ate. Of course, he believed the world would be a better place if people ate less meat; they'd be healthier and happier, and it would slow deforestation and lessen the impact of industrial farming—the pesticides, antibiotics and concentrated manure—on the planet. But change was personal; it had to come from an informed choice.

He believed the best way to move people off meat wasn't to lecture them; it was to show by example. And let them try delicious vegan food.

But it wasn't that easy to find vegan food. What was available in health food stores wasn't very tasty, especially the waxy cheese. Almost no restaurants had anything other than the default salad with oil and vinegar dressing for vegans, or French fries, even though sometimes those couldn't be trusted. He probably wouldn't be a vegan, couldn't be a vegan if he wasn't a chef and knew how to make his own food. He hoped that changed in time. But given how entrenched most meat-eaters were, it wouldn't be in his lifetime.

The whole vegan thing started because of Sophie. After his time tree-sitting five years ago, he developed a deep connection first to her and then to all living things so that now eating sentient, suffering creatures was no longer even an option. That was one of many things he discovered about himself as he listened to the wind in the leaves and the birds settling on the branches.

"Did they let you eat rabbit food in prison?" Rob asked.

Roz looked over at him curiously, and Hudson felt a flash of embarrassment.

"You know, they were pretty good about it, really," he said, absently touching the scar on the back of his hand.

That wasn't exactly true.

The first few months were rough. He got beat up twice and cut pretty badly once. One guard made sure he only got meat on his tray when he was recovering in the hospital wing. Prisoners and guards alike soon tired of it though, when he just smiled and starved, leaving meat uneaten on this tray and doubled down on sad vegetables and stale dinner rolls when he could. He was already thin but lost fifteen pounds in the first four months.

"I didn't know you were in prison," Roz said.

He nodded, reaching for the vegetable stock for the soup.

"Everybody makes mistakes, right?" he said.

She nodded thoughtfully—he didn't see the immediate judgment most people had—and then she carried her soy lattes into the dining room.

"Did you cook before prison?" Rob asked. He was peeling a crate of carrots for tonight's second soup option—carrot lentil with mini-lamb meatballs.

Hudson added the vegetable stock to his kettle and watched as the liquid came to a boil. He then slowly stirred in a blob of roux, waiting for the Hungarian mushroom soup to finish simmering and thickening.

"No. I learned there."

At first, he worked in the laundry, but when they lost a cook, the prison bosses figured Hudson was not much of a threat and, therefore, was a good fit for handling a knife.

"You picked up some real skills," LuRon said.

"Thanks, man. They have this great incentive program where if you don't cook good food, someone will beat you to death with a lunch tray."

There was a long, awkward pause.

"I'm kidding," Hudson said, reaching for a gallon of whole milk and slowly stirring it in. "No one got beaten … not to death anyway."

LuRon laughed. "You're all right, Hudson."

"What were you in for?" Rob asked.

LuRon looked at Rob and shook his head.

"What?" Rob said. "I don't know the etiquette. I've never worked with a felon before. Just like, regular old petty criminals and dope fiends."

Hudson ignored Rob and grabbed a clean spoon and tasted the soup, then adjusted the seasonings, adding more salt. "It tastes good, but I can feel my arteries hardening from that one bite."

"You can't make a soup taste that good without all the fat and cream and butter," LuRon said. "I mean, it's nasty, but it's good-nasty. Like eating a bowl of Alfredo pasta sauce without the pasta."

"I bet I could make a vegan version of this soup that tasted just as good, with like a quarter of the fat," Hudson said, stirring in the spices.

"Just as good? No way," LuRon said.

"I don't know, I got pretty creative inside. They let me have a copy of the *Moosewood Cookbook* and *Laurel's Kitchen*."

"Are there a lot of vegans in the joint?" LuRon asked.

"No," Hudson said. "But there were two Hindus and a Buddhist. I think the warden was worried about some kind of freedom of religion lawsuit. They let me make special meals for them. By the time I was let out, lots of people were requesting them."

"What would you use instead of the sour cream and

whole milk and butter?" Rob asked. He had ladled up a bowl for himself and snagged some day-old rolls from the salad cart as Dave-two rolled by to reload.

"I'd have to play around with it a little," Hudson said. "Maybe coconut milk and cashew cream with some potatoes."

"If you can make a granola version of this soup that tastes even halfway decent, I will stop eating meat for a month," LuRon said.

"You're on," Hudson said with a laugh.

"Okay, a week. I need to be realistic." He pretended to think about it. "Definitely a day."

"Fair enough. Speaking of eating, I'm going to grab something before the lunch rush," Hudson said.

He grabbed a plate from the salad bar and loaded it up with greens and veggies and marinated tofu, then sat down in the back dining room.

Roz walked by and asked if she could join him. He smiled and nodded. She slid into the booth across from him.

"You were in prison?" she asked.

"Yeah. Sorry, I thought you knew. I thought everybody knew. I wasn't trying to hide it."

"No, it's not that. I just …" she paused.

He leaped into the pause. "Look, I got tangled up with the wrong people. That's not an excuse. I don't want it to define me, but I can't hide from it. It's part of who I am now."

"I get that." Roz was quiet for a time. "Was it awful?"

He nodded. "Pretty bad, yeah. It changes you at a core level."

She seemed on the verge of tears, and he felt a flush of concern for her.

"Does it have to be like that?" she asked. "You know,

change a person?"

She seemed weirdly serious, so he chose his words carefully. "It's hard losing your freedom. And maybe it was even a little harder for me because I was innocent. I'm in the process of being exonerated, fingers crossed. I never should have been there. Still, no matter what, prison leaves a mark."

"I hope not a permanent one."

He wanted to tell her that it did and that the permanent change was how his life was pervaded now by a constant sense of uncertainty, like a low-level background noise. His life had changed dramatically with no notice, everything gone in an instant. Once that happened, you never get over thinking it could happen again, and that made it harder to connect with people other than superficially. But he didn't say any of that because, for inexplicable reasons, he felt it would upset her.

"Are you okay?" he asked. "This conversation seems to be hitting you hard." She wasn't crying, but she radiated a sense of quiet despair that lived in the same neighborhood.

Roz stood. "I'm fine. It's all fine. Just means I'll write some especially tortured poetry tonight."

"You're a poet?"

Roz nodded, embarrassed. "Well, I try. I'm not sure I'd call myself an actual poet. I haven't been published or anything."

"That's cool. I'd love to read your work sometime."

"Do you read poetry, or are you just being nice?" she asked, now leaning on the back of the booth.

"I read a lot of everything in prison, including poetry. It was the least popular subject, so you could always count on checking out a few from the library. They had all the classics: Blake, Rilke, Shelley, Dickinson, Plath, Lourde, and some out-there stuff like Szymborska. It got me through some hard nights. I like how poetry condenses so much emotion into a tight space."

"That's quite a list. You have unexpected layers, Hudson. Enjoy your salad," she said, turning to walk away.

"Still waters run deep," he said. "Wait, you didn't say yes," Hudson called after her. "Can I read your poetry?"

If she heard him, she chose not to answer, but he felt like she was smiling.

I'll have to ask again, he thought, taking a bite of tofu and feeling an unfamiliar sparkle of something like joy. He wasn't exactly sure because it had been a long time since he had felt anything like it.

7

Nov. 15, 1995—Five and a half months before the protest

The Rose and Thorn restaurant

When she was drinking, Roz hated working breakfast. Dragging herself out of bed at the crack of dawn, hung over with a headache like a deep stabbing wound to her brain and a case of desert mouth, to walk the ten blocks to the restaurant unsteadily and then barely making it through the shift.

But sober, mornings were different. Now, the walk to the restaurant was filled with everyday magic—playful squirrels, scolding crows, the rattle and clatter of trash trucks. She didn't even mind it when it was raining.

At the restaurant, she loved the dreamy quiet of the unopened dining room. The first cup from the espresso machine tasted like chocolate clouds and the fragrances from the kitchen as the cooks got the grill going, priming her appetite for a breakfast special.

But what Roz loved the most about the early mornings was when she happened to be alone in the restaurant with Hudson.

As the lead lunch chef, Hudson was also responsible for the early morning prep routine. Most days, he opened the kitchen at six o'clock on the dot. Later, just before eight in the morning, a line cook would come in, usually the Greggman, but sometimes LuRon or Rob, to help with breakfast orders, but in those first two hours, the kitchen usually belonged to Hudson alone.

On the days their morning shifts overlapped, Roz came in even earlier to set up the dining room so there would be extra time to hang out and talk with Hudson before any customers arrived.

She was growing fond of him. While she was used to feeling an instant attraction to hot guys—and Hudson was definitely hot—this one was different. She felt an uncharacteristic nervousness talking to Hudson, even just being around him. Typically, men did not make Roz feel nervous, it tended to be the other way around.

Today, she was resolved to act. She would get over this stupid, unexpected nervousness. She was going to invite him to her poetry reading.

She finished rolling the last silverware wrap, brewed another pot of coffee, and walked to the front door to turn on the neon *open* sign Molly had installed last month. The red light flashed and pulsed, and Roz felt a tiny sizzle of joy as if, somehow, she was the one electrifying the day.

She nodded at Tess, sitting at a booth in the dining room, working on the shift schedule.

"Let me know if a table comes in?" Roz asked. "I'll be in the back."

"Sure thing," Tess said with a smile.

Roz headed to the kitchen.

Hudson was chopping off the head of a salmon to add to the dozen or so heads already on the counter. He looked up and smiled at Roz, and she smiled back but her expression turned into a grimace when he held up the fish carcass as part of waving hello.

"Sorry," he said, putting it down. "Not the best way to

say good morning, I suppose."

Roz laughed and pinched her fingers around her nose. "You know, not so long ago I would have up-chucked everywhere with that smell."

"Congratulations on your vomit control," he said, then paused. "I shouldn't joke about this topic. What I mean is congratulations on your sobriety."

"Thanks," she said. "That means a lot coming from you. I know you understand."

"I have to admit something," he said. "I'm not really in recovery. I know I said that a while back. I don't like to drink, hate it actually, it makes me feel stupid and sick."

He stopped talking and shrugged.

"But you don't want to be hassled by everyone to drink. I can hear it now. *Come on, buddy, have a drink, just one, hey, why not, do you think you're better than us?*"

"Exactly. Drinking is such a huge part of restaurant culture, and it gets old fast telling people *no* all the time, plus it gets you pegged as a weirdo. Being a vegan is weird enough for most people. But I don't want it to be read like I don't respect your struggle and success. I do."

She thought about what he was admitting for a minute. Did it bother her that he told her and everyone else a lie about being in recovery? No, not really. A convenient fiction, as they say. Besides, she wanted to be around people who didn't drink, whatever their reasons.

She shrugged. "It's nice to have an ally. Drinking is a constant here and in every restaurant I've ever worked at. And drugs. Can't forget the coke and yellowjackets."

He nodded. She leaned against the metal scrub counter and watched as he began gutting and then deboning the pink flesh with a small set of pliers.

"That's a yucky and smelly part of your job," she said. "How come the fish don't come to you already cleaned?"

"If you buy them from a supplier, they do, but we got these beauties from a Native American family. A late fall run."

He tilted his head toward the fish he was working on. "Salmon are such magnificent, mystical creatures. A whole bunch of them are now swimming upstream in the Columbia River, coming in from the Pacific to lay and fertilize their eggs at the very same spot they were born."

"How do they know the way back home?" she asked.

"Nobody knows, it's a scientific mystery," he said. "But each one of them will die in the same place they were born unless they get caught along the journey, like what happened to these guys," he said. He bowed his head toward the fish. "Brother Salmon, I honor your sacrifice."

"You what?"

Hudson shrugged. "Just trying to be one with nature and all. Wish these guys could have made it home."

Roz could feel words swirling around her mind. There was a poem begging to be written about this moment. She promised herself to work on it later this afternoon.

"Do you fish?" Roz asked.

Hudson laughed. Roz was crazy about his laugh, it felt like home somehow, like she had been hearing it her whole life.

"No. I used to. And hunt. I could never do that again, now that I don't eat meat or fish. Molly has a deal with this family. These fish are part of their allotment that they sell to her each year. This is likely the last of the season."

"What's that mean, their allotment?"

"Treaty fishing rights. They have the right to fish using their traditional ways, with nets, and are allocated a certain number to catch each season. I drove up to Cascade Locks yesterday after work to pick them up. Just two days ago, these fish were swimming free in the river."

"That was a long night for you."

"I got to watch the sunset over the Columbia River Gorge. It was amazing," he said.

The poem was going to write itself, she thought.

She let her mind wander to what it might be like to sit next to him, shoulders leaning together, watching the sky slowly turn pink as night crept over Mt. Hood and lit up the river's craggy lava cliffs. Even though she missed seeing the Pacific Ocean from her childhood in Coos Bay, sometimes, the beauty of this part of Oregon, the mountainous part, blew her away.

"It's so goddamned beautiful here," he said, putting the scraper down for a minute.

"You're reading my mind," Roz said.

"Yeah, and it's pretty scary in there."

She punched him on the arm just as there were three loud knocks at the back door. "I'll get it," Roz said. "You have your hands full."

"It's probably Jason from Cisco. The delivery is canned goods, just sign for it and have him leave it by the door. I'll get Dave-two to shelve it when he clocks in."

Roz hadn't met Jason, and when she opened the door, she was surprised by how handsome he was. Dark, tall, broad shoulders, sexy trucker sideburns and a baseball cap pulled down low. He looked like a country music star. "Jason, is it?" she asked, brushing back a strand of hair, automatically slipping into flirt mode.

It was her default style, a way to take control and put some emotional distance between her and men, sometimes women. At first, when she was younger, it was a defensive response to the constant come-ons she had to put up with, but as she learned to control it, she found that flirting was a very effective way to put everyone at ease, more or less. It didn't have to mean anything. It was like a romance language of its own, particularly useful in restaurants where no one took anything seriously. Especially relationships.

"I'm at a disadvantage here," Jason said. "What's your name, little lady?"

He even sounded like a country music star.

"Love that hat," Roz said. "I want one like it. It's smoking."

"Well, now, you have good taste, don't you?"

"I definitely have good taste," she said.

He tipped his hat, and they flirted back and forth, and after a few minutes, Roz half-expected him to ask for her number, but then she noticed he was wearing a ring on his left hand. She was relieved he didn't take it too far.

Still, he winked and waved goodbye. "See you next time, sweetheart."

"I'll be watching for you, Jason," Roz said with a smile.

When she turned around, Hudson was standing directly behind her, listening.

"Already done with your mystical fish?" she asked.

"Wow, you are quite the flirt," he said, grinning.

At first, she was taken aback. Was he spying on her? But his voice was gentle and coaxing, maybe even a little flirtatious.

"Jealous?" she asked.

"No, not jealous. But I could use a refresher on flirting. How about some lessons? I'm out of practice."

"From being in prison and all?"

He nodded. "I was never very good at it to begin with, but prison knocked it right out of me."

"I guess I could show you a few tricks."

"Great," he said, looking at her expectantly.

"Right now?"

"Why not?"

She laughed and felt uneasy, and that nervousness

roared back. "I can't just turn it on."

"I'm not buying that," he said. "Like, that Jason guy was, what, fifteen years older than you? And I'm pretty sure he's married, but you had him smiling like a lion cub, like something was going on between you."

She didn't say anything.

"There's not, right?" he asked. "Nothing is going on between you?"

"No, of course not. Flirting is a way to pass the time. A kind of communication style, a language that can only travel down lines of attraction. People who do it know it's a game." Most of the time, she thought. Until it isn't.

"So, teach me," he said. "How can I turn it on when I want to, you know, pass the time with someone I like?"

"Well, Hudson, the first lesson of flirting is, I mean, you . . ." her voice trailed off.

Unexpectedly, flirting now with Hudson felt awkward and weird. But flirting was her thing, and she *was* good at it. With Jason, she had just lapsed into automatic pilot. So why did this feel so strange?

"You what?" he asked.

Okay, she thought, try that again. Slip right into auto-pilot.

"The first thing is to pretend you're already friends, that you already have some intimacy."

"So, fake intimacy. Good. What's next?"

"Identify something you like about the person."

"Like Jason's hat," Hudson said.

She felt her face flushing and realized that explaining the rules of flirting was impossible, like trying to explain why a joke should be funny. Even more so because this was feeling a little too real, and she tended to use flirting for the opposite of what it was intended for—to keep herself distant.

"Okay, no, I can't flirt on demand. Especially if there's no object to turn it on with."

"Are you saying I'm not worth a little flirting?"

"No, that's not what I mean," Roz said. The words were coming out wrong. And sideways.

"How would you flirt with *me* then?" he asked. "If you didn't know me and wanted to dial it up a little."

She was starting to feel a little overheated. "Maybe you might be better at flirting than you're letting on."

"Definitely not," he said, grinning that lopsided grin that made her heart flutter.

Here goes nothing. I will ask about the poetry reading, if I can make the words work with my mouth.

"Come on," Hudson said. "Show me how you'd flirt with me."

"I'd probably ask you to come to my poetry reading," she blurted out, then dropped her eyes quickly with a shaky laugh.

The back door burst open. LuRon and Rob came in, arguing about something related to the start of the NBA season.

Then the dining room door flew open, and Ione walked in, holding her stomach. "I'm fucking nauseous. Is there any Pepto-Bismol in this place?" Ione put her hand over her mouth. "For god's sake, do something about that fish smell. And the pile of heads. Gross. Roz, you have two tables, get your ass out into the dining room."

"On my way," Roz said.

Hudson caught her arm lightly. "What if I say yes?" he asked. "Is that still flirting?"

"It's a gray zone," Roz said. "Depends on if you are serious."

"When is it?" he asked.

"For real?"

He nodded.

"I'll get you the details," Roz said.

Roz scattered out of the kitchen into the dining room, her heart doing mini-somersaults. Passing the bathroom, she heard someone violently throwing up inside. A minute later, as she was taking the order from the skinny anthropologist whose heart Kristoph—the longest-serving waiter at the Rose and Thorn—had recently broken, she saw Ione coming out of the bathroom, pale as a ghost.

8

July 4, 1991—Four years and ten months before the protest

Old-growth forest near Veneta, Oregon

A month had passed, and Hudson was still living high off the ground, up in the boughs of Sophie. He was filthy, his hair was greasy and an inch longer, and he was pretty sure he smelled like something dead or dying, a rotting mushroom or a mouse corpse.

He had never been happier in his life.

Axonic, the timber company, decided to wait him out. After an initial burst of attention from the media, the reporters were long gone. The company left behind two guards who traded shifts to watch the tree-sit. One, whose name was Bill, was there for the paycheck, was largely indifferent to Hudson and left him alone. The other, whose name Hudson never got, made it clear, shouting from the base of the tree up to Hudson that he hoped Hudson fell out of the tree and died. He wasn't there for the paycheck. He was there to vent some anger. Probably a former mill worker, Hudson thought.

Axonic was in no rush to cut the tree down; they had plenty of other properties to harvest. But the second Hudson came down from his perch on the old-growth tree, they would make an example of him, lock him up, and lock down the premises so the tree could be cut, and her century-old wood turned into planks and plywood.

Not on Hudson's watch.

The activist ground crew from the college green club kept him supplied with water and food through a system of ropes and baskets he dropped down whenever anyone could sneak on the property. Two weeks ago, he pulled up two new pieces of plyboard his buddy Pinecone snuck past the sleeping guard, so Hudson's living space had doubled. It still wasn't comfortable, and he tied himself to Sophie's limbs at night to keep from tumbling out of the tree. She hadn't let him down yet.

Hudson felt alive in a way entirely new to him. In the deep of the night, watching the moon and the stars, he felt connected to the tree, his Sophie, to the entire forest—the other trees, the animals, the birds, the sky, even the breeze.

After the first week, a bird—a little finch of some kind—landed on his platform. Hudson tried to be nonthreatening, but the bird flew off when he moved. The next day, it came back and brought others, and now birds regularly landed on the platform as if he were a part of the forest. Chipmunks visited, too, rewarded with nuts from his dwindling supply of trail mix.

The experience was mystical, as if he was connected to the entire universe through his place in this tree. Being alone with Sophie in her world was changing Hudson fundamentally. He wasn't sure how it would play out once he left the tree—if he left it alive—but for now, he was content to bask in the simple joy of this existence, at least when the guard was yelling at him from down below.

When Moon arrived two days ago, though, the birds stopped coming. It was okay. They would eventually get used to her and come back, although Hudson wasn't sure he would. Right now, she was on the far side of the platform behind a blanket holding a limb while she squatted over the edge, taking a shit or piss. The blanket didn't minimize sounds or smells, but it helped them get along with a bit less embarrassment.

Moon had been sent to relieve him, even though Hudson didn't want to leave the tree. But he understood the rationale. It had been a month, and if they were going to go the distance against the timber cartel, they needed to rotate people on and off. He would take a break and then rotate back on.

Moon said it had been easy to sneak past the night guard. She walked right up to him and said she was going up. She was really pretty, so maybe the guard couldn't help himself, or maybe she bribed him somehow, or maybe the guard's indifference went so far that he looked the other way. All that mattered was that she was here now and dedicated to Mother Earth—a fellow foot soldier in the war to save the planet before humans destroyed it.

Moon pulled back the blanket and moved to the center of the platform, her weight causing it to tilt and shake, then sat down. He followed her gaze up to the sky. Clouds were gathering, and it looked like they might be in for a light rain tonight. Hudson strung up the tarp for shelter above their heads.

After she helped tie the tarp down on her side of the platform, Moon sat down and pulled a bag of nuts from her pack. She smiled wide, and the dimples that appeared on her cheeks made her look almost angelic, Hudson thought. But even though he was a little lonely for human touch, and they found themselves in the most intimate living conditions possible, something between them hadn't clicked, not in that way anyway.

He sat beside her cross-legged, pulled out an apple from the provision's basket, opened his pocketknife, and sliced it into wedges. She handed him a camp plate, and he arranged them like a flower petal to share.

"You handle a knife well," she said, adding a pile of nuts to the communal plate.

"I like to cook," he said. "Though this isn't much of a meal."

"Apple slices and cashews. Totally gourmet."

"What else can I tell you about tree-sitting?" Hudson asked. "You feel ready to take over?"

Moon picked up an apple slice and took a bite. "Sit in the tree and try not to fall off and die," she said. "Seems pretty straightforward."

He laughed.

"Alpine, can I ask you something kind of related?"

He nodded. Alpine was his code name. Moon didn't know his real name, and he didn't know hers. It was one way to help protect other members of the eco-resistance from the cops and the informants who were forever trying to infiltrate their work.

"Sure," he said. "Anything."

"What are we accomplishing by sitting in this tree?"

He was taken aback by the question, given its obvious subtext. Why was she here if she didn't think this was a valuable thing to do? But then he reconsidered. After a few days of living rough in a tree, pooping over the platform's edge in front of a tattered and filthy companion, who wouldn't have doubts? That's what he was here for, to help her, to train her.

"We're saving this tree. Her name is Sophie. She's at least two hundred years old, maybe three hundred, and she's worth saving, worthy of human respect."

"I think you're in love with this tree," Moon said.

"Okay, let's be practical then. Scientific. We have to stop the carbon in her from being released into the atmosphere. She's got a ton of carbon sequestered inside her. That's how Mother Earth keeps things in balance. The trees take in carbon, trap it, and breathe out oxygen. If she goes down, if Sophie is killed, that's hundreds of years of stored carbon that goes out into the atmosphere."

"Not to be flippant here, really, I'm asking for honest. It's just one tree. Shouldn't we be doing more?" She took two nuts and chewed on them. "I mean, look at all those selfish idiots in the world driving around in their gas-guzzling SUVs. That's spewing out a ton more carbon than Sophie is storing."

He picked up a single salty cashew and savored it. A light breeze moved through the tree. Hudson listened for the delicate shudder of the needles on the tree as it passed. Above, he heard a distant hoot from an owl.

"I understand your point, but if everyone on the planet, or even just a tenth of everyone, is inspired to save or protect one thing within their control, one tree, one stream, one animal, taken together, it all adds up," he said. "Big time."

"Nobody even knows you're here," she said, her voice tinged with defiance.

"They will. We got some good media coverage when it started. Yeah, it's died down a little, but we're beating the company at the waiting game. Eventually, when they come for me, or you or whoever is guarding this sacred tree, and try to drag us out, that will make news. Hopefully, eco-warriors around the country, maybe even the world, will be inspired, emboldened, to fight against the system."

"I admire your optimism but I'm not sure I share it," Moon said quietly.

"We have to be patient and smart in our defense of Mother Earth," he said. As the words came out, though, they sounded clichéd and hollow even to him. But it didn't matter. He was committed to this tree now and would do anything to save her. In the deepest part of night, over the past four weeks, he had let out all his longing, his loneliness, his hopes and dreams for life and love, and Sophie understood.

"Don't worry," Moon said. "I'm not wavering." She rustled around in her bag. "I have a surprise for you." She pulled out a can of beer and grinned. "It's warm, but we can split it if you're game."

"Even warm, an IPA tastes great."

They drank the beer in silence, trading the can back and forth. Darkness fell around them, and along with it came the night sounds of the forest. The chirp of insects, the rustling of small ground animals, the trilling water in the stream below.

The threat of rain had passed, so Hudson pulled back the tarp. They lay down on their backs and watched through the branches as stars flickered to life.

"So beautiful," Moon said.

Hudson felt tipsy; it had been a long time since he'd had alcohol, and his stomach was mostly empty. In the distance, they heard the boom-boom of fireworks going off in the nearby town of Veneta.

"Happy birthday, America," Moon said.

"Oh, yeah, it's the fourth of July," he said, then laughed.

"I want to tell you something," Moon said. "Promise you can keep a secret?"

"I managed to get into this tree and set up a platform without anyone in authority knowing my plan in advance," he said. "So yeah, I'm pretty good with secrets."

"I'm joining a direct action to fire-bomb the SUV dealership in Eugene," she said.

Hudson sat up too fast. He immediately felt dizzy. He waited for the vertigo to pass. "Don't do that. Please."

"How can you be against direct action?" she asked. "Tree-sitting is a direct action."

"Nobody gets hurt in a tree-sit, except maybe the sitter. But no innocent bystanders. With arson, you never know. You could get hurt, or someone else, someone innocent. Fire-bombing is going too far."

"I don't agree," she said. "There are no innocents in the fight to save the Earth. Just two sides, and if you're not on our side, you're the enemy. We need to take out the car culture, get those fat cats to stop driving their SUVs."

"You said you'd take over for me here. You committed to staying here for the next two weeks."

She took his hand. "Don't worry, Alpine, everything will be fine. I'll stay for the two weeks. But remember, we all have our roles to play in defense of the Earth. Mine is to destroy the machine so people like you can build something better to replace it."

"That thinking will land you in prison," he said.

"We have to make sacrifices in defense of Mother Earth. That's what you always preach," she said.

Moon was giggling again, and in the light of the now-rising real moon, she seemed like a lost girl playing a dangerous game. They had talked some since she arrived at the tree-sit, but nothing serious, until now. Hudson asked a few times about her family, but Moon deflected his questions. He stopped asking because she was entitled to her privacy, but she talked in her sleep the past two nights, an anguished kind of talk. He found it heartbreaking.

"Oh, come on," Moon said. "You look so serious now, like my dad or something."

"Promise me you won't do this, Moon. These people won't be there for you if, I mean when it goes bad. They can't be. It's every person for themselves."

"Alpine, I don't need anyone to be there for me. I'm

capable of taking care of myself. Plus, they're friends. They'll have my back."

"Look, you are helping the cause by what you're doing here, protecting Sophie and this entire forest," he said. "It's important."

He wanted to keep her here, be sure whatever was going down in Eugene happened before she left Sophie.

"I know, now stop worrying!" Moon said, reaching for the safety ropes. "I'm going to tie myself in and get some sleep. That half-beer went straight to my head."

Hudson watched as she slipped the safety rope around her waist, knotted it tight and snuggled into her sleeping bag. He did the same and then lay down next to her, back to back.

"Good night, Alpine, sleep well and see you on the flip side," she whispered.

At first, Hudson had trouble sleeping. The booming sounds of the fireworks and distant flashes disrupted the quiet he had grown used to in the forest. Eventually, he drifted off and dreamed of doors opening and closing. In the morning, when he woke, he was alone. The sun was rising, and he rolled over to see an unopened can of beer in the middle of the platform. There was a note under it.

Hopefully, I'll be back by nightfall. If not, the whole beer is yours. Love, Moon.

"Shit," he said out loud to no one. "Now what?"

Hudson snuggled back into the sleeping bag, thinking. A jay landed on the platform. He wondered if he should slip down from the tree that night without anyone noticing and try to stop her. He shook his head. No, he was staying with Sophie. He would see this through. Hudson made his peace with the thought of never seeing Moon again.

9

July 7, 1991—Four years and ten months before the protest
Coos Bay, Oregon

Roz watched her mom busy herself over the stove making pancakes.

When the phone rang, Susan dropped the spatula and snatched the handset from the receiver hanging on the wall. "Hello?" she asked hopefully.

There was a long, silent pause. Roz kept watching her, drawn to the anticipation in her mom's eyes, but it faded quickly.

"Oh, hi, Mother. Yes, of course. I'll stop by later. Okay. Bye."

She hung up the phone and rested her head against the wall for a long second.

"Grandma okay?" Roz asked.

Her mother nodded, then returned to the stove.

It had been more than three months, and no one had heard a word from Camille. No calls, no letters, not even a postcard. Every time the phone rang, every time the mailman dropped off the mail, hope temporarily returned, only to steal away seconds later.

Camille's departure broke them all in different ways.

Her mother, Susan, was devastated but pragmatic. She

had another daughter at home, a house to run, a husband to look after. Plus, her own mom needed help. It seemed to Roz that Susan was compartmentalizing her grief, shutting it away in the junk drawer of her mind so she could function throughout the day. But at night, in the quiet hours, Roz sometimes heard her sobbing in her bedroom and trying to stifle wails that sounded like a wounded animal in a trap.

Susan picked up the spatula and returned her attention to the pancake, flipping it. It was burned and trailing tendrils of smoke. "Goddamn it," she muttered, squeezing her eyes tight to try and stop the tears. "I'm sorry, I burned your pancake. I ruin everything."

"No, Mom," Roz said, standing quickly. She put her hands on her mother's shoulders. "You don't ruin anything. You have to stop blaming yourself. Camille left because …" She couldn't even bring herself to say it. "You didn't hit her, Mom."

She looked at Roz with grief-stricken eyes. "But I married him." She was shaking. "That's my fault."

Roz didn't have a good answer. "Sit down. Let me take over."

She guided Susan to the yellow linoleum kitchen table and poured coffee into a chipped ceramic mug with a cartoon of Mickey Mouse, then added two teaspoons of powdered creamer and a sugar cube, blending it with a quick stir. Susan took the cup from Roz and wrapped both hands around it, sipping slowly.

"How could she be this cruel to me, to you?" Susan asked. "She must know what we're going through. I'm sick with worry."

"I don't know," Roz said. She sprayed oil on the skillet. "What did Grandma want?" she asked, hoping to distract her mother.

"She needs help getting her Halloween decorations out of the attic."

"Seems a little early," Roz said, spooning batter into the pan with a sizzle.

"You know her. The planning is her favorite part. She likes to get organized."

"Couldn't Dad help?" Roz asked. She watched the edges of the pancake start to bubble and turned the heat down slightly. She picked off a single strand of red hair on the stovetop. Finally, she thought, my hair is starting to grow out.

"You know he still can't legally drive," Susan said. "And he'll likely be at church all day."

"He's at church every day," Roz muttered, watching as the bubbles on the uncooked side of the pancake proliferated like reverse raindrops, and then she flipped it. "What the hell does he do there all day?"

Her mom shrugged. "Handyman stuff, I guess," she said, looking out the window. "Pray. And not drink, that's all that matters."

Stan, Roz's stepfather, blamed himself that Camille was gone. His first response had been to drink even more to the point of potential permanent harm. A new DUI saved him from almost certain death. Court-ordered treatment was next, and through that process, he found a different kind of drug, religion, that was helping him cope. By outsourcing responsibility to the creator, to his mysterious plan in which everything was unfolding as God intended, Stan was able to make it through the day sober.

When he wasn't at the church, he was on the phone, calling the police for news about Camille and calling local hospitals and newspapers across Oregon in a vain attempt to track her down—so far, not a single lead.

Roz slid the pancake onto a plate. Her mom spread

margarine on it and reached for her special syrup—sugar water flavored with maple extract.

With Stan unemployed, things were tight. Even with income from Roz's waitressing job and her mom's part-time job at the Chamber of Commerce, they didn't have enough to cover the bills. Their small savings account was gone, and things seemed increasingly hopeless.

Nothing made Roz sadder than eating the wretched sugar syrup or drinking real milk mixed with reconstituted powdered milk to stretch the savings. Her mom wasn't saying anything, but she was pretty sure they were using food stamps now.

These days, Roz looked forward to her shifts at the Treetop, where she could eat a decent meal with actual store-bought syrup. That syrup wasn't real either, but it was better than what she got at home. Or drink whole milk. Or eat a burger with cheddar cheese instead of pale, waxy slices of American.

Sadly, today was her day off.

After breakfast, her mom headed off to see Grandma. Roz tidied up the kitchen, grabbed her notebook and favorite pen—with a smooth nib and purple ink—and walked to the town's public library.

Everyone had different ways of dealing with the loss of Camille. For Roz, it was poetry.

She knew she wasn't a very good poet, not yet anyway, but the release she felt from channeling her emotions onto paper, of trying to organize and tame her feelings by carefully using language, of capturing the most powerful images and moments from her life and turning them around into something universal, then polishing them until they sparkled, felt cathartic, healing.

She was focused on improving her writing, and she had a powerful ally: Mrs. Gault, the librarian.

Mrs. Gault was eager to help Roz learn more, constantly encouraging her to read other poets and practice her craft. She took Roz seriously, and that meant something.

Today, Mrs. Gault looked up from her desk and smiled when Roz entered the library—a small building that used to be a real estate office.

"Roz, dear, how nice to see you."

"Hi, Mrs. Gault."

"Any word on your sister?"

Roz shook her head, and the librarian frowned.

"I'm sorry."

"Me, too," Roz said. "It's hard not knowing."

"I've been thinking about you, hoping to see you soon. I have a few books you might like. Poets that might speak to you because of your grief over Camille and maybe inspire you and even teach you. One is by Mary Oliver. Her book won the Pulitzer Prize a while back. The other is by Robert Frost. I want you to promise me you'll read *Nothing Gold Can Stay*, especially. It reminds me of the poem you shared with me last time. *The Waiting*, I think you called it."

"I'm flattered you remember," Roz said.

"You have real talent, dear," she said. "This town can be tough on those who have a creative heart, a sensitive heart. Your gifts need to be nurtured and protected. I'm pleased you feel comfortable sharing with me."

"I've been writing a lot," Roz said, embarrassed. "I'll have more soon, I hope."

Mrs. Gault opened the top book and motioned to a folded paper. "I happened to see a poetry contest for the journal *Electric Muse*. I copied the information. Maybe you'd like to submit to it."

"I'm not that good."

Mrs. Gault smiled at her. "You are that good. I've read this journal. Your work is as good or better than anything it has published. Just tell me you'll consider it."

Roz nodded, checked out the books and sat at a table by the window. A group of little kids came in, laughing and shouting, delighted to be around books and each other. Roz put on headphones and pressed play on her Walkman. It was a bootleg tape of a new Pacific Northwest band, Bikini Kill, and she let the music and lyrics wash over her as she sampled the poetry.

The Frost poem so moved her that she felt the urge to cry and scribbled the title line, "nothing gold can stay," in her notebook.

Later, the music still playing, she left the library and walked up to the train bridge to be alone and write. She had a poem in mind, something about using flavored gloss to soothe lips bruised from an unwanted kiss.

It was turning into a beautiful evening, golden sunlight stretching the shadows of the trees around her. Warm and peaceful. The poem wasn't working, though. It was childish and angry, and that was making her agitated. Or maybe it was that she wanted a drink, needed a drink, to relax the noise in her mind.

Everyone in her family had ways to cope with Camille's leaving. Hers was poetry.

And also, drinking. A lot of drinking.

She dug in her bag for the fifth of whiskey and took a deep pull. The warmth instantly spread through her like a sunset on the inside.

This was the last of her stash.

Turns out, she thought, the fruit doesn't fall far from the tree. She was just like her old man, a drinker. Roz hadn't seen him in years. He was probably in Alaska now, working on a rig up there. Or could be anywhere, really, anywhere there was oil to get out of the ground. Her mom told stories about his blackout drinking. And apparently, she was also a little like her stepfather, although that was less genes and more bad example.

I guess mom likes men who drink, Roz thought, or maybe she liked the pain they had in them that drove them to drink.

Roz was still underage, barely, and couldn't buy booze. Luckily, she was pretty. And, because of the circumstances, increasingly adept at how to use that to get what she wanted. A little flirting, along with some follow-up if required, went a long way.

She had an arrangement with Ned, who worked at the liquor store. He was a few years older than Roz and was willing to keep her stocked up on cheap booze in return for a look down her shirt, no bra. So far, he hadn't pushed her to go farther. That probably wouldn't last, though. It hadn't lasted with Tommy, who bought her booze before Ned started working at the liquor store. He was a lot older, thirty-something, married with a kid, and very specific about what he wanted in exchange. In the back seat of his Toyota, with her back up against the car seat. It was disgusting watching him jerk off.

Roz looked at the bottle, eyeing the small amount remaining, finished it off, and threw it onto the train tracks below, where it shattered in a spray of shards that momentarily caught the light of the dying sun like gemstones.

"Nothing gold can stay," she whispered.

She wondered if Ned was working tonight. She heard car engines, then excited voices. There was an abandoned quarry pit nearby, where local kids met up to drink, fool around and shoot bottles and beer cans. By the time she made her way down, there was a bonfire going. She saw someone she recognized. Connor. Camille's boyfriend. Ex-boyfriend now. He hadn't heard from her either. He had a bottle of Jägermeister and smiled when he saw Roz walking up. On the other side of the quarry, Tommy held up a beer.

She wanted a drink badly, but the dread of his tongue down her throat or his hand under her shirt forced a quick recalculation. She waved and veered back toward the main road her mind made up. In the corner of her eye, she saw Tommy's face fall. She tried to forget about drinking and forced herself to admit she had to stop as she walked home. Beer was okay, but this full-flung rush into the hard stuff wasn't good.

Her mom was making tea and sorting through the mail when the phone rang. Her mother picked it up, and Roz saw the familiar expression of anguish mixed with hope spread unevenly across her face.

"Hello?"

"Yes, this is she," she continued, voice flat. "Who is this?" A moan slipped out.

Roz suddenly felt very frightened.

"She's what?" Susan asked, her free hand fluttering up toward her mouth. "Oh, good Lord, oh no," she cried. "Where? What jail?"

10

May 1, 1996—May Day protest

Across the street from Fleet Motors

Two dozen or so protestors were still chained to each other and the door handles of eight shiny new black SUVs while the rest of the group milled around the lot—twenty or more by Hudson's count—marching with their signs and chanting.

Three uniformed police officers were talking with the same clutch of car salesmen, all men, all smoking. A fourth cop was on the radio in the squad car, the red and blue lights flashing color across the lot, but the siren was off. Two more officers were standing along the perimeter of the dealership, keeping gawkers at bay while also chatting them up.

These were the only cops left behind after the first wave had rushed onto the scene and then, mysteriously, just gone. For the moment, the police had stopped demanding the protesters leave. It was as if they were trying to decide how to handle it all. Hudson wondered who they were waiting to hear from, who had authority over this situation. Portland's mayor was known for her patience and tolerance for dissent. Maybe she had put the brakes on. Maybe she would keep it all under control.

But Hudson doubted that. Once a cell was committed,

it rarely pulled back.

The sun peeked through the clouds for the first time today, and Hudson looked up at the sky. A crow circled and then landed on a telephone wire, oblivious. Hudson thought about his life when he was tree-sitting and the way the birds trusted him there in the quiet of the forest. If only things had turned out differently and he hadn't been forced to leave Sophie. But then, he would have never met Roz.

A city bus lurched to a stop to let off passengers, exhaust streaming out the pipe as it idled, temporarily blocking the view of the dealership. One of the passengers dashed across the street to join the protest. The remaining passengers looked down at Roz and Hudson curiously. Hudson made eye contact with an old woman on the bus, gray hair coiled on top of her head. She smiled, curious and kind. The bus pulled away.

Roz was slumped against the metal rail, giving up—for the moment—yelling for the police, although she still refused to listen to Hudson's explanation. In fairness to Roz, he hadn't said much because he wasn't exactly sure how to tell Roz that her sister was a liar.

"Why does everything always turn to shit for me? What did I do to deserve this?" Her voice was so low that Hudson could barely make out the words.

"It doesn't have to," he said, hoping he sounded supportive. "We can leave now, and this will not turn to shit."

She didn't respond except to dig into her army surplus canvas shoulder bag, pull out a pair of dark Ray-Ban sunglasses, and slip them on.

"There are things you don't understand, Roz, you have to—"

"Look!" she said, interrupting him. "The press is here! That's what we need."

A television truck pulled into the SUV lot. The red and white logo of Channel KLIN, the local NBC affiliate, was splashed across the side of the van. A blonde woman in a sky-blue pantsuit jumped out of the front passenger seat, followed by two men who, working in unison like synchronized dancers, opened the back doors and pulled out equipment—a video camera, microphones, coiled cables, batteries, power cords—as the woman walked briskly to the police and salesmen.

"That's Caroline Bentley," Roz said. "The evening news anchor. If she's here, this is big and will get serious coverage. I have to talk to her."

Roz looked at him again. She smiled. She took off her sunglasses.

"Hudson, let's start fresh, okay? I'm sorry I've been a bitch. I need to talk to that reporter. Please. Unlock the cuffs. I know you have the key. And then we can go back to your place and talk all this through. Patch things up."

She was all sweetness now, patting his knee, and he almost believed her, but he knew Roz too well. There was no way she was coming back to his place. Not today, and probably never. Even so, he wavered.

He had seen the communique with his own eyes, faxed, faded and written in overly dramatic terms. It had been light on details, but he'd seen his share of such missives and could interpret the veiled meaning. As could anyone who was part of a cell. But not the people gathered today—Roz's cool and kind eco-collective friends. They had no idea their peaceful protest was about to be hijacked.

Hudson owed it to Roz, owed it to her family and her sister, to keep her safe from what was coming.

After his stint in prison and after the recent high-profile attacks at the homes of scientists and two more fire-bombings earlier in the year at an SUV dealership in Salem, he knew the feds would be in no mood to coddle protestors. With her sister already behind bars for eco-terrorism, the slightest misstep could bring suspicion—and ruin—straight to Roz.

That meant when things turned violent, the police would be looking to make an example of anyone who stood out in this rag-tag group of poet-pot-smoking-protestors. The story for the press would be all the stronger if that someone was the sister of a convicted eco-terrorist. Or an ex-con on early release still trying to clear his name.

A tall man in a cowboy hat walked out from behind the front entrance of Fleet Motors, a wall of glass and brushed aluminum facing the busy street.

"That's Crystal's ex-husband," Roz said. "He owns that dealership. He's the one who put her in all those *if it's fast, it's fleet* commercials." She stood, dragging Hudson along with her.

"Who's Crystal?" he asked.

"Clay's first wife, the one who cheated on him, broke his heart until Kassi came along. Crystal married that guy after she left Clay but then left him to go to New York."

"Sounds complicated," Hudson said.

They watched as the cheating ex-husband-car-salesman walked directly over to the reporter, pulling her into a bear hug, one hand dipping down quickly.

"Did he just—?"

"Yeah, he grabbed her ass," Roz said.

"Does he know her?" Hudson asked.

"Presumably, but you can't be sure with some men," Roz said. "She didn't object, but in her line of work, objecting might make it hard for her to get the story."

"There goes any chance of fair coverage," Hudson said. "It will be slanted in favor of the SUV dealership now."

"You don't know that. Could be the opposite, to get

back at him. If I could get over there, I could talk to her, tell her my sister is innocent, get her to write a story about Camille."

"You go over there and talk about your sister, and I guarantee you will become the news."

"She *is* innocent. She is in prison because you lied. That's why *you* got such a short sentence, why you got out early."

"That isn't what happened," Hudson said.

"Here's what I think you're up to today, this cuffing and shit. You're trying to keep me from talking to anyone by pretending this protest will be violent, the same way you wanted to prevent my sister from telling the truth about you by smearing her. I don't know what you're still hiding, but you can't hide it behind me," Roz said.

Roz started waving and shouting, hoping to get Caroline Bentley's attention, but the reporter didn't glance their way. She was smiling and joking with Crystal's big-shot ass-grabbing ex and the policemen.

"Before the shit hits the fan here, and the chance is forever gone, I'm going to tell you the truth about what happened to your sister, at least the part I know about. She's not the person you think she is," he said.

"That's bullshit. You'll say anything to keep on fucking me," she said.

Her words hit like a punch to the gut. "You know that's not true."

Roz shook her head and then wiped away a tear. "I don't know anything about you anymore. It was all a lie."

Hudson remembered she cried when they first kissed, too. Just over six months ago, right after her poetry reading. With that one kiss, Hudson had been sure he had met the one, that he and Roz would be together forever.

He was still sure she was the one, but it didn't seem

likely he could ever make it right between them. Why wouldn't she believe her sister over him? Roz didn't have many people she loved. Or trusted. Maybe none, really, beyond her sister.

"Roz, I didn't rat out Moon, I mean Camille. It was the opposite, Roz. Someone lied about *me*."

In his peripheral vision, Hudson saw three people slip onto the car lot from the side street, positioning themselves quickly on the ground next to two SUVs, blending in with the group. The cops were too busy chatting up the sexy reporter to notice. The three carried milk jugs and had black skull caps pulled down only to their ears. Balaclavas. When their moment came, they would pull them over their faces so they couldn't be identified. Black bloc.

Shit, he thought. It's happening. Exactly as he had been warned it would.

11

Nov. 15, 1995—Five months and two weeks before the protest

The Rose and Thorn restaurant

Roz was finishing her shift side work at the Rose and Thorn, filling caddies with sugar and artificial sweetener packets. It had been a long day, and she was exhausted in that special food service kind of way.

A customer had spilled an entire cup of Hungarian mushroom soup on her, staining her white shirt with a wide stripe of pink-puke gray. Another swore he got the wrong order, twice; he ended up getting both comped. A kid kicked another much younger kid in the playroom, prompting a full-fledged, top-of-his-lungs screaming meltdown with flustered parents converging from all corners of the restaurant. And she was pretty sure she gave the "Are you sure this is decaf?" woman caffeinated coffee—something that would undoubtedly come back to bite her.

She was tired *and* distracted. She told herself that was because of the poetry reading later that night, but she knew better. She was trying her best to stay out of the kitchen because she felt weird about Hudson coming to the event.

Why on Earth did he say yes? Did he pity her or something? Why did she think floating her emotions out there like some giant, needy weather balloon for Hudson to see was a good idea?

She'd read her poetry in public before many times, but tonight would be different. And not only because of Hudson. This was the first time she'd taken the stage sober. Not that she was ever stumbling drunk, but a drink or two gave her the right amount of temporary courage, the emotional armor she needed to be brave and open on stage.

After a shot or two, the scared part of her got to crouch down and hide in the corner while tipsy, fun, extravagant Roz showed the world a buoyant, confident face—the face and voice of a poet—someone who could enchant, bewitch and inspire with her words alone.

Today, though, she wondered if, like the booze, poetry was just another way to hide—a crutch to keep her own emotions at bay.

Ione walked up carrying cleaning supplies and looked at her suspiciously.

"Your expression is weird. Is everything okay? Are you sick? If you're sick, you need to go home right now. I cannot catch the flu. Two of my three lovers are sick, and I am a terrible caretaker."

Roz shook her head and mustered up a good-natured fake giggle. "I'm not sick. Everything is fine."

"You're not drinking again, are you?" Ione asked. "Are you drunk right now?"

"For fuck's sake," Roz said. "Does everybody know my business?"

"Yes," Ione said. "You, of all people, know there are no secrets in a restaurant. Everyone knows you got drunk and tried to seduce Clay multiple times, even though he was not into you. And now you're developing a serious crush on Hudson."

"I did not try to seduce Clay multiple times," Roz said, reaching for a pot of coffee. "Just the once. And I am not developing a crush on Hudson."

"Oh, please," Meredith said, walking past with a tray full of dirty plates, her brown ponytail swinging behind her like a windshield wiper. "You are so into Hudson. It's sweet. And obvious. And he seems like a nice guy."

Roz rolled her eyes. "I am not getting involved with someone with such a complicated past."

"Yeah, no, that makes sense," Meredith said. "Because our pasts are all so simple." She pushed past Roz into the kitchen and then poked her head back through the door. "He's awfully cute, though, as far as felons go."

Roz laughed and stuck her tongue out at Meredith, who grinned and disappeared.

"He is cute," Ione said. "I know he's not supposed to talk about it, but Molly said he's working with the Portland Justice Project lawyers. Pretty sure he's about to have his conviction overturned." She paused. "He is a vegan, though. They're weird. I wouldn't want *that* in my life."

"That part I kind of like about him," Roz said. "Means he cares. You know, about the planet."

"Oh, my god, you do like him," Ione said. "Please, please learn from the Kassi and Clay debacle. Don't get romantically involved with someone you work with. Sexually involved is fine, but keep your heart out of it. Good kitchen help is hard to find right now."

"Hey, what about servers?" Roz asked.

"You're a dime a dozen," Ione said. "Someday, we'll probably use robots to deliver the food. But we'll always need cooks to make the food, and Hudson is good."

"Hudson is good at what?" he asked, walking up to fill his glass from the soda fountain.

"Good at minding his own fucking business," Ione said.

She turned to Roz, glaring. "You remember what I said." Ione walked to the front of the restaurant, where a four-top was waiting to be seated.

"What was that about?" Hudson asked, filling his glass with sparkling water.

"Nothing," Roz said. "She's just … intense."

"I'm picking up on that," he said. "Hey, listen, I wanted to check in about your poetry reading tonight."

Roz felt a flush of heat creeping up her neck. She hadn't blushed because of a man since, well, maybe never, she thought.

"Is it still cool that I come?" he added.

She nodded. "Sure. Okay. It will be boring, and I probably won't go on stage until late …"

He looked at her closely. "If you don't want me to come, please just say it."

"No, it's fine," she said. "I mean, if you *really* want to. Don't just do it to be polite."

He nodded. "I really want to. And what's wrong with polite?"

"Nothing," she said, feeling clumsy and clammy. "Except it can send the wrong message."

"Maybe it's just the prison talking, but I've found polite can keep you out of trouble," he said.

"You think spending time with me is trouble?" she asked, hand on hip.

"Are we flirting now?" he asked.

"Definitely not," she said.

"Damn, I need more practice," he said with a quick lopsided smile. "I could have sworn that's exactly what we were doing."

She looked away, blinded by the flash of heat connecting them. "Revolution Bookstore. It starts at…"

"Eight o'clock. I saw it in the *BridgeCity Bimonthly*. I'll see you there. Looking forward to it." He returned to the kitchen, sipping his soda.

Roz watched him disappear behind the swinging door. He had looked up the poetry reading in the events section. He did want to come. And he was trying to flirt. She felt a little happy and a little terrified and a lot confused. There had to be something wrong with him, something beyond being an ex-con.

When she got off shift, she clocked out and walked past Ione, who was at the cash register and glaring. "Remember, keep your heart out of it," she hissed. Then she put her hand over her mouth and turned quickly, heading to the bathroom. Is Ione pregnant? Roz wondered, then laughed. Like she would get pregnant with three lovers.

When Roz got home, she had a cup of tea with honey and read through the three poems she selected for the reading, making a few minor edits in purple ink on the printed pages. She got out her notebook and jotted down a few lines about robotic waitresses, intrigued by what Ione said earlier.

She checked her watch. She was feeling increasingly nervous and jittery. She wished she could have one drink, a single shot, a small glass of wine, or even half a beer—anything to take the edge off. For so long, it had been part of her ritual.

Roz fought back the urge and went to get ready. She showered and then blow-dried and straightened her hair. She picked something cute, but not too cute—no sense making Hudson think she was trying too hard for his sake—and checked her look in the mirror. Okay, I'm not trying quite hard enough, she thought.

She dialed up the cute level, defaulting to her lucky jeans, the ones that hugged her hips and ass, a creamy camisole top and her favorite flannel shirt, open and tied at the waist. Then she did her makeup, swooping on pale blue eyeliner and a little color on her cheeks.

Roz took another look in the mirror. She had managed to reconstruct the exact outfit she wore that drunken night she tried to seduce Clay on the dancefloor at Dante's.

She stayed with the jeans but switched to a tight, low-cut T-shirt with a delicate blue flower pattern and pulled a faded jean jacket over it. Bingo.

The bookstore wasn't far from her apartment, so she walked. Her favorite bar, the Eclipse, was on the way. She was thirsty and ducked in for a soda.

Even though it was a quiet night, the air was thick with cigarette smoke. She took a seat at the bar across from the small army of whiskey bottles standing shoulder to shoulder in front of the mirror. In the dim light, the bottles of amber liquor gave off a warm, welcoming glow as if lit from within. She let herself sink into the memories of numb happiness associated with whiskey.

One shot, she thought, on a special night—that wouldn't hurt too much. It had been four months. Wasn't that enough to prove she was okay, that she could drink like a normal person?

"Hey Roz, long time no see," the bartender said. He was wearing a short-sleeved shirt rolled up to show off bulging biceps. He reached for a bottle to pour two shots for the waitress standing nearby.

"You look great," he said. "I haven't seen you since that night those two guys got into a fight over you. Remember? About the dart game."

"Don't remind me," Roz said with a fake groan and deflecting giggle.

"That one guy damn near lost an eye," the bartender said. "What a night. What are you drinking?"

"Whatever it is, make it two," Hudson said, sliding onto

the barstool beside her. "Hi. I saw you from outside. Hope you don't mind me barging in like this."

Roz, startled, stammered at the bartender. "A sparkling water with bitters. Two, I mean."

"Easy enough," he said, turning away. "On the house. Let me make up for the unpleasant memories."

"Here's to poetry," Hudson said, raising his glass after the bartender delivered the drinks.

Roz clinked hers into his.

"To poetry," she said, taking a hurried sip. She felt a flush slowly ricocheting up her chest and into her neck.

She drained her glass, rattled the cubes, checked her watch and smiled. "We should go."

Inside the bookstore, a crowd was gathered, mostly young people, with a few older hippies dressed in tie-died clothing milling about. The rich, spicy smell of pot—cut through with patchouli and a little body odor—hung heavy in the air.

Roz and Hudson found a window bench toward the back and sat close to each other, waiting for her turn on the stage.

"Are you nervous?" he asked.

She wanted to say yes, she was very nervous, but not because she was about to read in public. She was nervous because he was so close, and she could feel heat and strength emanating from him. And he looked really good tonight: comfortable, confident and so handsome. "No, I'm not nervous. I've read at a few of these before."

"I'm excited to hear some poetry," he said, looking at the crowd. "I'm a big fan."

"So you said earlier. Who's your favorite poet?"

"I think it might be you," he said.

"You haven't read my poetry," she said, leaning in and nudging her elbow into his ribs.

He felt solid and warm and smelled like peppermint soap, and she stayed close. He seemed to feel that as well, keeping their shoulders touching.

"I'll get back to you at the end of the night then," he said.

Six poets read their works, and the crowd was cheering and supportive.

Roz was half-listening and half-enjoying the feel of her body pressed into his, how comfortable it felt and how it also seemed to release a small tornado of clumsy butterflies in her stomach, their big, soft, trembling wings jittering her insides.

When it was her time, she stood, and he did, too, giving her a hug for good luck. She slipped her arms around his waist and held herself against him for a beat too long, then looked up into his eyes and smiled.

He followed her to the rickety stage to get a closer view, cheering and hooting with the crowd the whole way.

"Thanks, everyone," she said, squinting into the spotlight as the spectators settled down in anticipation. She adjusted the mic, pulling it closer to her lips. "I'm reading three poems tonight. And for once, I'm not fucked up …" the crowd roared in appreciation. "… so it's gonna be hard. But we'll get through it together. I hope you like them."

The first was a long, rhymed piece written in a classic pentameter called *American Heartsick*, about growing up as an outsider in a small, conservative town. The second was shorter, more experimental and stream of consciousness, called *Without Her*, focused on losing her sister to prison. The third was a new piece she'd been working on, *Metamorphosis*, about finding yourself in the eyes of another.

When she finished, the room was utterly quiet. Hudson watched from the front, his eyes locked on hers. In the silence, she was confused and then embarrassed. Then people started clapping and cheering.

She made her way down from the small stage as the next poet stepped up. He was a young man with wild hair that looked like it may not have been combed in a year. "Tough fucking act to follow," he muttered.

"You were amazing," Hudson said to Roz.

"You think so?" she asked, still flustered.

"Oh, yeah," he said. "I feel, I don't know how I feel. Off balance and … changed, just from listening to your words."

Roz felt elated. And confident.

"Is it okay if I kiss you?" she asked.

His eyes widened, and then he nodded. She leaned forward and slid her hands around his neck to pull him close. Standing on tip-toe, she stretched up to press her lips against his, closing her eyes and letting herself slip into the feeling of intimacy, the feeling of falling. He placed his hands on her hips, holding her with tender strength.

Roz's heart was thudding behind the kiss, her lips were tingling, and when she darted her tongue into his mouth, he pulled her in tighter, pressing his hips against her gently, turning a leg slightly so that it slipped between hers. She could feel him getting hard, and it sent pulses of pleasure racing up and down her spine.

When they stepped back from the kiss, the poet on the stage was saying something about oranges, Christmas lights and Halloween. Hudson gazed at her with what felt to Roz almost like reverence, and then he touched her face, wiping away a tear.

"You're crying," he said.

"I am?"

She felt her cheek. It was wet. She was crying—or something like crying—only from some weird mixture of hope, relief and desire, not sadness. She could feel more drops building in the corners of her eyes and then spilling down her cheeks.

"I don't know why I'm crying," she said. She wiped her cheeks with her sleeve, and Hudson pulled out a clean bandana. She took it from him and wiped some more. She took a deep breath, trying to stop it, and then the crying turned into laughter. Hudson started laughing, too.

"That was amazing," he said, hands on her shoulders lightly.

She wiped some more tears away.

"It's been so long since I've even, you know, kissed someone. I'm kind of rusty."

"You did just fine," she said. "More than fine. Hence, the tears."

"I don't know what I'm supposed to do next."

"Walk me home?" she said, taking his hand and leading him toward the exit.

12

Nov. 20, 1995—Five months and two weeks before the protest

Forest Park, Portland, Oregon

Hudson waited at the entrance to Forest Park. The day was chilly but sunny and dry. He had picked this park for the hike with Roz because he wanted to introduce her to a stand of protected old-growth trees, more than a century old, about a mile up the trail.

He clapped his hands together and blew warmth on his fingers. He should have worn gloves. A raven landed on the wooden fence bounding the creek that snaked through the middle of the grassy park entrance. The bird and Hudson stared at each other, sharing a moment, until it flapped its wings and flew off. Hudson marveled at the beauty of the jet black against the cloudless cerulean sky.

He checked his watch. Ten minutes to three. She would have finished her lunch shift and hopped the bus by now. He looked up. Any minute, she should come around that corner.

Hudson had never been in a relationship that lasted more than a few months. He told himself it was because he never met the right person. More likely, it was because of the example he had as a child.

Romantic love, or whatever it was between his mother

and his married-to-someone-else-father, looked punishing from Hudson's vantage growing up. Even though his parents were miserable apart, they seemed almost as miserable together.

According to his mom, his dad wouldn't leave his wife, couldn't leave his wife, because he believed divorce was a sin. An ironic justification, Hudson thought—years later, when the hurt dulled a little—given that cheating was also a sin. Hudson eventually came to see it in a kinder light, as a misguided notion of loyalty. His father immigrated from Mexico with his wife and two small children well before he met Hudson's mother and wouldn't desert his wife and their kids in a foreign country, no matter what his heart wanted.

But small towns are cruel, especially the kids, and the open secret about Hudson and his mom being a second illicit family meant Hudson received endless torment, taunted as a bastard and with racist slurs—his father was Mexican, his mother white.

It took him until the sixth grade to understand half of the insults. It took him until the tenth grade to confront his father. That was right after his mom's funeral and just before he was pulled into Idaho's foster care system. To this day, he never met his half-siblings and didn't speak more than a few words of his father's language.

A childhood like that leaves a mark, a bruise that hurts to the bone. For Hudson, it solidified the link between love and pain, and he wanted nothing to do with that kind of suffering. More accurately, he didn't want ever to hurt anyone the way his father hurt his mother.

What kind of man did that?

Because of this, before prison, he'd kept his distance from women. No one made it close to his heart, only his bed, and even then, rarely. Prison had taught him lessons that made romantic love seem even more unlikely. Prisoners with someone on the outside who loved them suffered the most behind bars, really suffered. Inmates who no one ever visited, who no one missed, like him, made it through the ordeal more easily. He was looking only to build a solitary life when he was released.

Then he met Roz.

When he first saw her, he was immediately stricken. He hadn't been around women in such a long time, and he hoped that if she reciprocated his attraction, it might lead to a few nights here and there until she moved on to someone better, someone who wasn't damaged or prone to being whisked away in the middle of the night by an FBI van. He kept telling himself that even as they got closer and the attraction deepened.

The kiss at the poetry reading changed everything.

At that moment, he felt a power surge that stopped his heart from beating and flooded him with white, lifting light. When he came back to his senses, back to the planet, every cell in his body was aligned around a simple truth—they were meant to be together in the past, the present and the future, together in a forever that streamed both ways in time.

He also knew if he told her, she would take off in the other direction like a racehorse that had thrown its jockey. Any sane person would. Normal people don't fall in love so fast, or ever, he thought, even in the movies. It takes time, patience and concentration.

He saw Roz walking toward him and waving. Her hair was loose, and she pushed the strands away from her face, blowing carelessly, caught by the wind.

"I've been waving for like two blocks," she said.

"Sorry," Hudson said. "I was kind of spacing out."

"No, I'm sorry," she said. "I'm late, the bus was packed

and had to let off people at every stop, it took forever—"

Hudson leaned in and kissed her. Lightly, on the lips. Just a hello.

"Oh, I guess we're just kissing whenever now," Roz said.

"Gosh, I'm sorry. Is that okay?" he asked.

"I think so," she said. "Let me check." She kissed him again. "It's more than okay." She looked over his shoulder. "Wow, what a great park."

Hudson stepped back. "It's awesome. Have you been here?"

"No, but I've meant to come forever," she said as they walked up the trail. "I read an article about it. It's one of the biggest urban parks in the country. The same guy who designed Central Park in New York City built this one."

"Learn something new every day," he said. "How was work?"

She smiled and started talking about her day. "It was super busy, but it always is. I dropped a bottle of ketchup. It shattered everywhere. Luckily, it was only half-full. Miguel was on top of things and got it cleaned up so fast. Ione was feeling crappy all day, and oh, get this, Molly blocked the door when a customer was leaving because she thought he hadn't paid. But he had left cash at the table and told me to keep the change. I hadn't rung it up yet. Molly had her entire body slammed against the door, and she is not tiny. The guy was terrified. It was hilarious."

She stopped and blushed. "I'm blabbing."

"I like it," Hudson said. "Please, don't stop."

They chatted more as they walked along the creek for a long stretch. The temperature dropped in the shadows of the large trees away from the clear, sunny sky. Leaves and twigs crackled underfoot. Hudson took her hand in his and was happy when she didn't object. They walked for a mile or so, stopping once after a particularly steep incline.

"Smoking all those years wrecked my lungs," she said with an embarrassed laugh.

"They'll come back if you stop."

"I'm quitting," she said. She pulled a box of Marlboro's from her coat pocket, crushed them, and handed it to Hudson. "Throw these away for me."

"Gladly." He tucked the crushed pack in his pocket, took her hand again, and continued walking. "This is one of my favorite places," Hudson said as they approached a stand of four giant trees.

"Why?" she asked.

"There are not many old-growth trees like this in our city."

They stopped and gazed up at the towering trees, soaring hundreds of feet in the air, massive trunks more than 20 feet in diameter at the base, their delicate branches swaying in the breeze far above.

"These trees have been here longer than Portland. Before cars, before the Great Depression, before World War II, before—"

"Before bikinis," Roz said.

"Bikinis?"

"Yeah," she said, rubbing her gloved hands together for warmth. "This weather makes me think about being on a beach in a tiny bikini."

He imagined a sandy tropical beach with Roz in a yellow polka-dotted bikini. A tiny yellow polka-dotted bikini. She looked amazing.

"I know what you're thinking," Roz said.

"I doubt that," he said.

"Was it a polka-dotted bikini?" she asked.

"How on Earth did you know that?"

She smiled and then sang a few lines from the song *Itsy*

Bitsy Teenie Weenie Yellow Polka Dot Bikini. "It's like Pavlov's dog. Everyone always goes there."

"You said that knowing where my thoughts would go. That's sly."

"I can control you with my mind," she said, looking up again at the towering trees. After a short silence, she said, "I have to admit something to you."

"You don't have a bikini?"

"That is true, but what I was going to say is I kind of hate these fucking trees," she said.

"What? Why? I mean, who hates trees?"

"I do," Roz said. "Well, not really, but do you know about the spotted owl thing? Those birds that live in these old-growth trees?"

Of course, he knew about the spotted owl thing, as she called it. He wanted to tell her the truth, that he was arrested while trying to protect the spotted owl habitat, but he couldn't, not yet.

"Some. It was all over the news for a while."

He hated being evasive, but his lawyer was clear: He was not to discuss anything that might jeopardize the work to exonerate him. He doubted there was a "falling in love" exception to his lawyer's strict instructions. He couldn't risk alienating the people working so hard and doing it pro bono to get his record cleared.

"The spotted owl, cute bird, I'll give it that," Roz said, interrupting his spinning thoughts. "It lives deep inside the branches of old-growth trees like these. When that cute bird was declared threatened under the Endangered Species Act, it destroyed my town, turned my dad into an alcoholic, got me started on my road to alcoholism, and broke up my family."

"That's a lot of damage for a bird," Hudson said.

"That's not even the half of it. My family was one of

hundreds, thousands probably."

"Your dad was a lumberjack?" he asked.

"Worked at the mill. After the courts declared no more timber cuts on federal land in owl habitat, which was most of southern Oregon, Dad was out of work. He was too old to move, or so he said, maybe too poor. He's been out of work ever since, although the church gives him odds and ends, and he gets a government check for disability, but it's not much." She looked up at him with her wide eyes. "I mean, I don't *really* hate old-growth trees, but that bird and these trees did a number on rural Oregon."

Hudson nodded in what he hoped was a sympathetic fashion. From his standpoint, the effect of that conservation victory had been nothing short of miraculous. Thousands of trees, acres of forests had been saved from the axe by declaring the spotted owl's habitat off-limits. Intellectually, he always knew that the ruling wrecked the economies of small towns that depended on timber harvesting. Still, he never actually met anyone who had been directly harmed by it. Certainly not someone he cared about.

"How did that ruling make *you* drink?" he asked. "Were you also a lumberjack? A tiny, child lumberjack?"

She laughed. "No. The ruling dropped a couple of bombs on my family. Drinking turned out to be a fairly effective short-term method of blocking the pain."

Hudson reached for both of her hands. "I'm sorry," he said.

"It's not your fault," she said. "And I came around, to be honest. I'm on the side of the Earth and the trees and the owls now."

"Like your poem last night?"

"Yeah," she said. "I even joined the Portland Eco-Artist Collective, people who use art to protect the environment, as naïve as that might sound. That doesn't mean I don't still love my family and the few friends I have left in Coos Bay, but we've grown apart in our thinking."

"What made you come around?" he asked.

"I'll tell you," Roz said. "When you're ready to tell me why you were in prison."

"Deal," he said. "And that will be soon, I promise."

"The guys in the kitchen said you couldn't talk about it because you are in the middle of possibly having the conviction overturned."

"That's right."

"There are no secrets in a restaurant," she said.

"So I am learning."

"Okay, back to the other topic. Here's a gross fact for you to chew on, pun intended. Before the ruling, a restaurant in Coos Bay served barbecued spotted owl wings," Roz said.

"Did you eat a spotted owl?" Hudson asked.

"Will you hate me if I say yes?"

He shook his head. "I can't think of anything you could say or do that would make me hate you."

"Really?" she asked.

"Really."

"You should never admit that," she said, leaning in.

She closed her eyes and brushed her lips against his. He pulled her in tight, wrapping his arms around her waist. She fumbled her gloves off, slid her hands underneath his thick jacket and hooked her fingers inside the waistband of his jeans. He thrilled at the feeling of her chilly fingers brushing his bare skin. He brought his hands up to her cheeks and held her face as they kissed deeply, and the longing he felt for her was nearly overpowering. He pulled back slightly, wanting to keep himself under control. His hands still on her cheeks, he kissed her forehead, then moved to the furrow between her brows, her cheeks and the tip of her nose, lightly brushing her lips before kissing her chin. She sighed and rested her head on his chest. He had never felt more peaceful.

"It was chicken," she said. "The town wanted to piss off some tree-huggers, so they pretended it was an owl. I ate it to make my dad feel better."

"Did you know it was chicken?"

"I did," she said. He felt her stiffen, and then she took a step back. "But there are plenty of stupid things I did for real I should tell you about. Honestly, Hudson, I'd rather know now before this goes further if my past will scare you off."

"I know everything I need to know," Hudson said.

"You don't," she said. "Men can get weird about women who, well, women who, how shall I put this, women who are comfortable with sex and—"

He held up his hand. "Stop. Seriously, everything that happened before this moment made you the person you are. I'm pretty crazy about the person you are."

"You are?"

"I am."

They began to walk back down the trail, holding hands and not talking.

"Did I say too much?" he asked at last. "I don't want to scare you off."

"You don't scare me," she said. "The opposite. Come back to my place. I make a mean hot chocolate."

An hour later, they were sitting on the futon couch in Roz's living room. He admired how she had made the attic apartment feel so homey. His basement studio apartment didn't contain much beyond a bed, and the table and chairs scavenged from the city dump.

It turns out she didn't make a mean hot chocolate

because she didn't have any soy milk. So, instead, they sipped steaming cups of tea.

"Sorry I overpromised on the hot chocolate," she said, folding her legs beneath her on the couch. "Tell me, what do vegans do for Thanksgiving?"

"Piss people off," he said, and she laughed. "Or mold tofu into something that resembles a turkey."

"Will you go to Idaho to visit family for Thanksgiving?"

"I don't have any family."

"None?"

"My mom is dead, and I have a dad somewhere, but I haven't spoken to him since I was in the tenth grade," Hudson said. "I'm an orphan by choice," he said, hoping his tone would come across as him making light of his circumstances.

She took his hand. "I'm sorry, that sounds hard."

"What about you?" he asked.

"I don't know my dad either. I think he's in Alaska, fishing or drilling for oil; who knows?"

"What about other family?"

"They're in Coos Bay, down on the Oregon coast. That's where I'll go for the holidays. I leave the day before Thanksgiving, and I'll be gone until a few days after Christmas."

A month, he thought? That was a long time to go without seeing her.

"I'd invite you to come with me," Roz said. "But I doubt LuRon would give you the time off. The holidays are really busy. I'm only getting it off because I put in the request months ago, and my mom is having some health issues."

"Will she be okay?"

"I think so. It's mostly, well, to be honest, she suffers from pretty bad depression."

"I've been there," Hudson said.

"In prison?"

He nodded, not wanting to go into that now. Hudson felt such a heady mix of joy and optimism being this close to Roz, talking like this, the intimacy, and he hoped they could avoid talking about prison.

"Let's not talk about that now," Roz said, putting the cup on the tiled table in front of the couch and scooting closer to him. "I want to make sure you miss me while I'm gone."

"I already miss you," he said.

"I mean, really miss me," she said, moving closer and straddling his lap, her hands on his shoulders. She leaned forward and kissed him. He slipped his hands under her shirt, marveling at the feel of her smooth skin.

"We should probably get an AIDS test before we go too far," she whispered.

"I haven't been with anyone in four years or more," Hudson said, voice ragged.

"Well, I haven't been in prison," she said, raining light kisses on his lips and running her fingers through his hair. "I'll do it before I leave," she said. "It takes a while to get the results anyway. In the meantime…"

"Yeah?"

"In the meantime, there's plenty of pleasant stuff we can do without clothes," she said, pulling her shirt off.

13

Aug. 31, 1991—Four years and eight months before the protest

Old-growth forest near Veneta, Oregon

The hunger wasn't the worst, not anymore. That had long since faded from a piercing and periodic need into a constant dull ache in his belly. It was Hudson's resting state, his new normal. The part that sucked the worst was the confusion, the growing disconnect between his mind and body, between his sense of self and the world around him.

It had been almost two weeks since he'd received a supply restock. Six days since he ran out of food. Two days since he took his last sip of water. He'd caught some dew from his makeshift condenser that morning, enough to stay alive, and was hopeful there would be more later because the sky looked like rain. The rain would help, but it wouldn't be enough, not without food. And he was battling a cough that wouldn't quit.

His support network had abandoned him. Probably arrested. He wondered about Moon and whether she had made it. It was not looking good for him or Sophie. He put his hand against her trunk and felt a ripple of sadness.

It's an okay death, he thought. Here in this tree. Dying for what he believed in. He hoped the press found out. He thought about his mom and wondered if he would see her after he died. What would he say to her? Before she died, they had barely been on speaking terms.

Back then, he blamed her for making his childhood so difficult. But here, now, impaled by hunger and with the clarity of impending death, he knew that wasn't fair. She was chasing her happiness. Trying to find some respite from a dark, pointless world. How could he have begrudged her for finding joy in the arms of another lost but married soul? He'd been cruel to his mother.

Was that why he was committed to Mother Earth? As a way of making amends to his own mother? The dusty revelation made his head hurt.

Hudson dug in his pack for a piece of paper and a pen to write his dead mother an apology letter. Somebody could read it as his funeral. That's how he could make it right. Maybe some reporter would print it in the newspaper. Everyone would know how sorry he was for being such a bad son—everyone in that tiny, shitty, judgmental Idaho town.

It was growing dark. He turned on his headlamp. The batteries were failing, like his body, and the light flickered in the gloom. His hands felt like useless lumps of pumice.

She tried to give him a good life. Waffles on the weekend. Store-bought snack cakes in his school lunches. Handmade sock-puppet shows. Walks by the reservoir, skipping stones. The puppy she got from the neighbors, even though she was hesitant to take on the responsibility. She needn't have worried.

He named the puppy Cinnamon. She thought it was because the dog was reddish brown, but Hudson picked that name because the puppy made him as happy as the cinnamon toast she made whenever he was feeling down, which was often. She used lots of margarine and a thick dusting of cinnamon mixed with sugar, then browned it to a delicious, sweet crust in the toaster oven. He could practically taste it now, and his stomach gurgled at the memory.

Cinnamon was hit and killed by a high schooler on an ATV when Hudson was in junior high. For a brief period, they stopped teasing him about his mom's affair and started calling him Dead Puppy. It didn't last long. Soon enough, he was "that bastard" again.

Before moving into the tree three months ago, Hudson ran into someone from his high school. Keith something. A football player. A jock. He was happy to see Hudson and excited to catch up. He didn't remember how cruel he had been. Only the wounded carry scars.

He stared at the paper. Maybe I should write about Cinnamon, he thought. A poem. It was hard to concentrate. His headlamp flickered again, casting crazy shadows into the swaying branches.

Last night, Hudson almost fell from the platform. He woke shivering, achy and confused. In his head, the distant lights of the truck where the security guard sat looked like the nightlight that used to be in the bathroom of the double-wide trailer he grew up in. His body still remembered the exact steps and sequence needed to walk from his bedroom toward the nightlight and step over the little runner into the bathroom to get to the toilet.

He realized at the last second that he was standing with one leg out into space, about to step into forever. With a curse, he grabbed a limb, caught himself, and then hunched down on the platform's edge. He'd forgotten to clip in his harness. The fall would have killed him.

The guard was back again tonight. The night guard was nice enough, even though they were on opposite sides of the fence. Once or twice, when he was bored, the guard—

Bill—would lean against Sophie's trunk and they'd talk about the Trailblazers, all the girls he'd loved and lost, and his favorite TV shows, Home Improvement and ALF. Hudson had never heard of either.

No doubt Bill was sitting in his truck now enjoying a thermos of coffee, a turkey sandwich, some Hermit cookies like Hudson's mom used to make, and probably a beer. Hudson's stomach gurgled again.

Sophie had stopped talking to him a while ago. It was puzzling. They had shared so much, and he had given so much, but in the last week, she had grown quiet and detached. Was she punishing him for his inevitable failure?

Rain! He tipped his face up to catch some of the drops, then pulled on his slicker. Water started collecting on the flap of the tarp he slept under. He creased it to catch the rainwater. Soon, almost an inch was in the bottom of his water bottle. He drank it greedily, quickly, then put the bottle back.

The water helped soothe the discomfort and fever in his brain. Humans can live a long time without food, but not without water.

Sleep would help. They would bring him food tomorrow, he was sure of it. Shivering, he crawled into his damp sleeping bag. His body was stiff, but he drifted into uneasy sleep anyway, lulled by the patter of heavy drops on the tarp.

He was dreaming about cheese when Sophie finally spoke to him again.

"Wake up, Hudson," she said.

"I don't want to," he mumbled.

Her voice was sad but strong, exactly like a tree should be. "You must. It's important that you know this is not a failure. Your courage was not in vain."

"What isn't a failure?" He was having trouble keeping

his eyes open.

"All of this. It mattered, it was for a reason," Sophie said. Her voice was calm and expansive now, like wind over a river. "No matter what happens, you tried. And when you try, it's because you have hope. Never forget that."

"I don't understand," Hudson said.

"You will," Sophie said. He felt her branches trembling in the wind, felt the sharp edge of every needle and the raindrops slipping through them.

"Love means always doing the right thing, even when it might hurt you," Sophie said.

It was hard for him to stay awake, to stay focused. "You're scaring me, Sophie," he said. "Am I dying?"

"No," she whispered, her voice suddenly rich with scents of sunshine and pine, radiating evergreen hope into every miserable corner of him. "You're just beginning."

Hudson closed his eyes. He wasn't sure for how long—all night, a few seconds, a lifetime. He felt content, whatever happened. Suddenly, bright lights were everywhere, people were yelling, and rough hands grabbed him. The tarp was yanked away. It had stopped raining, and a gaudy splash of stars leered down. People dressed in black—guns strapped onto their backs, lights crisscrossing their chests—were dropping onto the platform from above.

They dragged Hudson to his feet. "Run, Sophie," he whispered, confused, as he tried to make his legs work.

They were shouting and shoving. Handcuffs were clapped around his wrists, his hands twisted behind his back.

"Hudson Destry, you are under arrest for the suspicion of domestic terrorism," a looming face said, hidden behind a mask. "You have the right to remain silent. Anything you say can and will be used against you in a court of law. You have the right to an attorney."

"I don't understand," he mumbled.

They kept shouting and shoving, the words tangling up in his fevered mind into an unintelligible cloud of anger. Sophie was hunched in sadness and defeat, her boughs closed around him like angel wings.

Someone buckled him into a harness, clipped himself to Hudson and jumped out and away from the platform. They fell together toward the ground like a shooting star.

They landed with a jolt and Bill was standing there, shining his flashlight into Hudson's face. He looked unexpectedly worried at the sight of his longtime nemesis brought so low.

"Jesus Christ," the FBI agent said, unclipping the rope. "He's skin and bones. We're going to need a doctor. And a sandwich."

Hudson watched Bill sprinting toward his truck. "I've got an extra turkey sandwich in my cooler," he called over his shoulder.

14

Sept. 26, 1991—Four years and seven months before the protest

Correctional Facility for Women, Salem, Oregon

The engine clunked and clanged and sputtered. Great, Roz thought, just what I need. Thankfully, the noise didn't last long, ten seconds tops, but the car gave one final act in its performance, belching dark smoke from the exhaust pipe. Roz sighed, looking at the cloud of black soot through the rearview mirror. A man in a cowboy hat walked by, staring. Roz slumped down in the driver's seat, but not before shooting him a quick what-are-you-looking-at-asshole stare. He shook his head and kept walking.

Hopefully, the car had enough life to get her back to her hotel and then home. She could barely afford the gas to drive over from Coos Bay, much less any major repair. Or minor repair.

It was almost four o'clock. Her visiting time with Camille was in thirty minutes. It would be the first time Roz had seen Camille since she was sent to prison.

From the driver's seat, Roz took a good look at the place. The Salem Correctional Facility for Women was a large rectangular building with guard towers at every corner. The front entrance was brick, crumbling in a few places, but the rest of the compound was concrete, dotted with modest windows. She heard it was built nearly a century ago as an insane asylum, now repurposed as a prison.

Roz hadn't seen Camille since the night she ran away from home, not even after the family found out what she was accused of—fire-bombing an SUV lot in Eugene. An eyewitness placed her definitively at the scene, along with two others. He saw her light the wick—a twist of cloth stuck into a plastic one-gallon milk container filled with gasoline—shove it under a new SUV and run. Run quite fast, they said.

It made sense. Camille had been on the track team in high school.

The following day, reporters swarmed the lot, and within hours, the news came out about a teenager who had been passed out under one of the SUVs after drinking too much at a nearby frat party. He was severely burned. The doctors said it was touch and go.

The police arrested Camille and two accomplices the next day at a homeless shelter downtown where they were hiding out. Photos and names of the two men were splashed all over the media, in Oregon and across the country. Not Camille though, something Roz couldn't understand. The police wouldn't tell her or her parents why, only that they should talk to the FBI or the district attorney.

Roz tried, but the DA wouldn't take her calls. Once, when she happened to reach his assistant, he told Roz that she should stop making things difficult for her sister.

Since Camille was an adult, there was no way to demand to see her, unless she insisted on her side, which Camille did not. They were denied all contact and given no information about a trial. Even the lawyer they hired, draining their slim savings, could make no headway.

After a few months, her mom got a collect call from Camille. She was incarcerated at the Salem Correctional Facility. She had been given a ten-year sentence for eco-terrorism. Roz checked the papers at the time. It was substantially less time than her compatriots who were arrested along with her received.

Sitting in the car outside the prison now, Roz lit a cigarette and pulled a flask from the trendy leather purse fringed with turquoise beads she found at Goodwill last week. She took a long swig from the flask. The whiskey spread through her chest like an electric blanket on a frigid day, and she felt calmer.

Looking up at the blue sky, she watched a line of pigeons teetering along a telephone wire. She remembered the time she and Camille played along the railroad tracks that stretched from the sawmill to the main line outside town. That day, a bunch of pigeons, or maybe they were seagulls or even crows—it seemed so long ago now—were perched on the line, and she and Camille stood under them, jumping around and waving their arms to make them fly. The birds were uninterested, at least at first. Then suddenly, as if they voted on it and came to a collective decision, the birds rose simultaneously and flew off, releasing a shower of shit on the two girls. Stinky, funk, slimy drops of white and grey bird poop splattered them. It was in their hair, on their faces, running down their shirts. At first, they were shocked, then grossed out and then hilariously amused. Still laughing, they ran to the bay, stripped down to their underwear, and washed off in the cold water.

Roz smiled at the memory, took another long swallow, and tilted her head back as the last drops burned down her throat. She should have stopped at a liquor store but if she missed this visiting slot, it would be another month before she could get approved to see Camille. She'd stop on the way home.

With the windows closed, the car was heating up. She stubbed out her smoke, pulled her driver's license from her wallet, and put the flask and purse in the glove compartment. She shoved two pieces of Dentyne in her mouth.

She didn't bother locking the car. Who would steal anything from a junker car in a prison parking lot? Go straight to jail, like on the Monopoly board. She felt a little buzzed, just enough to take the edge off her nerves.

Roz walked into the door of the brick administrative office. A short line of people stood in front of the reception desk. She took her place at the end. She tried to catch the eye of the woman with a flowered headband in front of her, holding the hand of a wide-eyed child, but the woman kept looking straight ahead, silent, as if she were the prisoner. Roz watched as each person in the line gave hushed and humbled answers to the guard's questions, handed over their driver's license and got the once-over, and then followed a prison guard down a darkened hallway to a closed, forbidding door.

It took about five minutes before she reached the front of the line.

"Prisoner?" the woman asked.

Roz was nervous. She hoped she didn't smell like booze. "I'm not a prisoner," Roz said, stammering. "I'm here to—"

"Ma'am, what prisoner are you visiting?"

"Camille Smith," Roz said.

The room was humid, and the window-unit air conditioners struggled to keep up with the late afternoon sun beating through the barred windows. Roz felt a sheen of sweat collecting on her forehead.

"Your name?"

"Rosalyn Anders."

"Relationship?"

"Sister. Older sister. I mean, stepsister, that's why the names are different."

The woman smiled faintly, making it clear she didn't care. Her long, manicured cherry-red fingernails scratched across the paper as she scanned the printout. She crossed out Roz's name and asked for identification. Roz handed over her driver's license.

"You've got forty-five minutes. The guard here will search you and then take you into the community room. No hugging, no touching. Do not give your sister anything. Hands on the table at all times. If you do not follow these rules, you will be escorted from the room and denied future visiting privileges," she said. She nodded to the guard standing next to her. "Next."

Roz moved away from the desk. The guard motioned to follow. He was tall, with broad shoulders and blond hair, handsome in a cruel sort of way.

At the end of the corridor, in front of the operations room where three other guards monitored a bunch of video banks, the guard ran a hand-held metal detector over her and then patted her down lightly.

"I usually save the heavy petting for a second date," she said, her nervousness joining forces with her natural inclination to flirt.

"This way," he said, ignoring her.

Roz's cheeks felt warm, she hoped they weren't red. Why had she said such a stupid thing?

They buzzed through the first door, and her eyes fixated on the holstered gun at his waist. Her throat constricted. She followed him down another corridor as he turned a corner. He slipped a skeleton key into a massive metal door. It squeaked open, and he motioned her through. She jumped a little at the heavy clang when it closed behind them.

Her breath came faster. She accidentally bit the inside of her lip. She spit the gum out into her hand but, not seeing any place to get rid of it, kept it balled in her palm.

They rounded another corner, and the narrow space opened into the community room. About twenty square tables, each about four feet from the other. Prisoners, women of all shapes, sizes and ages—the sole commonality being orange jumpsuits—leaned close across the tables, whispering to loved ones. Some cried. Tears of joy and despair, both. A graying mother hugged her daughter. A tall guard separated them and pointed at the exit.

"Please," the mom begged, "don't make me leave. I'm sorry." He gave her another chance.

Roz saw Camille at a table on the far side of the room. Even from a distance, Roz could tell she had lost weight—a lot. Camille waved. Roz waved back and crossed the room, making her way around and through the tables.

She sat in the chair across from Camille, desperate to hug her. Camille's beautiful curls had been shaved into a buzz cut, and her scalp showed patches of white skin. A spray of acne pocked her forehead. Her eyes had lost their defiant sheen.

Roz forced herself not to gasp out loud, or cry.

"Are you okay?" Roz asked. She stuck the gum in her palm on the underside of the table.

"Hands in sight," the guard called.

Camille rolled her eyes and then offered a delicate shrug. "As okay as possible."

"Tell me everything, please. Everything," Roz said.

"They tape these visits," Camille said. "I'm not going

to talk about what happened."

"I don't need to know what happened. I don't care. I want to know how you are, and how things here are for you." Roz did want to know the details and how Camille could have let this terrible thing happen, but she knew that was pointless. Now, her job was to help Camille get through this ordeal. The rest would have to wait.

Camille's lower lip trembled. She was a beautiful girl once, Roz thought. She'd get it back, someday, once she was out of this shit hole, in ten years. The weight of that truth sagged her shoulders.

"Your hair is getting longer, finally. I liked it short," Camille said.

"I looked like an elf. Now I look like a Raggedy Ann doll. I am determined to grow it long, at least to the middle of my back."

That got a small smile from Camille. "How's Mom? And what's happening at home?"

Roz wanted to tell her about the bouts of depression and how they were getting worse. Instead, she kept it on the surface, telling her about their mom's disastrous new perm, which girls from their high school were pregnant (again, in some cases), who was divorced (again, in some cases), and who had wrecked their car (again, in some cases).

"And Dad?" Camille asked.

"He's pretty broken up. Blames himself. Truthfully, he spends most of his time at the church. Half repenting, half doing handyman work. At least he's making some money."

Camille sighed. "I wish I could blame him. I can't, though. Tell him that for me, will you?"

Roz nodded.

They talked some more; the words were about nothing in particular, but the emotion underneath them spoke volumes. Then, they were quiet for a while until Roz checked her watch. "We're running out of time, but I can come back next month. I'm thinking about moving to Portland so I can be closer."

"That would be nice," Camille said.

"I'll leave money in your commissary account," Roz said.

"Thanks. It would be nice to eat some Pringles."

"Is that all they have?"

"They have other good stuff too. Pop-tarts. Coke. Cigarettes."

"Don't make me jealous," Roz said. "For reals, Cammy, how is it in here?" Roz asked, unsure if she wanted to hear the answer.

"Awful."

Camille looked to the side quickly, then put her head in her hands and cried, shoulders jerking with silent sobs. Roz was again desperate to reach out and touch her, but when she looked up to see if the guard was watching, he was. He shook his head slightly.

"How is it awful?"

"Well, let me count the ways. No, wait. It would take too long," Camille sat up straight again.

"I want to know everything," Roz said.

"Someone ratted me out, so I told the DA about him, told the DA how to find him," Camille said

"That's what you should have done. Anything that gets you out of here sooner is good," Roz said.

Camille's face was wet with tears. She reached across the table to take Roz's hands. "Anything?"

"No touching!" the guard yelled.

15

May 1, 1996—May Day Protest

Across the street from Fleet Motors

"Fuck," Roz said, rattling her Walkman. The batteries were dead, slowing down and then finally silencing the Soul Coughing song that had been mostly drowning Hudson out.

Hudson looked at her. "Now, will you listen to what I have to say?" he asked.

She rattled the cuffs. "Let me go, and you can say whatever you want."

"That's not the same as listening," he said. "Look, I keep telling you, I didn't set up your sister."

"That sounds exactly like what a lying, scheming tree weasel would say."

"Tree weasel?" he asked, his voice somewhere between hurt and amused. "Have you been saving that up?"

"It just came to me. I'm a poet, remember? I'm good with words."

"No argument there. But you've got it backward. Moon is the one who gave *me* up."

Roz felt her pulse quickening, felt the anger and betrayal and disappointment coursing through her all over again. "Her name is Camille. Camille Smith. You only know her as Moon because you pulled her into your fucked up nature cult and gave her a goddamn code name."

He looked pained. She felt a flush of vindication. She'd landed something that hurt. Her victory was tinged with a shred of unwelcome sympathy, so she focused her anger on it until the sympathy twisted away like the cloudy tendrils from the cigarettes the cops and reporters were smoking reaching them courtesy of a tricky breeze.

She looked over at the protest. People were singing, and someone was playing bongos. The cops looked bored and impatient. The media had finished their interviews of the protestors and car sales reps. Now, they were waiting, like everyone else. For what, she wasn't sure.

"She was just a dumb kid," she said softly without looking back at him. "You were the ringleader. You should have looked after her."

"Roz, I did." He put his free hand on her wrist, over the metal of the handcuff, and she spun around with a glare.

"I said, don't touch me."

He withdrew his hand. "I tried to stop Moon. I tried to talk her out of it. And I wasn't the ringleader."

"Camille. Stop calling her Moon. She's a real person with a real family who loves her. She's not some spy," Roz said. "Her name is Camille. Camille."

"I did try to stop Camille. You have to believe me."

"Why would I believe you?" Roz asked, incredulous. "You've been fucking me for how long now, months, while conveniently failing to mention you sent my little sister on her suicide mission."

"Don't," he said. "Please don't cheapen what we have."

"Had," Roz said. "What we *had* was pretty good sex. End of story." That wasn't exactly true, she thought. The sex was incredible. Life changing. Even the thought of it now made her feel like a kitten basking in a ray of sunshine. She knew no one would ever compare. She sure wasn't going to let Hudson know that.

"I never hid that I was, I am, an environmentalist. But I've never been involved in any violence. Roz, you know me better than that."

"I thought I knew you," she said. "But that was before I learned who you really are. An eco-terrorist who recruited my sister and then persuaded her to plant that Molotov cocktail."

Hudson shook his head. His dark eyes were pained and stunned. "That's not what happened."

"Unbelievable," Roz said. She turned her head angrily back to the protest. "Free the eco-warriors!" she screamed but couldn't stay focused. She swiveled her anger back on Hudson.

"I'm glad she gave you up if she did," Roz said. "But what I don't understand is why the fuck she's still in jail, and you're out here walking around free?"

"I'm not exactly free," he said. "I'm an ex-con. What kind of opportunities do we get? I can't even vote. But my conviction might be vacated thanks to the people at the Portland Justice Project."

"Because you lied to them, just like you lied to me, and you lied to Camille."

The drumming at the protest was getting louder.

"I never lied to you," he said. "I wasn't involved in that arson."

"Oh, for fuck's sake, you're like a goddamn echo chamber."

She wanted to believe him. She wanted to hit rewind and go back to when she didn't know any of this, when they were together under the covers, skin on skin, when it felt like they were inside a poem, when everything fit, everything was magical and loaded with promise.

"You're the reason my sister is in prison," she said, her anger giving way to the exhaustion lurking below the surface. “My sister, Hudson. My baby sister.”

“I’m not,” he said quietly.

“You led her astray, like you led me astray. She was just a kid, a naïve kid, and you talked her into throwing her life away. And for what? The planet is still dying, they’re still cutting down the trees. Nothing has changed, not a goddamn thing, except my sister is slowly rotting behind bars, and the person who put her there and pretended to love me is now making my life hell.”

Hudson’s expression looked stricken.

“You’ll pay for this stupid stunt,” Roz said. “Sooner or later, this protest will be over, and you can bet I’ll be talking to your attorneys to tell them about what you’ve done. You can kiss that exoneration goodbye.”

16

Dec. 31, 1995—Four months before the protest

The Rose and Thorn restaurant

New Year's Eve was typically a slow night at the Rose and Thorn. People who were going out wanted to go somewhere fancier. People who were okay with celebrating in an un-fancy place didn't want to deal with the people going out, so they went home early. This year, the fact that New Year's Eve fell on a weekday made it worse. The dinner "rush" was over before eight o'clock.

Roz was getting a head start on her side work and also feeling a little bruised by Molly, who had rampaged through the kitchen and the dining room earlier to find something, anything, on her never-ending list of tiny things that were wrong.

She yelled at Roz for not logging the last time the coffee maker was cleaned. She yelled at Meredith for sticky fingerprint smudges on the pastry case. She yelled at Ione for letting Roz and Meredith slack off. Roz knew it was Molly's way of dealing with the disappointing customer count and the associated flagging sales overall, but it still stung. Luckily for them all, Molly's usually boundless ire burned out early, and she was already gone.

Roz was polishing silverware and splitting her time

between pretending to listen to Ione—sitting at the tiny bar, halfway through a club soda and with a splash of orange soda—while also sneaking longing glances at the kitchen where Hudson was working.

This would be their first New Year's Eve as a couple. Roz was nervous and excited. For most of her life, the holiday was a slow-cresting disappointment followed by a bout of blackout binge drinking that usually ended up with her in a stranger's bed—or worse, a car. This year promised something better, although her past was a low bar.

She was on the precipice of an actual relationship, even though this would only be their second official date and they hadn't yet had sex, though they came pretty close after the hike in the park last time. It had been five weeks since that wonderful night, and they hadn't been in the same room together since.

After the walk in Forest Park and a long, lovely night of exploring each other's naked bodies, Roz went to Coos Bay for a month. Unlike anything she had ever experienced, they agreed—by phone—to be exclusive. To her great surprise, she kept up her side of the deal.

Tonight, her first night back in town, was also New Year's Eve. They were definitely doing it, even if she had to tie him to the bed. She wondered if the sex would be good at first. He hadn't been in many relationships. None since prison. She would be patient, she told herself, and not put too much pressure on him to last. Not the first time, anyway.

"Oh, for goodness sake, just go back there," Ione said.

"What?" Roz asked, drifting back into the present with a pleasant, tingly feeling inside. "Why? And anyway, I can't leave you out here alone."

"You are practically dripping desire," Ione said.

"You shouldn't have let Meredith leave," Roz said, fake pouting.

"Don't tell me how to manage the restaurant and besides, Molly almost made her cry," Ione said, taking a sip of her drink. "I miss wine."

"She yelled at me, too," Roz said.

"Meredith is not tough like us," Ione said. "And she's my second-best server. Don't want to lose her."

"Ouch, where am I on that list?" Roz asked.

"Number three," Ione said. "You took a pretty big jump up when Kassi left."

"She was a table hog," Roz said.

"But a supremely skilled table hog," Ione said. "Go, seriously. I'll let you know if I need you. Just don't, you know, break any health codes back there. God knows Molly doesn't need anything else to yell about. Bring me some fries when you come back. I'm starving. Also, an order of pasta alfredo."

Almost skipping, Roz made her way to the kitchen. Hudson smiled when she walked in.

"Order?" LuRon asked, his tone somewhere between hope and dread.

"Nope. It's dead out there, except for Ione. She wants fries and an alfredo."

"We really should just flip the sign and go home," LuRon said, reaching for the fry basket. "Because you know what's going to happen. We're gonna be all cleaned up and broken down, and some sorry ass shit bird will flap in, all sad and lonely, and stay here until almost midnight because they got no place to go and no one to love them, so why not punish all of us who *do* have someplace to go?"

"That's harsh," Hudson said. He was prepping enchilada sauce on the counter near the steam kettle. "Why are you so cranky?"

"I'm pissed at Clay. I wasn't supposed to work tonight, but he had another 'emergency.'" LuRon made dismissive air quotes. "And the emergency was that he wanted to spend time polishing his fucking food truck."

"I'm sorry, man," Hudson said. "What did you and Dara have planned tonight?"

LuRon stared at him with a bewildered look. "She's six months pregnant, and we are already parents. Do you understand what that means?"

Hudson shook his head. "Not really."

"She's uncomfortable and tired, and no matter what we'd *like* to do, what we're gonna do is have some sparkling apple cider and watch *Free Willy*, for the millionth time, until the kids fall asleep. Then we'll put them to bed and swap out DVDs for a romantic comedy with sad, confused white people doing a bunch of dumb stuff until the very end when everything magically works out. All while I rub Dara's feet until *she* falls asleep and then I'll sit there drinking my apple cider until she wakes up enough for me to take her to bed."

"That sounds pretty nice," Roz said.

"It's not bad, honestly," LuRon said with a smile. "Wouldn't have it any other way. But I am already late to the party."

"That's not a party, that's a cry for help," Rob said. He was sitting on an unopened case of broccoli, flipping through a pamphlet for the Bondage NW Expo coming up in January. The cover featured a black and white close-up of an impossibly thin waist in a cinched corset, shot from the back to show the hint of a shapely, androgynous behind, with hands tightly cuffed. The title was *Resolve to satisfy your darkest desires in the New Year.*

"I'm sure you have something weird planned," Roz said.

"Absolutely," Rob said. "Meredith is coming over, we've got champagne and a cheese platter with some charcuterie."

"That sounds normal," Roz said.

"Then, just before midnight, we'll play rock, paper, scissors to see who gets tied up and who has the whip as the new year rolls in," Rob said.

"Gross," Roz said. "I mean, I'm glad you two are trying to work things out, but gross. The foot rubbing sounds a lot better than being whipped."

"You've probably never been whipped correctly," Rob said. "I can teach Hudson in ten minutes. It's all about keeping your wrists loose and thinking about where the tips of the lash hit …"

"I'll pass on that, all the same," Hudson said.

Rob shrugged. "Your loss. Actually, her loss. So, what big night do you two have planned?"

"Why would you think we have a big night planned?" Roz asked. "We're just friends."

She shot a glance at Hudson. He had stopped his prep work, and his left eyebrow was raised.

"Friends?" Hudson asked, grinning.

"Oh, yeah, friends," LuRon said with a laugh.

"It does seem like you two are more than friends," Rob said, his expression getting serious. "You seem emotionally close in that gross, conforming-to-social-stereotypes kind of way. I worry about you."

Jon, the dishwasher, poked his head out of the dishpit. His oversized glasses, held together at one temple with duct tape, were steamed up and his vinyl apron was beaded with water.

"Researchers still struggle to define the evolutionary benefits of romantic love," Jon said.

"Enough," Roz said, blushing, looking at Hudson. He

nodded. "Okay, we're more than friends, but please don't make it weird."

"You're the one making it weird," LuRon said, pulling the basket of fries from the hot oil of the deep fryer. "Sneaking around here grinning at each other secretly like we're all wearing blindfolds."

"I mean, especially tonight," Roz said. "It's New Year's, which is already a weird holiday if you're used to being single. And for those of us who aren't drinking, including you and Dara, it's rougher. We haven't even planned anything. We'll be staying in and chilling out. I'm just glad I have someone nice to spend it with," she said, smiling at Hudson.

"Oooh, she called you *nice*, H-train," LuRon said. "That's the worst thing your new girl can say about you. You better have something double special planned."

"Stop it, LuRon," Roz said. "We're going to have a simple, lovely night, watch the ball drop on TV, and probably have some sparkling cider."

Hudson grinned at her in that low-key lopsided way of his, a noncommittal expression that hid his thoughts but didn't feel defensive or elusive. She wondered if he learned that in prison.

Despite how great—and slowly—everything was going, she was feeling a little weird about the night. She hadn't been in a relationship for New Year's Eve in a long time … she tried to remember. Was it since Frank?

She shook her head at the memory. They were *so* bad for each other. She had a flash of that New Year's Eve when he drunkenly tried to seduce her, and she drunkenly tried to let him. They fell off the porch of his house. He fractured his wrist but didn't discover it until the morning.

Ione poked her head in. "We've got a one-top."

"We got ourselves a shit bird," LuRon groaned. "We'll

be here all night."

"I got it," Hudson said. "Seriously, go home and crack open that cider. Get to work on the foot rub. Dara deserves some special attention."

"You mean it?" LuRon asked.

"Yeah," Hudson said. "You too, Rob. Get your whip hand loosened up."

They were out of their aprons and clocked out in less than two minutes.

"That was nice of you," Roz said.

Hudson slid Ione's plate of fries and a bowl of pasta alfredo, extra cheese, into the window.

"I'm not leaving until you do anyway. No reason to make them wait," he said.

When the shit bird finally left and Ione flipped the sign to closed, they rushed through their closing work and, by 11:30, were on the way to Hudson's place.

She slipped her hand in his. "I'm glad I'm spending New Year's with you," she said, feeling uncharacteristically shy. "Even if we don't have anything special planned."

"Who says we don't have anything special planned?" Hudson asked, unlocking the door.

Inside, a bouquet of wildflowers in a red glass vase sat on the table, next to a bottle of sparkling apple cider chilling in an ice bucket and a decanter of dark liquid. Candles were burning, casting a romantic glow.

Roz was so surprised she squeaked and held her hand over her mouth.

"What? How did you do all this?" she whispered.

"I bribed a friend with vegan chocolate chip cookies to come by."

"That's who you called before we left the restaurant?"

"Yep," he said.

"No wonder you were walking so slowly."

Hudson took her hand and led her inside. He spent the month she was away making his basement studio apartment suitable for her to visit, and hopefully sleep over. He had a genuine sofa, a television, a two-person dining room table with matching chairs, and a nice mattress and box springs in the sleeping alcove.

He pointed to the decanter sitting on the new table. "That's a spiced ginger syrup to spruce up the cider. Who says you need booze on New Year's?"

"Pretty much everyone," Roz said. She couldn't stop smiling.

He turned on the stereo. A soft, slow song started playing.

"Who is this?" she asked.

"A British band called *James*. The album is *Laid*, but don't read anything into that. It's just a great song." He looked at his watch. "We better get started if we want to eat before midnight."

"There's food?" she asked.

"A special holiday menu. Black-eyed pea fritters with cashew cream aioli and collard greens. Black-eyed peas are supposed to bring you luck in the New Year. Collard greens bring you wealth. And for dessert, vegan Mexican wedding cookies. Again, don't read anything into the name. I just like them."

He helped her out of her coat and hung it on the rack by the door.

"This is so sweet of you. What would you say to eating *after* midnight?" she asked, taking his hands and pulling him close.

"I could probably be persuaded," he whispered as she pressed her body against his.

"Dance with me," she said, lost in the moment and the slow song. She put her arms around his waist and leaned into his chest, feeling the heat building between them.

"This is nice," she whispered as he wrapped his arms around her. "Special. I feel cared for."

"I'm crazy about you, Roz," he said. "I've fallen for you completely."

She looked up and into his eyes, seeing that truth reflected there. The honesty and electricity of the moment was almost unbearable. Pulses of pleasure radiated throughout her body in rhythm with their dancing, bodies pressed against each other.

Roz kissed him and was immediately lost in the sensation of his lips on hers, the taste of him, the scrape of his stubble against her cheek as he cradled her head in both hands to hold the kiss for as long as possible.

When he at last pulled back, panting a little, Roz let her hands drift under his shirt to caress his rippled stomach and then up to his muscled chest, thumbs circling his nipples lightly. He closed his eyes and leaned one hand against the wall for support as she let her hands travel down to the small of his back and then lower, cupping his ass and pulling him into her with a velvet tug.

He softly moaned, his swelling erection pressing into her. She created space between them so she could dip both hands to the bulge, kissing him in a flurry on his lips, slipping her tongue inside his mouth.

He was moaning, or maybe that's me, she thought, moving her fingers up to unbutton and then slowly unzip his pants. She pushed the waistband down, dragging his boxers off with them. He kicked out of his pants as he gently pulled her shirt over her head.

She wasn't wearing a bra, and she saw his eyes widen as he dipped his head to lightly kiss her breasts. She ran her fingers through his dark, wavy hair, holding his mouth in place as he gently cupped and feather-touched her breasts.

Walking backward, she guided them toward the couch, stepping out of her pants along the way. Wearing a new pair of sexy black lace panties she picked up at Victoria's Secret yesterday, she sat on the couch in front of him, reached up, almost shyly, and guided him into her mouth. She could feel his body go rigid as she moved her mouth up and down him, and Roz reveled in the pleasure she was giving him.

But then he pulled back and knelt before her. "It's too much," he whispered.

"I want to make you feel good," she said, disappointed that he stopped her. The thought flashed through her mind: was she being too aggressive?

"I want to be inside you when the New Year comes," he whispered.

She nodded, understanding, and stretched out on the couch, making room for him. He positioned himself between her legs and with a breathtaking, delicious and agonizing slowness as they deeply kissed, he entered her, but only for a second and just partly, and then pulled back. He repeated that motion three more times until Roz was drowning in the electric anticipation and wild for him to be fully inside her.

"Don't tease, please," she moaned.

She closed her eyes, trying to memorize the precise feeling of him as he pressed forward. She felt a rush of joy and contentment as he filled her, inch by inch, until he was fully inside. She held him there, hands pressing his ass, and moaned as he pulled almost out, caught in a delicious sense of emptiness as he held back.

"Do it," she cried. "All the way. Now."

Hudson obliged and thrust deep, then began to increase the tempo as their mutual pleasure spiraled around them out of control. He had one hand on the arm of the couch, the other on her breast, and they could hear the chants of neighbors around them counting down to midnight.

3 … 2 … 1

"Let yourself go," Roz whispered happily, and then the fireworks began.

17

Feb. 20, 1996—Two months and two weeks before the protest

The Rose and Thorn restaurant

The dildo discussion was going downhill fast.

Ever since Clay quit, the kitchen banter—especially between Rob and Meredith—veered too often into the almost pornographic. Sometimes, Hudson wondered if Meredith was egging Rob on as part of her research for her PhD thesis on deviant sexual behavior.

The back and forth between them didn't bother Hudson. Nothing those two said could ever hold a candle to what he heard in prison, but he figured it bothered other people. He was thinking maybe it was time to speak up.

Rob was currently talking about his dildo collection and how Meredith was researching size versus length. Meredith was irritated because—apparently—he was explaining it all wrong.

"That isn't what I'm researching," Meredith said. "You have it so wrong it's ludicrous. And a little insulting. Do you even listen to me?"

"Please explain to everyone why you think size *doesn't* matter," Rob said.

"You're making it worse," she said.

"I say shape is the dominant consideration," Dave-two

said, holding up a bent cucumber destined to be stripped, sliced and moved to the salad bar. "It's the angle that matters if you want to put a little shimmy in the push to hit all the right buttons."

Hudson glanced up at Rizza, the newest dining room hire, and even though she was smiling, she looked irritated. That was something else he got from prison—he understood how it felt to be uncomfortable in a situation but unable to say anything, how it felt to pretend to get along.

No one had yet picked up the mantle of banter enforcer that Clay handled as head chef. Within days of Clay's decamping to California, the filters started to degrade, Rob's most of all. He seemed almost giddy with the new freedom, testing—and exceeding—the limits every day. Ione needed to hire a new head chef soon, Hudson thought, before someone quit. Or filed a complaint.

"If you ever listened to me, you'd know my current research is about how primary colors influence consumer patterns for women when it comes to sex toy purchases," Meredith said.

"Stop talking about sex toys, you degenerates," Ione said, walking into the kitchen. "Everyone, gather around," she shouted, clapping her hands. "Impromptu staff meeting. Gilroy, keep the grill going, and Rizza, handle the table in the dining room and stall any others that come in. The rest of you, eyes on me."

It was a half-hour before lunch, so everyone was clocked in except the two bussers and one line cook on the dinner-only night crew.

Roz came in from the dining room, and Hudson tried to keep the smile off his face, but it was impossible. For her, too, he saw. She beamed her spotlight smile his way, and he felt so good, like he'd just woken up and a fresh donut was waiting on the table next to the bed. She crossed over to where he was chopping veggies. He wiped his hands on a kitchen towel. They stood side to side, facing Ione. When their hands lightly brushed, he felt a full-body spark.

"I've got three announcements," Ione said.

When Molly entered the kitchen, all heads swiveled in her direction. As always, each employee was making a calculation. What kind of mood was she in? Who would be on the receiving end of a frantic rant about lunch specials, food delivery timing, the state of the salad bar, or even the state of the world? But today, she didn't start on her usual rant. Instead, she stood quietly in front of the swinging doors, hands clasped at her waist.

"What's going on?" Hudson whispered to Roz.

"Some shakeup or something now that Clay is gone is my guess," she whispered back, moving closer enough to him so their shoulders touched.

"You smell like oatmeal soap," he whispered.

"That was a supremely nice shower," she said.

His mind flashed back to six hours earlier. Clock-in for him at the restaurant was seven in the morning. but Roz didn't have to be on shift until ten today. He spent the night at her place and set the alarm for six, intending to slip out of bed quietly, but he woke up an hour before the alarm went off.

It was still dark outside. The glow from a streetlight lit the attic apartment she rented in a converted 19th century old-Portland brick mansion that once belonged to a wealthy newspaper family. Roz was sleeping with her head on his chest, and he watched her pale, delicate shoulder gently rise and fall with each breath. He marveled at the curve of her shoulder, her long, soft red hair spilling out across his chest like velvet fire, the freckles on her nose and her tiny, delicate snores.

As he was trying to figure out how to get out of her bed without waking her, she let out a little sigh and opened her eyes, momentarily confused and then happy at the sight of him. She trailed her hand down his chest and then gripped him lightly.

"You're awake," he said.

"You too," she said sleepily, squeezing him gently.

"How can it be you're awake when you were snoring like thirty seconds ago?"

"I do not snore," she said. "If I was, it was just pretend." She moved her hand with a careful rhythm.

He laughed softly and closed his eyes, relaxing into the pleasure of her touch.

"Do you like morning sex?" she asked.

"Apparently, very much so," he said.

"Well, come on then. I want you inside me before you leave."

She moved onto her side, and he cradled her body in a spoon position. He ran his hand over the curve of her hip and then reached over and slipped his hand between her thighs, feeling the warmth and wetness there.

He moved his fingers slowly, gently, and when she moaned, he nearly came just from the sound of her pleasure. He sucked in a breath to keep control and then, after asking if she was ready, pushed himself inside her, and they rocked together with electric slowness.

She pressed her back against him, and he kept his fingers busy, all the while pushing into her, then out again and in. It didn't take long before Roz shuddered as an orgasm began to overtake her. He held himself to shallow thrusts, waiting until she was on the trembling verge, and then pushed in deep as they climaxed together.

In the golden glow of the moment, they sank back into

the bed. Roz shoved a pillow under her head. Hudson tugged on the blanket that had slipped to the side, covered her with it, and wrapped his arms around her again, snuggling into their shared heat and blissful lethargy.

"For someone who says he has so little experience and hasn't been with anyone in four years, how can you make me feel so good every time?"

"You bring out the best in me," he said, kissing the back of her neck.

Later, they showered together. He used her oatmeal soap to lather up his hands and caress every square inch of her body. Now, the smell of that soap brought back all those heady feelings. He sensed the heat building in her, too.

She nudged him in the ribs to bring him back to the present. "We have to pay attention," she whispered.

"First announcement," Ione said. "LuRon is our new head chef. I can't imagine that's much of a surprise to anyone."

"Congratulations, LuRon," Molly said. Everyone started clapping. Standing behind the grill, LuRon smiled broadly.

Other than Clay, LuRon had been the biggest influence on Hudson since he started working at the Rose and Thorn, never riffing on him for being in prison and taking the skills he had learned there seriously. He was relieved LuRon was in charge now. Maybe the daily dildo conversations would decline.

"It won't be easy filling Clay's shoes, but he left me a few of his secret recipes. Between that and some ideas I have for new dishes focused on African American cooking, we're going to start a new culinary chapter," LuRon said.

"That leaves us down a line cook," Rob said, a hint of irritation in his tone.

Hudson wondered if Rob had expected to get the head chef job.

Ione paused, and her silence made Rob squirm a little. "Eventually, we'll add a new cook, but not immediately. And that brings me to my next announcement. I'm sure you've noticed the slowdown, and we are facing some harsh economic times—"

"Isn't Gilroy leaving too?" Rob interrupted. "That will put us two down cooks. That's a lot of slack to pick up."

"If you're not careful, we'll be down three," Ione said. She paused again, closed her eyes and put her hands on her hips. "That was uncalled for. Rob, you're a valuable employee even when you can't keep your mouth shut and talk about inappropriate things. Gilroy won't be leaving until the assignment from the Peace Corps comes through."

"Could be a day, could be six months," Gilroy said. "I requested a French-speaking country, so that constrains the options somewhat." He flipped a veggie sandwich on sourdough—spinach and mushrooms drizzled with aioli pesto—onto a plate, then added a side salad of pasta mixed with asparagus.

"Rizza, votre ordre est arrive," he said, ringing the bell.

"What?" Rizza asked.

"Order up," Gilroy said. "Just practicing."

Rizza carried the plate into the dining room. Hudson liked her, and he knew Roz did, too. She was on a student visa from Jordan, studying for a degree in nursing. This was her first time in the United States, and she worked at the Rose and Thorn as much to get a taste of the culture outside of college life as she was to perfect her English. She didn't need the money, a fact made clear because she always way over-tipped bussers and the kitchen staff. Hudson couldn't make out how she went home after each shift with much left.

"Second announcement. There will be no layoffs, but that means making do without any new hires," Ione said. "At least for now. For those of you in the kitchen who want to pick up extra hours, you'll get paid time and a half. It's not a requirement to pick up shifts, but it would help."

"I'll do it," Gilroy said. "Never going to turn down the extra money. Plus, you've been good to us."

"Thanks," LuRon said.

"I'm good with some overtime," Hudson said. He hated the idea of spending time away from Roz, but the extra money would help beef up his savings, and the lawyers at the Justice Project could maybe use the extra hours to demonstrate his good character.

LuRon, Gilroy and Hudson stared at Rob.

"What? Of course, I'll do it, you know I will. Bondage gear is expensive," Rob said.

"Thanks, everyone. With this team, we'll have a line around the block in no time," LuRon said.

"Okay, third announcement. I'm pregnant."

The men in the kitchen looked stunned. The women smiled.

Roz whispered to Hudson. "It's been obvious for a while. No alcohol. Hungry all the time. Puking."

"You and Dara will have babies about the same time," LuRon said.

"Looks that way," Ione said. "The pregnancy won't affect my work or anything about the restaurant. But since I'm beginning to show, it seemed best to say something."

Rizza came back into the kitchen. "The dining room is filling up. I need you out there," she said to Roz and Meredith. She noticed the charged atmosphere and added, "Did I miss something?"

"I'm with child," Ione said. "LuRon, what are my

specials?"

"We've got honey-barbecue chicken or soy curls with sweet potato fries and collards, and an asparagus pasta tossed in a pepper and lemon zest dressing, with garlic bread. Server samples ready in ten," he said.

The kitchen staff exploded into action, but the second Ione and Molly left the room, everyone stopped.

"I remember when Dara and I announced we were pregnant a while back, Ione said children should be banned. I thought she hated kids," LuRon said.

"She's gonna be one tough-ass mom," Rob said.

"She's a committed polyamorist and hates monogamy. How does a person get pregnant in that situation?" Gilroy asked.

"The same way as always," Roz said. "Just makes paternity a little less clear."

"Which has advantages," Meredith said. "And jibes with her polyamory because that whole approach is a rejection of monogamy and its offshoot, the nuclear family, both of which are patriarchal and meant to keep women under control."

"I sorta understand that," Gilroy said. "Kind of out there, but it's hard not to agree that women get the raw end of the deal in marriage and child-rearing."

"Marriage isn't for the faint-hearted, that's for sure," LuRon said. "Rob, got those sweet potatoes ready for the fryer?"

"Just about," Rob said, slicing the last of a mountain of peeled sweet potatoes. "That's some bullshit there. Marriage keeps women under control? Marriage is a ball and chain to men's natural sexual appetite."

"You're telling me that in all your sex-cons and fetish meetings, along with your own personal life," Meredith said, giving him side-eye, "you can honestly say women's appetites are less than men?"

"Okay, enough. We got to take this sex talk down a notch or two, and it starts now," LuRon said. "As the new head chef, I get the last word. Rob, I've been married eight years, and I can tell you, the sex has never been better."

Hudson smiled and returned to prepping a case of collards for the lunch special as Roz slipped back into the dining room.

"All I know is she's going be a bear to work with," Rob said. "All those hormones bouncing around."

"That's probably true," Meredith said as she took a bite of the soy curls LuRon placed in the order window. "Oh, wow. I love meat, but these are amazing."

LuRon smiled as he slid the plate of asparagus pasta into the window and waved for Roz and Rizza to come by. "I've been reading those cookbooks you showed me, Hudson."

"I wonder who the father is," Gilroy asked to no one in particular.

"When do you think she's due?" Rob asked.

"By the looks of it, I'd guess a mid-summer baby," Meredith said.

"Privacy, people," LuRon said. He was zesting a pile of lemons for the pasta special. "Ione is one of us. She'll tell us what she wants when she wants. Our job is to support her now. Agree?"

Everyone murmured their agreement. Hudson was relieved LuRon was reeling in the kitchen banter. He grabbed two bunches of collards and laid them on the cutting board, slicing them along their spine and then chiffonading the dark green leaves.

He could still smell the oatmeal soap and couldn't stop smiling.

18

June 18, 1992—Three years and ten months before the protest

A stranger's apartment, Portland, Oregon

Roz woke up to the sound of a bird. Harsh. Insistent. An avian jackhammer. A jay, likely. Roz opened her eyes, then squeezed them shut.

She should close the window and shut the curtains, stop the shrill cawing and block the morning sun. The insides of her eyelids felt like they were being blistered by the brightness, but the dull, relentless thumping in her head kept her immobile.

Her whole body hurt. She was face-down on the floor, her cheek pressed into a cheap fake oriental carpet that smelled like beer and dust and a little like urine. Her mouth felt like she had been chewing cotton.

"Oh, fuck," she whispered as her brain cells began to snap back into place. "What did I do?"

She sat up too quickly and had to steady herself to catch her breath. A quilt slipped off her body. She was naked. Well, not completely naked, she realized, lifting the blanket to check. She was wearing panties and one sock.

She looked around. The practical need to figure out where she was and assess her safety kept the rising panic at bay. This was not the first time.

Looking around, she didn't recognize the apartment.

She stood. Her head objected by throbbing even harder. She stumbled and leaned against the wall, waited for the worst of the vertigo to pass, then started looking for her clothes. She found her other sock and polka-dotted blouse on the back of the sofa and her pink bra on the kitchen table. She dressed silently, methodically, and then tip-toed down a short corridor, hoping to find a bathroom. And her pants. And shoes. And purse. Fuck, fuck, fuck, she screamed inside her head. Why do I do this?

She passed by a tiny bedroom where a man was passed out on the bed, face-down, snoring loudly, with two women snuggled in beside him. He didn't have on pants. His pale bottom jiggled with each deep, wet, ragged snore.

The bathroom was across the hall. She found her jeans next to the toilet, which was full of someone's puke. Shutting the door behind her quietly, not wanting to wake anyone up, she flushed and then peed and flushed again. With some relief, she realized she didn't feel tender down there, it didn't feel like she'd had sex, consensually or otherwise.

Roz pulled on her jeans and looked in the mirror.

The weave of the carpet was imprinted on her cheek. She picked bits and pieces of fiber from her hair, then smoothed down the tangles. She had cut into a super cute shag yesterday. Today, it was an unrecognizable mess. Her makeup was wrecked, and her mascara had run enough to give her greenish raccoon eyes. But there were no bruises—on her face or anywhere else, at least none that had bloomed yet.

She turned on the faucet and stuck her mouth under, taking a long drink. The cold water energized her, so she splashed some on her face and rubbed off the ruined makeup with a soggy towel draped over the shower rod. When she glanced down into the trash can next to the sink, she saw a used condom.

The last thing she remembered was having fun at Dante's downtown. A club on West Burnside. Dancing, but not drinking. Roz had been sober for a good six months, and last night was the first time since she started attending AA that she had ventured out. She felt strong. Her sponsor warned against it but didn't try to stop her.

She remembered looking and feeling great, reveling in all the attention she attracted on the dance floor, chatting up the bartender and the waitresses. In the middle of Heatmiser's first set, she saw Camille's high school boyfriend on the edge of the dance floor. She hadn't seen Connor since right after Camille disappeared. What was he doing in Portland?

She realized he was ripped when they slipped into a corner to talk—slurred words, dramatic gestures, forgetting his point in the middle of a sentence. He said he knew what happened to Camille, but Roz could only remember fragments of their conversation now in the morning light ... *your dad was an asshole, no wonder she got in trouble ... her fault for quitting school ... prison fucking hard.*

Roz had been in touch with Camille regularly since the first prison visit about a year ago. She moved to Portland to be closer so she could visit more often. They talked at least two or three times a month on the phone, and she mailed her a letter each week, often with a poem. She knew the prison read their letters and listened in on their calls, so she was careful. She also knew Camille was miserable, sad and terrified.

That knowledge, together with seeing Connor, derailed her. She had a drink—what was the harm in one—and then couldn't stop, didn't want to stop. It all felt so good and numb and comfortable and familiar. She couldn't remember anything from after the music ended.

Roz sat down on the toilet and put her head in her hands. Just as a sob threatened to tear loose, there was a knock at the door.

"Hello? I need to pee."

Roz wiped her eyes and opened the door. It was one of the girls from the bedroom. She was tiny and pale, with jet-black hair. Barely twenty, if even. Roz nodded and stepped into the hall. The girl closed the door behind her. Roz peeked inside the bedroom again. The man turned over, but the second woman was still passed out. Oh, for fuck's sake, she thought. It was Connor.

Did I really sleep with my sister's ex in a drunken haze? She had to get out of there. She scanned the living room for her purse. She found it in the kitchenette. She fished out Emma's number and punched the numbers into the wall phone with trembling fingers.

"Hello?" Emma said.

Roz paused, the words refusing to come. Six months of sobriety wrecked. And for what?

"Roz?" Emma asked. "Is that you? Are you okay?"

"I shouldn't have gone," Roz said, crying. "You were right."

"Where are you?" Emma asked.

"I … don't … know … where I am," she said, struggling for air.

"7413 Southeast Division," said the tiny girl, out of the bathroom now and standing behind Roz.

"I heard that," Emma said. "I'm on my way. Can you get yourself outside?"

"Yes, please hurry," Roz said. She took a deep breath, regained control and hung up the phone.

"You were really drunk last night," the tiny girl said.

Roz nodded. "Did anything, you know, happen?"

"Yeah, you threw up on me," the girl said. "I had to

practically carry you in here. Then, you danced around like some *Flashdance* maniac and took your shirt off. Said your boobs were like a poem, and you had to share them because that's what you do with art."

Roz felt an overwhelming sense of shame. Her head was still pounding, and she could feel the tears welling up behind her eyes again. She was such an idiot.

"I'm sorry," Roz whispered.

"Don't worry about it. You're a pretty good dancer. And you do have nice boobs."

Roz tried to smile but couldn't force it. She turned toward the apartment door, her body turned inward with self-loathing.

"And hey," the girl said. "Nothing else happened. You know, nothing like what you're worried about. Connor was drunk, too. He couldn't have done anything even though he wanted to. He sure did cheer you on when you took your shirt off though."

Roz turned back around and impulsively hugged the tiny girl. The girl squirmed out of the embrace. "You know, you should probably dump him. Doesn't seem like he's changed much since high school," Roz said.

"We're not together," she said. "I just dig his girl."

Outside the apartment, Roz sat on the bench near a bus stop. She was dying of thirst and doing her best to keep from vomiting.

Twenty minutes later, Emma pulled up in a light blue Ford Pinto. The right fender was dented. Roz got in. Emma, a woman in her fifties with warm brown eyes, short salt-and-pepper hair and turquoise dangly earrings, leaned across the seat to embrace her fiercely, protectively.

Pulling back, Emma said, "You okay?"

"Physically, yeah."

"I made some calls. I can get you a rehab bed today.

You should take it."

"Rehab?" Roz asked, startled by the thought of it.

"Honey, you need it. Give it four weeks, trust me. It's a nice place, a clinic in an old Portland house in a lovely neighborhood. You can come and go as you please, but you'll have support, decent coffee and meals, and twice-daily group therapy sessions. Let's get you through this rough patch."

Roz thought back to waking up on the floor less than an hour ago, mostly naked, with zero memory of the night before. The shame flowed over her again. She could feel her face burning. She had to change.

"How will I work, pay my rent, all that?" Roz asked.

"I have a friend. She helps fund things like this."

"Do I have to pay her back?"

"No. And it's anonymous. She won't know your name. But afterward, you may want to look her up. Her name is Molly. She owns the Rose and Thorn restaurant."

"Okay," she said. "I'll try."

"One more thing," Emma said. "This clinic is for artists, writers and creative types. Some of the sessions will focus on your art. Embrace that."

"I'm not an artist," Roz said.

"Sure, you are," Emma said. "I've read your poetry. I got you something for the next few weeks. Open the bag."

Roz opened the brown paper bag at her feet. Inside was a beautiful leather-bound journal with a graceful tree, a Douglas fir embossed on the cover, and a thick used paperback from Powell's Bookstore.

"What's this?"

"The book is the Best Poetry of 1990," Emma said. "Something to read and inspire you for a month. The journal is to capture that inspiration, process what you're going through, and dream of a different future for yourself.

There are a couple of pens in there, too."

"Do you think poetry can save me?"

"It's saved plenty of drunks before you," Emma said with a smile.

"Harsh," Roz said, tracing her finger over the tree on the blank journal. "But accurate.

19

June 19, 1992—Four years and ten months before the protest

Eastern Oregon Correctional Institute, Pendleton, Oregon

Hudson looked down at the knife wound in disbelief. Blood was pooling out from between his fingers. He felt a little unsteady.

"Shit, son, how did you cut yourself so bad on your first day?" Bernard asked.

Bernard, a tall man in his 60s, originally from Detroit, had five years left on a second-degree murder conviction. He was guilty and never disputed it. He killed his abusive stepfather with a hammer when the bastard hit his mom right in front of him. His mom, now 80 and hunched with age, came to see him once a month.

In Detroit, he worked at a busy sandwich shop. For the last 15 years, he ran the prison kitchen.

"I thought they were sending me someone who knew how to cook," Bernard muttered. "Turns out you're another junkie trying to get some pain pills from the doctor. Well, get on out of here and get your fix. I have dinner to prep and we're down two sets of good hands. Losing one more set of bad hands won't make a difference."

Bernard was not in a great mood. He lost one prep cook

to early release and his best cook through a transfer to another facility. He knew it was just because the warden there liked Pierre's hollandaise sauce.

Hudson shook his head. "No, sir, that is not the case, I did not cut myself on purpose. I want to learn how to cook. I want to learn something useful, something employable, for when I get out."

"Now I know you're lying," Bernard muttered. "Ain't nobody hire felons. Ever."

"Please, can we just pretend this never happened?"

Bernard glared at his finger, then shrugged. "I can't have you bleeding all over my mashed potatoes. Let's get you bandaged up. How the hell did you cut the *back* of your knuckles? That's some neat trick."

Hudson shook his head. "I was trying to rip the plastic off that cauliflower to cut it, like you asked, and my knife fell off the board and wedged against the wall with the blade up. When the plastic gave way …"

"You punched your blade," Bernard said. He shook his head. "You won't do that again, I bet. Don't look too bad." He carefully wrapped gauze around the sliced knuckles, taped them and then shook three rubber cots out of a box. "Slide these on, like finger condoms. They'll keep the germs out and the blood in, at least until we finish prep."

Hudson followed his directions and then stood expectantly. "Now what?"

"I guess I need to teach you how to use a knife without losing a finger and then maybe how flames are hot, and in a year or two, you might be able to scramble an egg," Bernard said.

"I look forward to eating that egg," Hudson said.

Bernard swung around, his chef's knife raised. "Are you cutting wise with me?" he asked incredulously, breaking into a grin. "Damn, son, I think you're making a joke." He pointed at the flat of cauliflower. "I still need that cut into florets. That's French for about as big as your dick head, which in your case, is pretty small. Now hold the knife the right way this time, in front of the handle." He showed Hudson how to choke up on the knife for control and safety.

Hudson laboriously made his way through the cauliflower, mangling more florets than cutting them, and then Bernard showed him how to slice mushrooms and aimed him at two flats of them. After that, he motioned Hudson over to show him how he was making gravy.

Bernard and his other prep cooks spooned mounds of mashed potatoes, peas and carrots, cauliflower and Salisbury steak smothered in mushroom gravy into the steam tables. He dished Hudson a serving and motioned for him to sit back by the walk-in to eat.

"One of the perks of working in the kitchen," Bernard said. "You always eat well. Or at least you go back to your cell full."

After his shift ended, Hudson was taken to the nurse station, where they cleaned up the wounds and put in two stitches on each knuckle.

The guard was escorting him to his cell, and Hudson asked if he could stop at the library. The guard, Hector, was relatively "kind" to him. In other words, he didn't play the power games most of the guards were so good at, finding a million ways to remind Hudson they were in control of every aspect of his life.

He picked up three cookbooks: *The Joy of Cooking*, *Mastering the Art of French Cooking* and the *Moosewood Cookbook*.

The inmate working behind the desk, heavy-set with a shaved head and a crude devil tattooed on his forearm, stamped the books. He tapped the Moosewood. "You into this vegetarian shit?"

"I've been thinking about it," Hudson said.

The man reached for another book. *Animal Liberation* by Peter Singer. "You might like this. I don't think it's supposed to be on our shelves, so read it fast."

"Thanks, Tiny," Hudson said. Hector walked him back to his cell and let him in. He nodded at his cellmate, Wayne, and crawled up to the top bunk.

"Dinner was good tonight," Wayne said. "Was that down to you?"

"I helped prep some of it."

"I heard you got cut," Wayne said.

"News travels fast in a prison."

Wayne snorted, a contorted sound due to a nose that had been broken three times that ended up in a brief coughing fit. "All we got is time and other people's business. You get any pills?"

Hudson let his breath out slowly. "No."

He wasn't exactly scared of Wayne, but he didn't trust him either. He missed Craig, his first cellmate. Craig talked a lot about animals and his belief that people didn't have rights to animals' lives or bodies, said he wanted to help usher in a new era of global empathy. Hudson didn't agree with everything Craig said—some of it was pretty out there—or his tactics, but his values seemed solid. Kind, even. Craig was in prison because he released a bunch of minks from a farm where they were destined to become fur coats. He got released from his own captivity a few weeks back.

Wayne, on the other hand, was doing time for aggravated assault and attempted murder. He beat up his ex and her boyfriend. Pretty bad to hear him tell it. Hudson knew people tended to exaggerate—in prison, the worse the reputation, the wider the berth—but Wayne had a weird smile when he talked about it. Hudson recognized that his cellmate was violent and unpredictable. Access to drugs, more precious than diamonds here, would make everything worse.

"Why the fuck not?" Wayne asked, kicking the bottom of the mattress above him hard enough to jar Hudson. "They'll give you pain pills for any-fucking-thing."

"I'm not a fan of the pharmaceuticals," Hudson said.

"Great," Wayne muttered, wiping his nose on his sleeve. "I have to end up with the hippiest dip-shit in the place. If they were doling out joints, you'd have your hand out then."

Hudson cracked open *Animal Liberation* and read the forward.

"You get hurt again, you ask for some pills. Trust me," Wayne said. "You could use some goodwill, some protection. People don't like you. You act like you're better than everyone."

"I don't think that at all," Hudson said. "I do think I'm innocent. I mean, I know I'm innocent."

"Yeah, aren't we all," Wayne said, kicking the mattress again.

"You brag about your crime. I actually didn't do what they accused me of."

"That's not what I heard," Wayne said. "I heard you got snitched out for being the ringleader. The feds got you."

He was too interested, Hudson realized. He was trying to learn something useful to trade up—better conditions, a shorter sentence, anything to lessen the burden. Dirt on other inmates, Hudson was learning, was only slightly less valuable than drugs.

"I was literally in a tree in a forest the night it happened," Hudson said.

"Who put the finger on you?"

"I don't know."

"You should talk to that group, that innocence group. What's the name? Oh yeah, the Portland Justice Project. I mean, if you're really squeaky clean, they could get you out of here. A handsome kid like you, even if you are a little on the brown side, that's right up their alley."

"Maybe I will," Hudson said. He put down the philosophy book and picked up the *Moosewood Cookbook*. "I want to learn how to cook before I get released."

"You're an odd one, Hudson," Wayne said. "I don't like odd. You turn down drugs again, you're gonna wish you had some painkillers, got it?"

"Got it," Hudson said.

He read the recipe for carrot soup with almonds, then closed the book and imagined himself eating a bowl of it while sitting high in Sophie, listening to the wind rustle the leaves and watching the stars wheel around in the sky.

So far, at least, a tree was his longest and most meaningful relationship. And it was unlikely she was even still standing. Someone down the hall screamed, jarring him out of his escapist reveries. He couldn't tell if it was a scream of anger or happiness.

"Keep it down, inmates," a guard shouted.

He opened the cookbook and read another recipe. This one was for Hungarian mushroom soup.

20

May 1, 1996—May Day Protest

Across the street from Fleet Motors

Hudson sat on the curb, butt cheeks numb and legs stiff from not moving. Close to two hours had passed, and Roz was still angry; he could feel it radiating from her like dark matter. She wouldn't look at or talk to him, maintaining a defiant silence since her earlier eruption.

He was starting to feel desperate. He hadn't thought things through clearly enough other than keeping Roz safe, but in hindsight, his plan was impulsive at best. And shortsighted. Now, stuck in the middle of it all, the endpoint was coming into view, and he didn't much like what he saw.

Even if this went exactly as he feared, even if the protest devolved into violence and his plan kept Roz safe and free of blame, things would never be the same between them. Roz was not going to be in his life in any form, not even as a friend. That revelation came with a pressing heaviness on his chest.

Roz was in an impossible spot. Choosing between him and her sister, she would always choose family because it was far easier to assume he was the liar. He probably would, too, if he had any family. He wasn't even all that angry with Moon. Maybe he would have done the same thing. Who knows? None of this would matter except that the woman he loved was Moon's sister. He was still blown away by the odds of it all.

After looking into his case, his lawyer uncovered that the DA had agreed to shorten Moon's sentence if she named anyone else involved. She was one of three people they arrested, but investigators found evidence that others helped plan the fire-bombing.

The way Hudson figured it, Moon was offered a deal. Finger her collaborators and get a reduced sentence. She was new to the direct action movement and likely didn't know anyone in the Earth Freedom Front, so she picked him. An easy choice for a scared young woman who was no doubt being leaned on heavily. Drop the name of some random activist guy she barely knew to knock some time off her sentence.

He imagined the conversation: *I'm telling you, it was Alpine, he was behind it all. He slipped down from the tree one night and showed us all how to make Molotov cocktails with plastic milk jugs filled with gasoline with a bandana shoved in the spout as a wick. A recipe straight from The Anarchist's Cookbook. Yeah, that's right, he picked the target and then snuck back to Sophie the next day without anyone ever seeing him.*

Hudson tried to tell the DA and anyone who would listen that he was in the tree the whole time the fire-bombing was going down, but no one believed him. The DA's office was intent on rolling up the Earth Freedom Front cells in Oregon to impress the FBI and the joint terrorism task force—plus, the DA was running for congress on a tough-on-crime platform—and Hudson got rolled up right along with it all.

Within a month, Hudson was in prison for arson and bomb-making. His first night behind bars was Halloween. He had never felt more scared or lonely than that night.

Although he was starting to feel pretty lonely now.

In prison, Hudson scoured the newspapers for information about the fire-bombing, trying to understand what happened and why he was taking the fall. There was nothing about him, which is how he knew someone cut a deal, and the deal included protection.

At that stage, the worst part of the entire ordeal was that no one noticed he was gone. No one visited him. There was no one for him to call. After getting locked up, he became an invisible man lost inside the prison system. A living ghost. It was terrifying.

He watched Roz take a sip from her water bottle, then put two sticks of Dentyne in her mouth. They didn't even look remotely alike, Roz and Camille. They were stepsisters, he knew now, but how could he have known they were related? What were the chances that he would not only meet but fall for the stepsister of the random girl who left him a warm beer that night years ago on the tree-sitting platform?

He felt bad for Camille, bad for how easily the Earth Freedom Front had pulled her in—a lost girl with a broken family—and made her feel like she was being heroic in the name of Mother Earth. The people in the EFF weren't bad, far from it. They believed in saving the Earth and committed only property destruction to make their points, never violence against people. But what they did was still illegal, and, in a way, that law-breaking was the glue between them; their willingness to risk their freedom—and the adrenaline that came with each direct action—bound them tightly. After Roz told him about her childhood in Coos Bay, he understood all too well how Camille might have wanted to belong to something bigger than herself.

He thought back again to that night in the tree with Moon. Was there anything else he should have done to keep her from leaving? He didn't think so, but what did it matter? He couldn't turn back time. Could he change the future? Maybe a way out of this mess was to find a path to help Roz's sister. Maybe his lawyer could help Camille.

"If you leave with me now, and we go far enough away from here that you can't ditch me and come right back, I'll uncuff us," Hudson said. "We can figure out a way to help your sister—"

"I thought you didn't have the key," she said, then stamped her foot.

"I can get a message to LuRon," he said.

"Why would I think you would help Camille? You can't prove anything you've told me. Where's the proof of anything?" Roz was biting her nails even as she chewed her gum angrily.

Hudson held his breath. There was an opening in her words. She was asking for proof.

His mind raced. How could he prove it? Any printed files linking to Camille as the confidential informant were heavily redacted, and even if he could track down the original FBI detective who arrested him or get his lawyer from the Portland Justice Project to talk to Roz, he didn't see much hope that Camille would change her story. Why would she? She had too much to lose, like years of her life.

This would always be Camille's word against his.

"I was right. You have no proof," Roz said.

"Not the kind you need," he said.

Hudson stretched out his long legs. He flicked away a few pieces of gravel stuck in his palm and pulled a pair of pocket binoculars out of his pack.

He looked at the faces of the protestors through the binoculars. Now that the initial adrenaline rush had passed, fatigue, or maybe boredom, had set in. Only one man was still thumping the bongo and without much conviction.

Their voices were tired from chanting, and some were probably getting hungry. The protest ringleader hadn't said it was okay to leave, so the hopeful, earnest members of the Eco Artist Collective milled around, those not cuffed delivering power bars and smiles to those handcuffed to SUVs.

"What are you doing?" Roz asked.

He shifted the binocular's focus to the reporters. Two more had shown up a little while ago from another station, and now along with Caroline Bentley, were chatting up each other, laughing and smoking on the sidewalk.

"It's about to go down," he said.

"Your imaginary violent protest?" she asked.

Hudson knew this was exactly the moment—tired protestors, distracted cops, but before the media left—when the Earth Freedom Front would act. Even though he was never a member, his first prison cellmate was. Craig had been involved in the part of the Front focused on saving animals—research rats, wild horses, minks. Hudson and Craig became friends.

The Front operated in a classic cell model, meaning no individual member knew the identity of any other, so no one could ever implicate anyone else. In theory, a member transmitted an order from an anonymous leader, almost always by fax, to an above-ground representative who served exclusively as a communication liaison and was never involved in any illegal actions. This kept their voice to the public safe from arrest.

That was the theory, but it wasn't really like that. There were too many anarchist types trying to burnish their anti-capitalist reputations in Portland to maintain that level of anonymity. In fact, Hudson recognized the wild orange hair of one of the three people he had watched slip into the SUV lot earlier. A guy he played basketball with at the state university. The other two were unfamiliar, but he was sure they knew each other. Probably carpooled to the protest.

"What's that?" Roz asked, cautious alarm in her voice. An acrid smell wafted above the protestors.

"Smoke bombs," he said. "Come on, let's stand," he said, dragging her up as he stood, the links of the cuffs dangling between them. Their hands brushed against each other, and even now, in this awful situation, Hudson felt the sparks.

They watched a black cloud of smoke billowing out from behind a red SUV on the far side of the lot. Seconds later, another cloud spread around the opposite side of the lot, followed by a third on the western edge.

He soaked a blue bandana with water and gave it to Roz. "Tie this around your neck and use it to wash out your eyes if they start to sting."

"It's not tear gas," Roz said. "Just fireworks."

"Please," he said. "This is about to get worse. You'll need it."

She yanked the wet bandana from his hand and turned her back to him, lifting her long hair. He knotted the scarf around her neck, loose enough so she could pull it over her face.

Two new cop cars roared up to the lot, sirens blaring, followed by a police van. The media team pulled out their microphones and hoisted video cameras, ready to roll again. On cue, the protest ringleader picked up his megaphone.

"What do we want?" he yelled.

"Free the eco-warriors!" the protestors shouted back.

"When do we want it?"

"Now!"

"It won't be long," Hudson said. "Get ready."

She turned to face him. "Remind me again how you

know all this protest stuff if you're not part of them?" she asked. "How was my sister so wrong about you?"

Across the street, there was a sudden whoosh, and orange flames lit up the sky—she could see it reflected off his face—followed by a brief haunting silence and then panicked screams.

"Shit," Hudson said, reaching out to shield her.

She struggled out of his embrace and swiveled her neck. An SUV was on fire. As they watched, a second explosion lit up. Hudson hoped the gas tanks weren't full. Protesters were scattering, and a girl was in flames, holding her burning arm in front of her and screaming. Two salesmen ran from inside the dealership and wrapped their sports coats around her to smother the flames. The police were shouting orders and tackling people as they ran past. The protestors cuffed to SUVs seemed unhurt, even though the fire-bombed SUVs were only two rows over.

"Good fucking thing you hippies have an alibi," a cop snarled as he lumbered past them, reaching for his baton.

Sirens wailed in the background as fire trucks sped toward the scene.

"You were right," Roz whispered.

Hudson pulled out a bright yellow snorkel mask from his knapsack. "Put this on," he said.

21

March 11, 1996—One month and two weeks before the protest

The Rose and Thorn restaurant

"Kind of a shit day, yeah?" Rob said, exhaling.

It was raining lightly but relentlessly, and a depressing fog blanketed the city. Hudson watched as the mist swirled and mixed with smoke from Rob's cigarette, creating a fresh, lacey web with each exhale.

"These are the days I can't wait to get to Haiti or Senegal or wherever the Peace Corps ends up sending me," Gilroy said.

Rob exhaled a final time, and the intricate floating pattern materialized again and then vanished almost as quickly.

"This weather makes me wish I was down in California with Clay. Maybe he'll hit it big and get a fleet of food trucks, need a new cook," Rob said.

"When do you think the Peace Corps will call?" Hudson asked.

"Any day now. I'm itching to go, ready for something new and to escape this weather. I for sure don't want to be in this city ever again when it snows," Gilroy said.

Two weeks earlier, Portland experienced a rare snowstorm. It didn't last long, melting in two days, but that didn't stop the entire city from shutting down. Schools closed, wrecks and abandoned cars clogged the streets, highways were backed up for miles, and power outages hop-scotched around neighborhoods. The Rose and Thorn closed early, and with city bus service curtailed, Hudson ended up walking to Roz's place, where they kept each other warm for the duration of the storm.

Unlike Gilroy, Hudson had fond memories of that snowstorm. He smiled, thinking about it.

"People around here drive like idiots when the roads are icy," Rob said. "I grew up in Minnesota. It's not that hard. Learn to drive or stay home."

"Seriously," Gilroy said. He rubbed his eyes tiredly. "I wish I smoked on days like this," he said, pantomiming Rob for a minute with an invisible cigarette.

Rob rolled his eyes.

"How come you don't smoke, Hudson? Seems like prison is the perfect place to pick up bad habits," Gilroy asked, ending the mimic by pretending to stub out a cigarette with his foot.

Hudson shrugged, a little surprised by the question. Gilroy was usually more sensitive about his prison time. They all were at the Rose and Thorn. Nobody ever asked him anything. At first, he was comforted by that, but now the silence was starting to feel awkward. Not that he necessarily wanted to talk about it. Talking tended to bring up memories he'd rather leave in the past.

"I smoked for a minute or two, it just never stuck," Hudson said. "But you aren't wrong. Almost everyone in prison smokes. Helps pass the time, I guess. It's not a place where anyone worries about staying healthy. Or living long."

The three cooks were outside, taking a forced break from the kitchen while the county health inspector did a surprise walk-through with Ione and LuRon. Hudson hoped nothing was wrong at his station. He kept everything squeaky clean all the time, but Molly swore she saw a mouse earlier in the week. That was a bad day.

"How do people in prison get money for smokes?" Rob asked. "Do they cage-fight for them? Trade sexual favors?"

Hudson grinned and shook his head. "Nothing so dramatic. You can buy cigarettes and other stuff, like Pringles, root beer and Milky Ways at the prison canteen."

"That's pretty specific," Rob said. "Are you a fan of Pringles, root beer and Milky Ways?"

"Not anymore, that's for sure," Hudson said. "Wives and girlfriends and family, whoever, are allowed to send money. There's a limit, ten dollars and some change a month. Also, inmates in good standing earn money at prison jobs."

"What kind of jobs?" Gilroy asked.

"Cooking, which is how I learned to cook, and laundry mostly."

"I hate doing laundry. Is that a service people like me can sign up for?" Rob asked. "Prison Clean?"

"It's not for individuals. It's for big places with tons of laundry, like hospitals. An 18-wheeler pulled up almost every day. The hospitals pay the prison a wage for the inmates' time, and then the prison takes a giant cut and pays the inmates slave wages to do the work. Ten cents an hour."

"Ten cents!" Gilroy and Rob shouted simultaneously.

"It's better than zero. Inmates save up and use it to buy snacks, smokes and other junk at jacked-up prices at the canteen. The prison makes a profit on incarceration from every angle."

"Cycle of capitalism," Gilroy said.

"Did you get paid piss-poor wages like that to work in

the kitchen?"

"Yeah, and I blew it all on Pringles."

Rob and Gilroy laughed, then returned to trying to stay warm.

Rob clapped his hands together, and Gilroy stamped his feet. Hudson put his hands in his pockets. None had a chance to grab coats before LuRon shooed them out of the kitchen.

"How long do these things usually take?" Hudson asked.

"Depends on what they find," Rob said.

"What happens if they find something bad? Like a mouse. You know, would a person get fired? I mean, I do my best and all, but accidents can happen and . . ." Hudson didn't like that his voice sounded nervous. He was feeling anxious, and he started breathing faster.

Gilroy glanced at Rob, then back at Hudson. "No one is getting fired today. You're doing a good job," Gilroy said. He reached out and put his hand on Hudson's shoulder. "It must be hard thinking you might have to go back there anytime."

"It is," Hudson said, trying to slow his breathing. "Everything was taken from me just like that." He snapped his fingers. "Once something like that happens to you, no matter what anyone says, it's hard not to think it could happen again."

"Hey, why were you in to begin with?" Rob asked.

Hudson breathed into his cupped hands, warming his fingers. So, here it was, the question. He felt oddly relieved. Maybe talking about it could help diffuse the anxiety and relieve the low-grade, relentless fear this new life he was building might vanish like it had once before. The last time they talked, his lawyer said everything was on track, and the formal notice of his exoneration should come soon. The lawyer seemed okay with him telling a few close friends about it.

But he hadn't told Roz yet, and she should be first. It wouldn't be fair to her if, after being so patient these past months waiting for him to share why he was in prison, she heard something about it during a random rant session in the kitchen.

"Your timing is funny," Hudson said. "Just this week, my lawyer told me it was okay to talk about it."

"Why wasn't it okay to talk about it before?" Gilroy asked.

"I didn't do it."

"No offense, man, but isn't what everyone says?" Rob asked.

"Sure, I get that, but it's true. I wasn't even there. I was, well, I was somewhere else when it happened." Hudson paused, searching their faces.

"Okay, whatever you say," Gilroy said. "You don't have to talk about it."

"I'm not trying to be secretive, and I really didn't do it."

"Tell us the category of what you didn't do," Rob said. "Murder?"

"No!" Hudson said. "Nothing like that."

"Robbery?" Gilroy asked.

"No," Hudson said.

"Was robbery warmer or colder than murder?"

Hudson laughed. "This is a terrible game. What's worse than murder?"

"A double murder," Rob said.

"Robbery is warmer than murder," Hudson said.

"Are you a spy for the British government? Did you commit treason?" Rob asked.

"Yeah, Rob, I'm James Bond," Hudson said. "And now, in a fate worse than prison, I'm forced to work at a restaurant in Portland, Oregon."

"Maybe the prison was just to help establish your deep cover," Rob said.

"Your brain is an interesting place," Gilroy said. "He stroked his wispy mustache. "Okay, so robbery is warmer … was it vandalism? Wait, were you some kind of activist?"

Hudson didn't respond.

"That's it, isn't it?" Gilroy said triumphantly. "You were some kind of eco-warrior."

"You weren't part of that whole Earth Freedom Front thing, were you?" Rob asked.

Hudson was surprised Rob knew about EFF. Best not to answer that question.

"Let's just say mistakes were made, all for the sake of someone named Sophie."

"Ah, the plot thickens," Rob said. "It was a woman. Was it a kink gone wrong?"

"That's your wheelhouse, not mine," Hudson said. "I'm sorry, guys, I can't say anything else. To be honest, I haven't told Roz, and she deserves to hear the whole story first."

"Ah, man," Rob said. "But we're your friends. We won't say a word."

"I told you in confidence about the dream I had about Ione, and she literally asked me about it the next day," Hudson said.

"Busted," Gilroy said.

"Look, she scares me too, all right?" Rob said. "I'll do anything to stay in her good graces."

"Not sure how telling her my dream helped with that, but whatever," Hudson said. "I'll tell you everything right after I tell Roz. And the important part is, I really am innocent. I'll be able to prove it soon."

"What did Molly know when she hired you?"

"All she knew when she hired me is what the prison told her," Hudson said. "Making it all that much cooler that she took a chance. She knows the Portland Justice Project is involved now and that my record is about to be expunged. She's been a real advocate."

"You know Molly is a lawyer, right? She's helping Roz on something right now, something about her sister being in prison," Gilroy said.

"I didn't know that," Hudson said, wondering why Roz hadn't said anything.

"Expunged," Rob said. "That's a weird word. Sounds a little bit dirty, in a good way. Like something sexy you'd do to someone else. Expunge all over them."

"Man, why do you always have to ruin a moment?" Gilroy asked.

LuRon pushed open the door from the inside. "Break time is over. Get your asses back to work."

"Perfect timing," Hudson said. "How did it go?"

"An A-plus score, of course. What kind of kitchen do you think I run?" LuRon asked.

"The kind with mouse sightings, apparently," Gilroy said.

LuRon stopped him with a glare. "There wasn't a mouse. That was Jon's pet rat, Casper. He stowed away in Jon's backpack for an unplanned take-your-rat-to-work day. That will not happen again."

22

March 17, 1996—One month and two weeks before the protest

The Rose and Thorn restaurant

Meredith walked by with a tray of beers dyed green for Saint Patrick's Day. Her long, straight brown hair was pulled back with a green scrunchie.

"This is way too much of the wrong kind of green, if you know what I mean," Dave-two said, dumping sliced radishes into their container on the salad bar.

Roz smiled and nodded. Pot wasn't really her thing. It tended to make her anxious and paranoid—two characteristics she didn't need help amplifying—but she had smoked with Dave-two plenty of times in the past. When she was with Frank and he worked at the Rose and Thorn, Roz occasionally hung around waiting for him to get off, pleasantly buzzed and making moon-eyes at Clay.

It seemed so long ago now. Things were going so well with Hudson, and she didn't want to jinx it by thinking about the past.

A few short years ago, St. Patrick's Day was less of a celebration and more of a personal challenge to see how hard and fast she could get wasted. She'd be downing green beer and shots of Irish whisky and kissing all the leprechauns. Now, she was sober and happy, and it was enough to wear a glittery green bowtie to mark the occasion.

She walked into the kitchen to pick up her order—two plates of corned beef and cabbage and a side of colcannon. Hudson smiled through the order window. It never failed to send a shiver of pleasure up her spine.

"Are you reading something tonight, Roz?" LuRon asked, tilting the sauté pan in his hand to slide a steaming portion of pasta alfredo with rosemary chicken into a bowl.

Molly was holding one of her famous fundraisers later that night, a St. Patrick's Day poetry slam. One of the morning servers was facing eviction from her family home due to unpaid taxes. Molly was determined to help her stay put.

"I don't think so," Roz said. "The stuff I've been working on lately isn't very, I don't know, right for sharing with coworkers."

"Gross," Rob said. "That means it's all sappy love poems because she's getting it regular from H-bomb."

"No, that's not it," she said, blushing slightly.

But there was some truth to what Rob said. Her poetry was starting to reflect a happier outlook on life, more hopeful. She had to keep telling herself poetry didn't necessarily have to be angry or depressing to be good.

LuRon sprinkled parmesan cheese on the pasta, then chopped parsley for color. "Roz, you don't sound very convincing there," he said.

"All right, let's not embarrass Roz," Hudson said.

"Tell you what," she said to Rob, picking up the plates and balancing them. "I'll read something if you do."

"Deal!" Rob said.

When the dinner rush ended, Ione clicked the neon sign to *closed,* and they set up for the fundraiser. The tip jar up front was already almost full, stuffed by patrons who added ones and fives and even a couple of twenties to the cause on their way out. Staff each paid $5 for a meal and a drawing for two days off with pay. Anyone who read a poem was entered to win a new personal pocket digital assistant.

In keeping with the day, LuRon prepared a family pan of Shepherd's pie with lamb and vegetables in a savory brown gravy, topped with creamy mashed potatoes, the peaks browned from finishing in the oven. Hudson added a half-sized pan of vegan Shepherd's pie with chunks of seitan instead of lamb. Rob, in charge of sides, cooked a big bowl of garlicky braised kale along with a platter of roasted carrots with a maple ginger glaze.

As the staff event kicked off, Roz sat next to Hudson and pressed her leg against his. Then, she took his hand under the table, their fingers interlacing.

Molly was talking about how important it was for Black Portlanders to be able to stay in their homes and resist the growing tides of gentrification. Roz was trying to listen and cheer at the appropriate times, but staying focused sitting so close to Hudson was hard. Her thoughts kept swirling away to earlier that morning when, sleepy and sensual, he spooned close and slipped inside her for a slow, delicious, explosive start to the day.

A tremor of remembered pleasure rippled through her as Molly wrapped up and turned it over to Ione to emcee the poetry slam. Ione was showing and, unsurprisingly, refused to wear classic maternity clothes. Tonight, she wore thigh-high leather boots, an oversized black satin mini skirt and a man's plaid flannel shirt. Roz thought she looked phenomenal.

Over the next half-hour, four servers and one prep cook shared poems to thunderous applause. When the action slowed, Rob stood up and looked at Roz.

"A deal's a deal, right?" he asked.

She nodded as he took the microphone.

"In honor of St. Patrick's Day, I have a very special poem to recite," he said. "A limerick." He cleared his throat and held the microphone close. "There once was a man from Nantucket…"

Ione grabbed the mic. "Absolutely not," she said.

"This is censorship," Rob said. "What about freedom of speech?"

"You should read the Constitution," Ione said. "Congress isn't making any laws prohibiting your free speech. But you work for us, and if you finish that gross little limerick, we're freely going to fire your ass."

"I changed it from the original. You don't know that my version was going to be X-rated," he said.

"Yes, we do," Meredith said. "He was practicing last night."

The room erupted in laughter. Ione handed the mic to Jon. "Cool the room down. Say some bland nerd things."

Surprised, he looked at Ione—blinking like a confused owl behind his oversized glasses—then stood.

"The term limerick refers to a verse of five lines with an A A B B A rhyme scheme and has developed a reputation for nonsensical subject matter, often with sexual innuendo. It is believed to be associated with either the town or county of Limerick, both in Ireland, but no definitive links have been established," he said.

Jon took a short breath and went on.

"Some think it was related to an 18th-century song sung by Irish soldiers. The song was called *Will You Come Up to Limerick*. As soldiers do, they changed the lyrics for the sake of entertainment and bonding. Another school of thought attributes limericks to a drinking game favored by a group of poets. Interestingly, the town of Limerick was founded by Scandinavian settlers in 812. It's located at latitude…"

Ione snatched the mic back. "Thanks, Encyclopedia Brown. That's perfect. Who's next?"

"I guess I have to do it," Roz said. "A deal's a deal, even if he did get thrown off the stage." She reached in her bag for her notebook, flipped through the pages until she found what she'd been working on over lunch, then stood and reached for the microphone.

"This is called *Sometimes the Morning*. It's … well, many of you know I've had my share of struggles with booze. Anyway, this is still a draft, so it's rough, but here goes."

Sometimes, you wake alone in a world of strangers.
It is cold and bright and you can't recall
exactly where you are or how you got there,
or really anything good about yourself at all.
But then sometimes the morning, when it arrives
dawns bright and clear and burns all traces of the past.
And you hold your breath and hope
that the moment can last and last.

She closed the notebook. "That's it. That's all I've got so far."

The room was quiet. She felt a flush of embarrassment rising in the ringing silence. She looked at Hudson. His eyes shone with some entirely unreadable blend of emotions.

"My limerick would have probably beat that, but yours was pretty good," Rob said at last.

The rest of the staff started clapping. Gilroy raised his green beer to toast her but then realized it might not be appropriate. He quickly took a sip and put it down.

"Leave your votes in the tip jar," Ione said. "We'll

announce the winner tomorrow."

LuRon came rushing out of the kitchen. "Dara's in labor," he said.

The room burst into cheers again. "Go, get out of here," Ione said. She threw Rob her keys. "Drive him to the hospital or home or wherever he needs to go. Do not leave his side until he's next to Dara."

LuRon was half-laughing and half-cursing, he was so excited. Rob steered him into the kitchen to leave through the back door.

After they helped break down and clean up, with Hudson taking over LuRon's duties, Roz and Hudson walked to her apartment, holding hands, chatting here and there, but mostly in silence. Roz was feeling awkward and anxious. Had she taken things too far, too quickly? She always did, it seemed, but historically, she had blamed that on alcohol, leading to faulty decisions. Now that she was sober, could it be that she just had a built-in self-defeating flaw? Was she destined to forever sabotage her happiness? What had she been thinking, sharing such a personal poem that was clearly about Hudson? Her public display probably mortified him.

He closed the door and hung up their coats on the hook behind the door

"Listen, Roz," he said, turning back to face her.

"I'm sorry," she interrupted. "I should never have read that stupid thing out loud. I didn't mean to make you uncomfortable. I was just feeling all happy from this morning, from everything …"

He put his hands on her shoulders. "Do you think I'm upset about that? The opposite. I'm … I feel so connected to you. I feel, I don't know, almost high." He kissed her, holding it for several long seconds, one hand cradling the back of her neck and the other pressed into the small of her back, pulling their bodies together. "I loved it. I'm in love with you," he said. "And I'm so turned on right now."

"I can tell," she said, breath ragged. She felt his hardness pressing against her belly and he pushed her gently against the wall to maximize the sensual pressure.

She closed her eyes and ran her hands through his thick, dark hair, tousling it and kissing his lips again and again.

"Bed," she whispered. "Now."

She pulled her shirt off, tossed it to the side, then took his hand and led him to the bedroom. She reached for his belt, but instead, he took charge, guiding her to the bed and leaning her down, her head against the pillows. He pulled off her sneakers, then tugged on her jeans until she was in her panties. He stepped out of his pants, yanked his shirt over his head and knelt between her legs. He kissed her ankles and her calves, moving up to the back of her knees, and then he nuzzled his head in between her thighs, kissing the soft skin there as she spread her legs. When he reached her panties, she moaned as he pulled them to one side.

She felt a wave of bliss surging behind every delicate touch and tickle of his tongue. A long, slow, rolling orgasm built from deep within, carrying her away as she gripped the bedsheets. He kept his tongue pressed tight against her as surge after surge of pleasure crashed over her. When the wave finally peaked, she relaxed her legs and released the sheets. He kissed his way up her belly and then to her breasts, taking first one, then the other nipple lightly between his lips.

"Are you ready?" he asked.

She nodded and held her breath as he propped himself up, hands beside her shoulders, and slowly entered her.

23

March 17, 1993—Three years and two months before the protest

Eastern Oregon Correctional Institute

Hudson watched a square of sunlight glow on the scarred surface of the table in front of him. The sun was west of the prison this time of day, lighting up the narrow window with a painful reminder of freedom. He had been waiting in the otherwise empty attorney-client room for almost thirty minutes now, although it was impossible to know for sure. There were no clocks anywhere.

The guard opened the door. "Looks like it's gonna be a no-show," he said.

"Please, Hector, give me a few more minutes."

Hector scowled but agreed. "Five minutes, that's it."

Hector was one of the few guards without a pathological desire to control or hurt people. At first, those impulses flummoxed Hudson. He always assumed people worked in prisons because they wanted to do something good for society, to help rehabilitate those who made mistakes. He was wrong—dead wrong, ludicrously wrong, downright naive.

Most people worked at the prison because it paid well and gave them the authority to threaten people, control them and inflict violence. Dead stop. And they did.

Frequently, and often for no apparent reason. When they had a reason, even a trumped-up one, it could get brutal. So far, Hudson had mostly avoided that, but it couldn't last. The probabilities were against him.

He worried his faith in humanity, his belief that people were inherently good but often misguided, while never strong, might not recover from this experience. It got a little more challenging with every bloodied nose or cracked skull, every petty instance of control and dehumanization he witnessed.

He hoped cooking would be the thing that helped keep him sane and safe. But no matter how good he got in the prison kitchen, what kind of restaurant on the outside would ever hire an ex-con?

The door opened again. It was Hector. "One minute to spare," he said. "You got lucky."

A woman, a briefcase in one hand and a purse slung over her shoulder, entered. She wore a plain black skirt and a white blouse. Hudson stood and held out his hand. She shook it with a crisp, firm handshake. Normally, no touching was allowed, but those rules didn't apply to the attorney relationship.

"My name is Alison Jennings," she said.

She seemed so young, younger than Hudson, practically a teenager. How could she be a lawyer, he wondered?

She plopped her briefcase—a black leather affair that looked like an oversized doctor's bag—on the table, clicked open the metal clasps, and pulled out a yellow-lined notebook and folder. She slid a pen from behind her ear.

Hudson watched curiously, still standing.

"Please sit," she said, motioning at the chair without looking up.

Deceptively pretty, Hudson thought, but understated. Her hair was pulled back into a tight bun. Still, she looked tiny. Breakable.

"I'm a law student at Lewis & Clark College. I'm working with the Portland Justice Project, and I'm here to review your situation. Please confirm your identity."

Law student. Well, that explained the age. She was like the Doogie Howser of the legal world.

"My name is Hudson Destry."

"Let's begin."

"You got my letter then?"

"We received your letter, yes. This is the first step of a process to assess your claim stated in said letter. Please start at the beginning."

Alison sat up straight and held her pen above the notebook, hovering, poised to stab the paper with facts.

"Okay, two years ago, or something like that, there was this bad arson in Eugene, someone got hurt, and then the police came and …"

"Not the beginning of the crime. I know all that. I've reviewed the files associated with your case, of course." She tapped the folder. "What I meant is start at the beginning of how you became enmeshed in this situation."

"I have an alibi," he said. It wasn't an answer to her question, but Hudson wanted to get that out right away.

"I know. We checked it. The security guard saw you in the tree that night."

Hudson leaned back in the chair. He was speechless. The guard vouched for him. His alibi was corroborated. He felt a surge of joy. Maybe this nightmare would soon be over, just like that.

"So, can I leave?"

"No," she said, tilting her head to gauge his reaction.

"But I have an alibi. I told them about it at the trial, before the trial even. I told everyone. They said they couldn't find the guard."

"That wasn't true. They had no trouble finding the guard. But his testimony was deemed inadmissible in your trial. He had performance issues. He'd been caught sleeping on the job and had a DUI. He wasn't considered reliable."

"But doesn't this at least introduce doubt?" Hudson asked, sitting at last. "Can't the judge call a mistrial or something?"

"This is real life, not the movies. You are a convicted felon based on sworn testimony. I visited the guard. He told me that he was not asleep that night, that, in fact, he remembers talking to you in the tree."

"He did. He told me a knock-knock joke, a really bad one."

She looked at him curiously. "Could be useful if you both know it."

"Knock, knock," he said.

"Who's there?" Alison asked, pen hovering above the pad.

"Nobel."

"Nobel who?" she asked, playing along.

"No bell, that's why I knocked," he said.

Alison mock-groaned. "That is indeed a terrible one. As it turns out, the DUI may not have been exactly by the books. And the performance issues appear to have been backdated. He is willing to swear you were there, but it probably won't be enough," Alison said. "We may need more. Your letter said you know who framed you?"

Hudson felt the always-present knots in his stomach tightening. He looked away from Alison's steady gaze, up to the ceiling and then at the barred window in the concrete wall, and let his eyes rest there for an instant. The sun was fading.

He still wasn't sure about saying out loud what he knew

had to be true. It had to be Moon. And even though he hated her for it, he still felt weirdly protective. Nobody in the eco-warrior circles cared for snitches, nor would other inmates if she was in prison. If it got out, Moon might face real threats. Could he trust this inexperienced law student to keep Moon safe?

Why did he even care? She sure didn't think about him when she lied about his involvement. It was likely he was here, in this awful place, because of her.

Even though he was angry, he could understand why she did it. She was just a kid, a confused kid, and they probably scared her shitless and told her she would spend the rest of her life in prison if she didn't play along. In the end, if she had stayed quiet and got herself a good lawyer, she might have gotten off with a light sentence without snitching, but how was she to know that?

He returned his attention to Alison. She was still staring at him, waiting, pen poised above the paper. The truth had to come out.

"I'd like this to stay off the record," he said.

"We are protected by attorney-client privilege," she said.

"Even though you're a student?"

"I am also employed by the law clinic."

Hudson nodded and then sighed. "Only one of the people involved with the arson knew I was tree-sitting," he said. "I knew her as Moon. She spent a couple of nights with me in the tree but left because she wanted to do something more direct. She specifically mentioned fire-bombing an SUV dealership in Eugene. I didn't know the other two who were arrested, the ones in the news. And I didn't even know what she had done, what they all did when I was arrested. I didn't know about the arson. It's not like I was getting the newspaper delivered to my tree. I didn't hear anything about it until the cops pulled me down and arrested me."

"Why do you suspect it was her?"

"Nothing was ever said about her in the media. Not a peep. I assumed she had become an informant. I don't even know the other two guys they arrested."

She was scribbling on the pad. "Either of those two might have known you were in the tree, though, correct?"

"I suppose. There was some media coverage at first, but it had dropped off by then."

"Why would Moon want you in prison? Were you lovers?"

"No, nothing like that. I assume it was because she got something from it, a deal, a reduced sentence. Maybe even witness protection, I don't know."

"What happened after you were pulled from the tree?"

He struggled to put it into words. "I was pretty incoherent that night. Half-starved and sick and cold, I was hallucinating—about my mom and my dead dog, Cinnamon. Things got chaotic. I was taken away in the back of a van. They gave me a turkey sandwich. I think Bill gave it to me, the guard. I threw it up in the van." Hudson paused. "Sorry, that was gross."

"No worries," Alison said. "Details matter."

"Anyway, after a pretty awful drive, they threw me in a county jail cell. When they gave me my phone call, I tried to call a college buddy, but he didn't answer. I tried a lawyer I remembered from my hometown, and the same thing happened. It was night, late. I didn't sleep. They gave me water and some saltine crackers. No toothbrush. I was in front of a judge that next morning. I looked like hell. They didn't let me wash or anything. The judge denied bail, the prosecutor argued I was a threat to the community. The lawyer they assigned to me didn't put up any defense, then or later."

She was scribbling furiously. "What next?"

"I was in a line-up the next day with five other men who looked like me. Sort of. A few days later, not sure how many, I lost track of time. I was being tried. Just a judge, no jury. The defense lawyer they assigned me barely spoke. He told me to plead guilty. I refused."

"What do you remember about the trial itself?"

"It was over in thirty minutes. The prosecutor said they had an eyewitness who placed me at the SUV lot, that I was the mastermind, and taught the 'terrorist gang' how to make the bombs. I remember that specifically. The judge called them a terrorist gang. The so-called eyewitness never testified. The attorneys met in the judge's chambers. I saw a TV with a video player hooked up before they closed the door. When they came back out, I was declared guilty. My lawyer didn't say a word, just packed up and left me there. Next thing I knew, I was in prison."

He waited while she kept writing, flipping the sheet to fill a fourth page.

"Did they try to get you to cut a deal?" Alison asked, looking back up at him.

"Yes, if I pled guilty I could get off with a year and then probation."

"You declined."

"Yes," he said, voice rising. "I was, I am, innocent. I didn't do it."

Alison flinched at the anger in his voice.

"I'm sorry," Hudson said. "I'm frustrated, but that's not your fault."

"I'd be frustrated, too," Alison said. "But I'm on your side." She put her pen down. "I'll be straight with you. I believe you. And what you say largely corresponds to what I've learned independently. What makes this tough, and

I'm just being honest, is that the person whose testimony placed you at the scene is considered a confidential informant, which gives them a lot of protection and cover. We may not get access."

"But it had to be Moon."

Alison sighed. "Three people were arrested for the arson in Eugene and imprisoned. Well, four, counting you. One of them is the woman you knew as Moon. But any of them could have implicated you. Your gut feeling that it was Moon is not evidence."

"But only Moon is invisible, she's the only one kept out of the media," Hudson said.

"That is true, and that means she is protected. But four others were also arrested and charged as accomplices for helping to plan the action, build the bombs and cover their escape, people who made deals for time served and probation. The prosecution, if they pressured her, won't make this easy. They'll say any one of those others could have identified you. They'll use every trick they can to drag this out."

Hudson felt a desperation settling in, the kind that drained his hope completely. "Where does that leave me?"

"We'll review their backgrounds and files, then conduct interviews, including the three in prison, but ..."

Hudson waited for the shoe to drop.

"...whoever implicated you is less important than the fact that the case against you was weak from the beginning. If we can demonstrate without a doubt that you were in the tree, their confidential informant doesn't matter relative to getting you exonerated."

"You'll take my case?"

She closed the notebook and slipped it into her case. "We already have. I am here to confirm we made a good decision. We're petitioning to get your conviction overturned. We're working the security guard angle. Be patient and stay safe. I'll be in touch."

She stood, put the papers and notebook in her briefcase and closed the clasps.

"I can't thank you enough," Hudson said.

"An aspect of our mission is to ensure people fighting for social justice, fighting to save the planet, get legal help when needed. This is a no-brainer." She walked to the door and rapped for the guard.

Before he opened the door, she turned back to Hudson. "The sad reality is the truth isn't always enough. We'll do everything we can, but it isn't always enough. It's often not enough. I hope you understand."

He nodded.

The guard opened the door.

"We'll do everything we can, though," she said. "I suggest you keep our conversation to yourself. You never know who might be listening."

"Thank you, Ms. Jennings," Hudson said, standing. "The world needs more people like you."

"Call me Alison," she said, then turned and walked away, the strike of her heels echoing on the hard floors long after she'd disappeared.

"Stay put," Hector said, "I'll be back for you in a few minutes."

The door banged behind them. A loud metallic sound followed by a clang of the lock as Hector slid the bolt into place. For the first time, the brutal sound of the door closing didn't feel like the end of the world.

24

April 1, 1993—Three years and one month before the protest

Correctional Facility for Women

Roz studied Camille across the table. She had been in prison for more than two years but looked healthier than in the early days. Her hair was longer, her skin had cleared up, and she'd put on a few pounds. Her appearance was still a far cry from before, though, and her time behind bars had aged her considerably. She once looked younger than a youthful twenty, now she looked almost middle-aged.

Doesn't matter, thought Roz. None of it matters. Overall, she looked good. Sad, but good. Except for the worrisome bruise on her forearm—mottled purple and green, like a thunderstorm under the skin.

"What happened there?" Roz asked, pointing at the bruise.

Roz sat across from Camille in the visiting room.

"Nothing," Camille said. "I fell. I slipped in the shower."

"Is that for real, or is someone hassling you? Are you safe?" Roz asked, worried and whispering.

Camille tried to smile. "For real. I did fall. I'm still clumsy. It's …" She struggled to find the words. "It's complicated here. Plenty of stupid little rivalries. But so far, nothing too weird has happened."

"I'm glad to hear it," Roz said. "You look good. Healthy."

"Bullshit. I'm getting fat," Camille said with a scoff. "It's the carbs and the meds."

"What meds?" Roz asked, leaning forward. "You didn't mention that last time."

"It's new," Camille said. "They have me on mood stabilizers."

"To make you more compliant? Why are you letting them put chemicals in your body?"

"You're one to talk," Camille said. "You put all the chemicals in the world in your body. You've got to get that shit under control."

"I'm fine. And don't switch topics," Roz said. "Should I tell a lawyer or something that you are being chemically restrained?"

"No," Camille said. "It's not like that. I want them. The drugs. The prison psychiatrist recommended them." She dropped her gaze, nervous. "Rizzie," she said, using the name she called Roz when they were little. "I was having weird dreams, nightmares where I'm always running away from something, but I can't see what is chasing me. And panic attacks." She paused. "I've done terrible things."

Roz shook her head. "Listen, Cammy, you were young and stupid and got caught up in some bullshit. Don't torture yourself. You'll be out soon enough."

Camille shook her head. "It's not that, not just the arson. Yeah, I was dumb and got caught. But that's not the worst of it. That's not what's eating at me."

Roz slipped her hand across the table to rest on Camille's wrist and saw her brighten momentarily at the contact.

"No touching," the guard called across the room.

Roz let her hand linger a second longer.

"I mean it," the guard called again.

"Why do they care so much about touching?" Roz asked, pulling back.

Camille shrugged. "They say it's to prevent contraband coming in. But mostly, I think it's just control. That's the name of the game here. Control and subservience."

"Is there a lot of contraband?"

Camille nodded. "I've seen weed, pills, phones, even a vibrator. There's a thriving little black market in here."

"A vibrator?"

"A quiet one, yeah. I mean, celibacy isn't easy. Especially if you're not willing to, you know, get out of your comfort zone."

"It's not forced or anything, right?"

Camille shook her head. "Highly encouraged, but most people are pretty cool about it."

"I want to help. Any contraband I should smuggle in?"

"Don't even joke, Rizzie," she said. "You'll get a full BCS every time you come back."

"BCS?"

"Body cavity search. All the cavities. And I've heard they let the guys watch."

"Eww, gross," Roz said.

They were silent for a moment, Roz thinking back to when Camille was little and how she used to play with toy horses. She wanted to be an equestrian, but the family never had enough money for lessons, much less a horse, although from time to time, she rode the ancient horse at the nearby dairy farm.

"Tell me why you're struggling so much?"

Camille shook her head. "I can't. I'm too ashamed."

"I'm your sister, you can tell me anything."

"Half-sister," Camille said with a smile.

"Full-pain-in-the-ass-sister. Seriously, get whatever this is off your chest."

"I don't think I can," Camille said. "I can't bear the thought of you being disappointed in me. More disappointed, I mean. You and mom. I can't do it. I won't do it."

"You know that would never happen," Roz said. She looked around the room. Conversations between inmates and their lovers, children and mothers were speeding up, and emotions were heating up as visiting hours wound down.

"We're running out of time. Talk to me."

Camille shook her head.

Roz fought back an urge to get angry. What was she hiding? After everything that had happened, what the hell was the point of any more secrets now?

"Two-minute warning," the guard called.

They stood, and Roz moved as close as she could without touching. Camille smelled like strong soap and faint mildew. "See you soon."

"Don't worry about me," Camille said, her voice sounding tired and hollow. "It's all going to be okay."

After she worked her way back through security to the parking lot, Roz got in her car and slumped down in the front seat. The forced cheer slipped away like a fog, leaving her sad, alone and defeated.

There was half a pint of Jim Beam under the seat, and she fumbled around for the bottle and took a sip, then another. She felt so tired. She closed her eyes. The darkness was welcome.

Three sharp raps at the window jolted her back awake, the bottle sliding from her lap and tumbling into the floorboard.

"Can't sleep here," a guard said, peering through the

window with a scowl.

"What the fuck," Roz said, started and momentarily confused. "I wasn't sleeping. I was resting my eyes."

"For an hour?" he asked, hands on his hips, near the pistol and baton. "Move along. Don't make me write you up. One infraction, and you can't come back. Not in this car anyway."

"Okay, already," she said, cranking the key and for once enjoying the coughing belch of black smoke that caused the guard to back up, shaking his head.

The drive from Salem to Portland usually only took about 45 minutes, but she was leaving during rush hour, and all the state workers who made the daily commute from Oregon's capitol were heading back to the City of Roses simultaneously. It was crowded but moving at a steady clip, at least until a wreck near Wilsonville snarled everything.

After she got past the Terwilliger curves, anxiously watching the semis weaving dangerously close to her lane, she checked her watch. Almost seven. Frank was getting off soon, so she might as well swing by his restaurant and pick him up. It didn't hurt that Clay would be there. He was the perfect package. He didn't have psychic powers, though, or he would have picked up on the constant mental images of them doing fun, inappropriate and naked things together. Too bad about his trashy wife, Crystal. Still, he was hot *and* loyal. That made him even hotter.

The Rose and Thorn restaurant parking lot was almost full, and she had to park near the back. Roz always felt a little weird coming here, knowing Molly paid for that little stint in rehab last year. That thought flew out of her mind when she caught sight of Clay outside talking to one of the cooks, the one with the thin, silly mustache, Godfrey or something; she couldn't quite pull up his name.

"Hey, Roz, how are you?" the man asked.

Gabriel, maybe, she thought. No, weirder than that. Gil … something.

"Doing well Gil … roy." Just in the nick of time, she thought. "Hey, Clay. Nice to see you." She shot him a low-key smile, what she hoped would be just the right amount of flirty but with deniability if Frank was watching.

Clay nodded. His long hair was pulled back, and he had taken off his chef's coat, so he was only in old jeans and a ragged T-shirt. His arms were crossed, and the muscles on his forearms were tight like cables. His shoulders were broad and solid.

She walked past, wondering what it must be like to have a man like Clay in your life, watching out for you and caring for you. Loving you. Fucking you.

Roz shook her head, trying to dislodge the naughty images. Frank was handsome enough, but he was a man-child. A boy in a man's body—well, not even a fully developed man's body—with a passion for weed, tequila, pizza pockets, and Dungeons and Dragons. At least he had a steady job, she thought.

She nodded at Ione, the manager, as she walked in. Ione scared her, but she tried not to let it show. "I'm just going to sit at the bar and wait for Frank," she said.

Ione nodded. "One beer. No more."

"Oh, come on," Roz said. "I apologized for that so many times already."

"One beer. I'll tell Frank you're here."

Ione walked back into the kitchen.

Roz wondered what working at the Rose and Thorn would be like. Probably would beat the diner where she currently worked in Old Town. Tips were pretty shitty because everyone who lived there was broke. Like, food stamps-level broke.

She wouldn't want to work with Frank, though, she thought. Now, if it were just Clay, that would be great.

Frank came out from the back and slid onto the stool beside her. "Hey, babe."

He kissed her. She smelled fish and weed. Dave-two must be working, she thought.

"How was your day?" Roz asked.

"It was good. Busy. I was on the sauté station. LuRon broke a plate near the steam kettle, and they had to throw away a whole batch of Hungarian mushroom soup. Molly was pissed."

He laughed too much, and she could tell he was super high. He ordered a beer and a shot.

"Aren't you going to ask about my day?" Roz asked.

Frank looked at her, puzzled. "I thought I already had?" He looked around furtively. "I'm pretty baked."

"I can tell," Roz said. "I went to see my sister."

"Oh yeah, your sister. How is …" he looked at her helplessly. "I want to say Candace."

"Camille." She stood. "For the hundredth time, her name is Camille. I'll see you at home."

"Hey, pick up some pizza pockets, will you?" Frank shouted as she stormed toward the front door. "The boys are coming over for some sick D and D action."

She stood on the sidewalk at the entrance to the parking lot, frustrated, and rubbed her eyes so long and so hard that lights and geometric patterns started flashing in the darkness.

"You doing okay?" Clay asked. She hadn't noticed he was sitting on an overturned milk crate reading a *Gourmet* magazine.

"Yeah," she said, turning on her flirty smile out of force of habit. "Thanks for asking. It's just, you know, relationships, right?"

He nodded. "They can get complicated, that's for sure. I try my best to keep it simple."

"You're happy, right?" she asked. She was aiming for nonchalance, but she could hear the unintended edge of desperation below the surface.

"I've got no complaints," Clay said, returning his attention to the magazine.

"Then there's hope for the rest of us," she said. "See you later." She waved and gave him another smile, but he never looked up.

25

May 1, 1996—May Day protest

Across the street from Fleet Motors

When the first fire-bomb first went off, for a few fleeting seconds, everything went quiet, as if all the sound in the world had been sucked up in the flames. Hudson could hear his breath scraping in and out and the deep thud of his heart. Time slowed down, and everything around them moved in slow motion until the present crashed back into reality, and suddenly, after the second explosion, it was all smoke, screams and shouting.

Then, he sprang into action. After handing Roz the yellow snorkel mask, he pulled scarves and small milk cartons from his pack. He hoped they wouldn't need them. Last, he grabbed a blue snorkel mask and tugged it over his face and eyes.

The cops already at the protest moved fast toward the first line of protestors, who were reacting almost as quickly. Protestors who weren't cuffed to the luxury cars raced from the scene, hurling themselves forward, anywhere, trying to escape the rising mayhem. As they ran, cops tried to grab them; most were too nimble and escaped their clutching, gloved hands, but they weren't faster than the pepper spray rolling in noxious clouds through the chaos. Sirens blared as more police arrived at the scene.

"What the hell is going on?" Roz yelled, her eyes securely covered by the yellow snorkel mask, as protestors reached their position panicked, with red-ringed eyes crying and blinking.

"Pepper spray," Hudson said, standing and still cuffed together, dragging her up along with him. He tossed milk cartons to the men and women running by.

"Thanks, man!" one shouted, catching the milk without stopping. The protestor opened the carton and poured the milk into his eyes, tossed the carton to the ground, and kept running.

Roz looked at Hudson, her eyes pressed into a question.

"Milk dilutes the pepper spray," he said. "Eases the pain."

Hudson was pepper-sprayed once at an anti-logging demonstration a year before he climbed Sophie. It took his eyes two days to fully recover. Even though his protesting days were long over, he made it his business always to be prepared, an ingrained habit. He was triple-prepared today since Roz was involved.

But milk didn't work on tear gas, which Hudson figured was coming next. He pulled four quart-sized plastic bottles of water with baking soda from his pack and shook them.

"What's that for?" Roz asked.

"Water with baking soda helps with tear gas."

"Tear gas, that's ridiculous—"

"Pepper spray is what they're using now, but the police need to reach a wider radius, meaning they'll switch tactics soon."

He pulled her in tight. They were facing each other now, close. Their cuffed wrists were between them, and he was holding her hands. He felt the warmth of her breath against his lips. He expected her to get angry.

"You won't go over there, right?" he asked.

"Do I look like an idiot?"

"You are about as far from an idiot as possible," he said.

Hudson let go of her arms and pulled a small key on a ring from his back pocket with his free hand. He unlocked the cuffs. She slipped her wrists from the metal and rubbed them. He threw the cuffs into his pack.

On the other side of the street, two protestors fell at the edge of the lot, both rubbing their eyes, likely having trouble seeing. The cops were close behind.

"You had the key the whole time," Roz said.

"Do *I* look like an idiot?" he asked. "I'd never put you at risk."

They turned toward the sound of a scream. One of the fallen protestors had recovered quickly, got up and kept running, but the other—her friend—was sprawled on the sidewalk, a cop raining blows methodically on her back with his baton.

He watched as Roz's face twisted at the brutality of it.

Her friend paused at the sound of her screams and turned, hesitating, but there was no point trying to help. Instead, she ran faster, disappearing out of sight within a block. That was the right decision, Hudson thought.

The tide was quickly turning on this scene. It was time to get out of there.

"I want to help. What should I do?" Roz asked. The plastic over her eyes was steaming up.

Just then, a cop wearing a gas mask tossed a tear gas canister at the group of protestors who hadn't run, the ones still linking arms and chanting in the middle of Fleet Motor's lot. Behind them, the black SUV burned. People were yelling. A police dog—an angry German Shepherd—was barking, gnashing and pulling at its short leash.

The remaining handful of protestors collapsed to their knees as the tear gas engulfed them, hacking and coughing.

The police, all in gas masks, pulled them to their feet roughly, spun them around and slapped them in handcuffs. A protestor tried to jerk away and was beaten with a baton, first by one cop, then another, before being dragged limply to a police van.

The TV cameraman came rushing out from the safety of the showroom, a bandana around his face, shooting video of the beating. Maybe heroes still exist, Hudson thought.

Hudson felt terrible for these protestors because the ones left behind, the ones who didn't run, were undoubtedly the most idealistic. They believed in non-violence, were passionate about their cause, and trusted that all it took was standing up and giving voice to the injustice against nature. They believed that with courage and conviction, people would care, would be shaken out of apathy, and could change the direction of the world.

Like he once believed.

Two fire trucks pulled up, sirens blaring. Responders poured out of the truck, loaded down with equipment, moving in a practiced rhythm. They rolled out hoses and connected to a nearby hydrant. Within minutes, they were dousing the fire.

Roz started coughing. Hudson leaned over to her to wrap a scarf more tightly around her neck. A few more protestors ran by.

"Here, take this!" Roz said, breaking away from Hudson and handing the water to a woman. "It's water and baking soda. It will help with your eyes."

Hudson could not let this go on much longer. If the cops saw, they might get picked up for aiding and abetting, which would defeat the whole purpose of this day: to give Roz an alibi.

After the fire-bomb went off, Hudson lost sight of the

three masked individuals who had joined the protest late, but he was certain they orchestrated the chaos. And either they weren't really EFF, or something had gone very wrong.

The SUV they targeted was too close to the protestors, cops and media, way too close. EFF was committed to damage only property, never people. They should have set it off on the far edge of the lot where there were no protestors, only SUVs. Maybe they just got rattled.

It took a cool head to set off a bomb.

Or maybe something else was going on, something deeper and more insidious.

Hudson hoped their alibi was secure. Two cops had talked to them, joking about them being lost protestors. Hudson had given each a muffin to make it memorable. Roz tried to tell them each time that she was being held against her will, but they were too focused on the protest—and the muffins—to care.

He also knew they'd been caught by the television cameras, multiple times. He made a point of waving often when he knew it was aimed in their direction, showing the handcuffs.

Two more cop cars screeched to a stop. Hudson shoved the leftover milk cartons and the remaining water bottle into his knapsack.

"We have to go," he said. "Now."

"I'll go when I'm ready," she said.

"Roz, wake up. It won't be good for Camille if her sister gets arrested at a protest where people got hurt."

"It won't be good for you either," she said.

"That's right," Hudson said, nodding. "In fact, it will be very bad for me."

"So, you go."

They faced each other, eyes covered with snorkel masks

and colorful scarves around their mouths. Her hair was wild and bunched up around the plastic, and they were surrounded by pure chaos. But he suddenly felt strong and peaceful.

He pulled down his scarf.

"Look, I love you. I will always love you. I understand we can't be together anymore, but that doesn't change my feelings for you or my desire for you to be safe and happy and live a good life."

She started to say something snarky, and he held his hand up.

"I don't have to be part of it, I get that. But trust me when I say, if you stay here, things will be worse for you, for Camille and your mom and dad."

The police were moving closer to them now. They would look like any other protesters in all the confusion and action.

The gas was getting to him. His eyes were blurring behind the goggles, and his lungs were burning. He coughed, almost doubling over. Roz reached out, touching his shoulder.

He straightened up and pulled his mask down to smile at her. "You should get going now," he said. "Don't take the goggles off until you're at least three blocks away. I'll stall them."

He covered his mouth again with the scarf and gazed at her for what he was sure would be the last time. She looked beyond them at the advancing police. They were in riot gear and in no mood for small talk.

There was another explosion, a big one, and the police scrambled for cover.

26

April 14, 1996—Two weeks before the protest

Hudson's apartment, Portland

"Ever notice how the shapes on your ceiling look like trees?" Roz asked.

She was leaning against a stack of pillows, snuggled up close to Hudson in his bed. Typically, she preferred to hang out at her place. It was bigger and cleaner, much cleaner. But the movie theater they went to the night before was closer to Hudson's apartment, and it had been—and still was—raining. A downpour, really. Roz liked the rain pelting the tiny windows while they were snug and dry inside. It made the day feel cozy and intimate.

Hudson looked up at the ceiling. "I see putrid gray water stains."

"Come on. Use your imagination." She pointed to the largest blob. "That looks like the crown of a giant Douglas fir, and the long stain to the left is its trunk."

Roz watched as Hudson's eyes followed her finger. He squinted and shook his head. "That's where a pipe burst last year. Only your beautiful poetic brain could see a tree in that."

He was so nice to her, always coming up with ways to say sweet things. Kindness wasn't something Roz was used to, but she liked it and was fast growing accustomed to it.

He made her feel special, seen, supported. It was new and wonderful and a little disorienting, like she had access to a special kind of emotional gravity that kept her floating a little bit higher than everyone else.

Whenever they were together, she felt safe and confident, sure nothing would ever go wrong for her again. At first, she didn't trust this feeling and was even a little scared of it, but being around him continued to erode the negativity in her life, mostly due to his almost bedrock certainty about them. The always-widening joy between them was now slowly erasing all traces of the emotional scars of her past.

She snuggled in closer. Roz loved Hudson's smell. It was some mad combination of earthy and sweet, like mud and mint or pine and brown sugar, and it always drove her a little crazy with desire.

She leaned over and kissed him on the lips, her bare breasts pressing into his chest. He pulled her in tight, and she felt him harden against her thigh. This would be their second time this morning, and she was ready all over again. Apparently, so was he.

"Turn over," he said. She turned onto her side, facing away from him, wiggling into the soft, sensuous spooning position where their curves matched. He slid his fingers between her thighs and began to stroke her gently. "Do you like that?" he whispered.

"Oh, yes," she sighed, relaxing into his touch.

They stayed like that for a few long minutes, Hudson softly stroking her, his fingertips teasing and pressing in all the right ways as she began to heat up under his careful touch. Unlike past lovers, Hudson was a quick learner and loved for her to tell him exactly what she needed or—better yet—show him, using her fingers to guide him to get just the right pressure and intensity. And he paid attention, noting how she responded and what she needed, eagerly replicating it the next time. He had learned exactly what she needed to release the deepest kind of ecstasy, a pleasure she never even knew existed. He was doing it perfectly this morning as she held her breath and leaned out over the sea of bliss, waiting to sink into it.

"You seem ready," Hudson whispered into her ear. "Are you ready to come for me, Roz?"

She nodded. Words failed her.

He applied more gentle pressure and slightly increased his rhythm, and she felt slow spasms rocking her.

"I want you to come for me now so I can slip inside you and fuck you slow and steady until we both lose ourselves," he said.

She moaned, both from his touch and his words. She loved it when he talked like this during sex. It was new, the first time was a few weeks ago, and like everything else, when he noticed it turned her on, he kept it up. The power of dirty talk during sex meant they had crossed some invisible but important boundary, she realized. That sex was now more than just two bodies seeking pleasure, there was an intellectual component to it now. He wanted her brain to enjoy sex, too. It was exhilarating.

"Do you know how much you turn me on?" he whispered. "How much you drive me crazy every time you are anywhere near me? I can barely function. I can't think about anything other than how hard you make me, how I want to kiss your breasts and touch you and slide inside you and give you pleasure."

His desire for her was electrifying.

She felt a spiraling bloom of pleasure emanating from around his fingertips. He clamped his hand against her and let the waves of bliss crash against the shore of the moment, his other arm under her so he could cup her breast. As the orgasm wound down into a series of tiny flutters, he gently parted her legs with his knee. Roz's thighs trembled, and she felt a nearly unbearable longing. She loved this beautiful, amazing man with all her soul.

"Say you're mine," he whispered, holding himself back. The heat of him, his hardness, was kindling something deliciously manic in her.

"Only yours, now and forever," Roz said. "Please, Hudson, I need you."

He pushed all the way inside in one slow, strong thrust, deep and full, and she pressed her head against his shoulder, then moaned with the agonizing pleasure of his achingly slow withdrawal. But this time, he didn't wait, didn't tease, and just began pressing in and pulling out in a slow, perfect rhythm that edged her closer to the cliff.

She held her breath again, then arched her back, and her entire body went rigid. Her muscles contracted around him, and they froze for an instant as their combined pleasure reached its peak. He let out a half-moan half-gasp, holding on to her hips as she felt him pulse inside her. She clutched the sheets as the wave passed, the biggest yet.

In the stunned, glorious silence that followed, he wrapped his arms around her upper body and held her as she tried to regain her breath and slow her delirious heartbeat. Finally, her hands loosened their grip on the pillow, and she took a deep breath.

"That was incredible," she said.

He let out a long breath. "Yeah, wow," he said. They slowly disentangled and rolled onto their backs, staring at the ceiling wordlessly. Roz had never felt so happy and complete.

"I see the trees now," he said. "And I love you."

"I love you, too," she said.

They remained still for a few more minutes until she

started to feel chilly and reached for the blanket. Hudson pulled it over her and handed her the glass of water he always kept next to the bed. Roz took a long sip and then handed it back to him.

"What did you think of the movie I dragged you to last night?" she asked, using the tip of her finger to draw a heart on his chest. She liked his hairy chest. Most men she had been with had bare chests. But Hudson was practically furry. Everywhere. And muscled. Manly.

"I didn't expect to like it, but I did."

"Why didn't you expect to like it?" Roz asked.

"I prefer *Pride and Prejudice*, to be honest, and I wasn't sure about the adaptation of *Sense and Sensibility*, but Emma Thomson and Kate Winslet were pretty great."

"You've read Jane Austen?" She was incredulous. "No way. Guys don't read Austen."

"Everything she's ever written," he said. "Remember, I had some spare time to fill the past few years."

Roz paused. Was this an opening? He never talked about his time in prison except to make jokes about youthful stupidity. The only serious comment he ever made was that a lawyer was working to overturn his conviction, so he couldn't talk about anything. He assured her it was nothing to do with violence or anything she might consider a red flag or source of danger. It was just a stupid property damage thing, and anyway, he was innocent.

She, of all people, knew what it was like to do stupid things. Really stupid things, many of which she couldn't even remember due to being blackout drunk.

Those days were over, finally. Roz had told him about her past, all the gritty details. Well, most of them. She felt it had been important to start this relationship right. When she offered to get the AIDS test early on, she was surprised he took one, even though, by his admission, Hudson had been celibate for years, including the year before he even went to prison. He told her again and again that nothing about her past bothered him because all of it made her who she was, and the journey had brought her to him. She was so grateful for the way he approached the world.

She lightly traced a scar across his knuckles. "That looks painful. What happened?"

"That's a little memento of my stay in prison," he said.

"You got stabbed?"

He looked at the pale scars and smiled. "I cut myself working in the kitchen. I wasn't a badass like that. I went to prison for tree-sitting."

Roz tried to slow her breathing. He was finally doing it, finally trusting her enough to share this story. "It doesn't seem like that usually results in prison time."

"Things got weird," he said, a pained look in his eyes.

"Tell me more."

"At first, it was one of the happiest times of my life," he said. "Except for this time with you. So, the second happiest time of my life."

"How so?" Roz asked.

He put his hand over hers. "It was just so peaceful, I guess. You'll think it's crazy, but I named her."

"Who?"

"My tree. Her name was Sophie."

"That's a beautiful name. It means wisdom, doesn't it?" Roz loved that he named his tree.

Hudson nodded. "Yes, and I learned a lot from her."

Roz listened as Hudson described the days and nights in the tree, the strong limbs of the Douglas fir, what he ate, the magnificent view of the stars at night, the birds and also the squirrel who came to treat him like any other non-threatening forest creature.

"I think Sophie thought I was a squirrel, too, at first. Just a big, noisy, graceless squirrel."

Roz laughed.

"I felt honored, I guess, being welcomed like that. At night, I learned how to tell what the sounds meant. Like how the strong, muffled flap of an owl's wings was always followed by the scurrying, scratching of mice and other critters hiding, worried they were about to be its next meal."

He turned on his side to face her. "It was a mystical experience like I was part of nature, not above it. I was breathing in the sun and exhaling moonlight."

"That's beautiful," she said. "How did you pick Sophie in the first place?"

"She was slated to be cut down. It just didn't seem right to me."

"How long were you in the tree?"

"Three months," Hudson said. "I didn't expect to be there so long, to be honest. The plan was people would swap out with me every few weeks so I could shower, get some hot food and stuff. And while people helped at first by bringing me supplies, no one was willing to stay with me. Well, one person came for a couple of days."

"Who?"

"Some girl, young, idealistic," he said. "I'd never met her before, and I don't know how she was connected with my friends."

"Was she pretty?" Roz asked, arching a suspicious eyebrow.

He leaned over and kissed her. "She was pretty, very pretty, but nothing happened. She was also pretty mixed up. Didn't last long. Said tree-sitting wasn't her thing. She wanted to do something bigger, more impactful. She called herself Moon."

"Moon. That's sweet," Roz said. "Did you have a code name?"

"Alpine."

"That's lovely," Roz said. "It fits you. I should start calling you that."

"Please don't," he said. "Those days are long gone."

"Is it okay that we're talking about this?" she asked.

Hudson nodded. "More than okay. I don't want to keep anything from you, ever."

"What brought you down from the tree?"

He sighed. "It's an ugly story. Are you sure you want to hear it now?"

"Whenever you are ready to tell it," she said. "We need to be able to tell each other anything. When you're done, I'll tell you something from my past, something I've never told you. About my sister, but I guess in a way it's about me because what happened put me on a bad path for so long."

He kissed her lightly on the forehead. It was almost chaste; he fluffed up the pillow under his head and stared up at the ceiling as he talked, not making eye contact. He felt okay telling her now that the attorney said they were only waiting on paperwork.

"I got dragged out of the tree by the FBI. I was in a bad way. Hungry, sick. They cuffed me, threw me in a van, and before I even knew what was happening, I was in front of a judge, being sentenced for taking part in an arson at an SUV lot in Eugene. They were wrong. I wasn't there, but some kid got hurt, and the whole state, the country really, was rabid to blame … Roz, what's wrong?"

Roz had sat up straight, rigidly. She pulled the sheet up to cover her nakedness. "Tell me that part again?"

"Which part?"

"The part about the arson in Eugene. At the SUV lot."

"I was framed. I was in the tree, but someone told the cops I snuck off for a night and helped them, that I was responsible for making the fire-bomb, helped get it set, and then high-tailed it back to the tree without anyone ever seeing me so I'd have an alibi."

"It wasn't the arson that happened on July 14, 1991, was it?" Roz asked.

"Yeah." Hudson looked up at Roz, and she saw an uncertain mix of concern and curiosity in his expression. "How do you know that specific date off the top of your head?"

Now, it was Hudson's turn to sit up, and as he did, Roz felt the quiet thud of her heart in her ears. Slow down, she thought. Think this through before you say anything else. Piece this together.

"Roz? What's happening? You look weird. You're scaring me."

"Remind me, how long were you in prison?" she asked quietly.

"About three and a half years. Roz, what is it?" Hudson said, reaching out to touch her arm. Roz flinched. She didn't mean to flinch; it was an instinctive response. Noticing her response, he pulled his hand back.

A memory came back from one of her prison visits, early on. Camille telling her about being in a tree a few nights, but she never said with who specifically. What was it she had said?

He thought he could change the world by hanging out in a tree all by himself. What kind of fool thinks that?

"Who was that girl in the tree with you?"

"Like I said, her name was Moon," Hudson said.

"Why did she leave?"

"Roz, why are you asking me this?"

"Please, just answer me." She knew her voice sounded cold and a little hard, but she couldn't help herself.

"She left in the middle of the night while I was asleep. She said she was going to Eugene to take part in a direct action at an SUV lot. I tried to talk her out of it ..."

Roz held up her hand for him to be quiet as she tried to remember more of what Camille had said early on, what she had told her parents. Her breath was coming in short pants now.

There must be some other explanation. Oh, please, Roz thought, this can't be true. She felt as if a bright light was taking over her eyesight, making it hard to see. A wave of nausea sloshed and swirled inside her.

"Why exactly did you go to prison?" she asked.

"Why are you grilling me?"

"Because Moon is my sister," Roz said, anguish in her voice.

She watched Hudson run his hand through his thick black hair, disbelieving. "Your sister? How is that possible? Moon is in prison."

"My sister is in prison. Her name is Camille, not Moon. I'm literally going to a protest in two weeks to try and get her released. Hudson, are you responsible for my sister being in prison?" Roz asked.

"This conversation is starting to get seriously fucked up," Hudson said.

He was standing now, pulling on his jeans over his bare ass. Roz sat on the bed, battling the competing emotions welling up inside. She was in love with this man, but if he hurt her sister, that meant he hurt her entire family. Her stepfather and mother were wrecked by what happened to Camille, their marriage destroyed, her mother heartbroken anew every day by Camille's imprisonment.

Was Hudson responsible for all this heartache?

"Camille always said someone set her up," Roz said.

Hudson pulled on his t-shirt and turned to face her. "That's possible. Maybe someone in EFF set her up. Some of them were real assholes, ready to take in anyone naïve enough to follow their orders for the good of the cause and also ready to shove any blame on them."

"EFF?"

"Earth Freedom Front."

"How do you even know that?"

"I just do," he said. "Maybe Moon, I mean Camille, was too trusting of them."

"She was too trusting, that's certain, but I don't think it was of them. Tell me why you went to prison if you were innocent, if you were in that tree the whole time?"

"No one would back up my alibi. The cops and FBI didn't even try to ask the security guard who knew I was in the tree. I was railroaded by the testimony of a confidential informant."

They stared at each other. Roz stood up. The sheet dropped to the floor. They faced each other. She stood naked. He was clothed, except his feet were bare. His toenails were bright pink. Two days ago, in a flirty post-sex bout of joy, she begged to paint his toenails. He happily agreed.

"This can't be happening," she said.

Her hands started to shake, and she wrung them in front of her body. Her brain was collapsing. She had been too happy, and this was her punishment. There was no way this was ever going to last and to think otherwise had been utterly stupid, and now it was just a giant humiliation. Her heart felt like a lump of jerky in her chest.

"I don't understand. What can't be happening?" Hudson asked, his tone almost pleading.

Roz was hurrying to put on her clothes. After zipping up her denim skirt, she twisted around to face him, still topless.

"Here's what I think happened. My fragile sister, who ran away from home, who we hadn't seen or heard from in so long, somehow landed in your tree. You told her about the plan to fire-bomb that SUV lot. She decided to go there. Or maybe you sent her. And you either used her to cover your own tracks or you ratted her out when you got nabbed."

"That's not true," he said. "It doesn't add up. I was in the tree a hundred miles from Eugene."

"I always knew Camille was innocent. I just couldn't figure out who would be manipulative enough to let an innocent girl take the fall. But now I see everything." She buttoned her blouse with trembling fingers, then realized she had forgotten her bra. She rummaged among the twisted sheets and found it, shoving the black lacy twist of fabric into her back pocket. She sat to pull on her boots. "You are a real fucking piece of work, you sick bastard. Did you know all along and fucked me anyway?"

He took a step forward and reached out his hand, ready to sit next to her. "Roz, you've got this all wrong—"

"Stop," she said, pulling back. "Don't touch me. You ratted my sister out, you told them she did it."

"I did no such thing, Roz. Please, this is crazy. Why would I go to prison, too, if I ratted her out?"

"You're out now, and she isn't. The math doesn't seem too fucking hard. You made sure someone could take the fall for you." A feeling of fight-or-flight had taken hold, and it was unclear which would win.

Hudson looked down at his pink-toenailed feet. He looked stunned as if he'd just been struck in the heart with a sledgehammer. "That's not true. None of it. *I'm* the one who should be mad."

"Oh, please," Roz said, her voice dripping with sarcasm. "My sister was not an activist; she was a child. Someone talked her into being there, and then someone talked her into taking part in that crime, and then someone told the authorities it was her. I think you did all three. Who else could it have been?"

She turned over the pillows, threw them off the bed, and stomped to the other side of the room. "Where the hell is my purse?"

Hudson followed her. "That isn't what happened. You have to believe me. I love you. You love me. Please, trust what we have."

She found her purse on the kitchen table and threw it over her shoulder.

"I wish there was another explanation," she whispered.

"Please don't go," he said. "Let's talk about this, it's a terrible miscommunication—"

"No, Hudson, this is not a miscommunication. It's discovering the ugly truth. There's a big difference." She jerked the front door open.

"I can help your sister; I have a lawyer," Hudson said. "She's really good, she's helping me. Roz, please, you've got it all wrong."

She could hear the panic in his voice as he reached toward her.

"Just a poor lost little boy without a family, desperate to ruin *my* family," she said, grimly satisfied at the hurt it seemed to inflict.

She slammed the door behind her, the harsh clap of its close sounding like the thunder of a prison door swinging forever shut.

27

April 25, 1996—Five days until the protest

The Rose and Thorn restaurant

It was a perfect Portland day—sunny and dry, warm enough to hint at spring around the corner and cool enough to feel fresh and new—but it was wasted on Hudson. He walked to work burdened by regret, his shoulders slumping under the pressure.

It had been almost two weeks since their terrible conversation, and he still hadn't talked with Roz. She wouldn't take his calls and her answering machine was turned off. She wouldn't answer her door, no matter how long he knocked. One night, he slept on her porch and never saw her come or go. In the morning, the other tenants in the building were not happy. They told him to get lost or they'd call the police.

He felt worse today than that first night in prison. The pain of her absence was nearly physical, like waves of dark electricity pulsing out of his cracked heart. He didn't know a broken heart could hurt like this. He had never been in love. It made him think about all the nights he heard his mother softly crying after she thought he was asleep.

Roz wasn't coming into work either, at least not on his shifts.

Hudson opened the back door to the restaurant, hung

up his sweatshirt, grabbed his chef's coat, and then glanced at the schedule pinned to the bulletin board. Sure enough, once again, her name had been crossed off this shift and switched with Meredith.

He clocked in and willed himself into auto-pilot.

Ione came up behind him, followed by a stranger—a woman in her mid-20s, with gleaming black hair gathered into a long braid and big, unusual eyes close to lavender-colored.

"If I had five dollars for every time some misguided workplace romance fucked up my schedule," Ione said, "well, I'd have a hundred bucks easy. And it sure didn't take long with you two. Maybe a record. You fell in love, or whatever the hell it was you were doing, and broke up before I even had enough time to finish making a baby."

She softly patted her belly. The dark-haired woman smiled awkwardly at them both.

"And don't come around here during her shifts. Roz made it abundantly clear she'll quit if you do, and I like her. More than you."

"I would never do that," he said, although he had considered it.

"Come on," Ione said, motioning the woman to follow her into the kitchen. "You too, Romeo. Gather round, hash slingers. This is Anastasia."

"Anzi, for short," Anzi said with a nervous smile.

"Anzi is our new pastry chef," Ione said. "All part of LuRon's grand plan to shake this place up and bring in a new class of customers."

"Uh, quick question?" Gilroy said. "What happened to Dino? I saw him like yesterday. Wasn't he our pastry chef?"

"Dino hasn't been here for a year. And he wasn't a pastry chef. He made cupcakes for the kids on the side," Ione said, shaking her head. "Anastasia, meet the kitchen crew. The man having a memory lapse is Gilroy. The sad, mopey-looking one is Hudson, that's Dave-two wheeling the salad by, and Jon—"

Jon poked his head out of the dishpit, his apron wet, oversized glasses steamed up and strings of hair hanging limply over his forehead, and waved.

"Jon is our dishwasher. You'll meet the others later when they clock in. Hudson, please give Anzi a kitchen tour, show her the recipe book and help her get going. We need muffins ready for tomorrow's breakfast and some fancy dessert for dinner."

Ione disappeared into the dining room. Anzi looked at Hudson expectantly.

"This is the kitchen," Hudson said, sweeping his arm around as if revealing some scenic national park vista. "The pantry is back that way. Over there is where you'll find the baking stuff. The walk-in is this way. Butter and cream and whatnot. And this," he patted a binder, "is the recipe book. This little space of counter is all yours, along with the mixer. And that's about it. Any questions?"

"Where do I hang my jacket and find an apron?"

He pointed. "In the back by the lockers. Feel free to grab whatever locker is open."

She headed toward the lockers. Gilroy arched his eyebrow. "Well, new-Dino is far better looking than old-Dino."

"Tone it down," Hudson said.

"Right, I guess you're not used to working with women in the kitchen," Gilroy said.

Anzi walked into the kitchen, shouldering into her chef's jacket, and stopped. "Did I just hear what I think I heard? You don't like working with women? What kind of sexist bullshit is that? I thought this was supposed to be a cool place."

"No, hold on, it's not like that," Hudson said. He shot a glare at Gilroy. "He was making a dumb joke. I learned to cook in prison, so yeah, there were not many women in the kitchen, zero to be precise. But we're not in prison anymore, right Gilroy?"

He shrugged. "Metaphorically speaking, the capitalist system *is* a prison; only the bars are made out of debt instead of iron."

Anzi smiled. "That's deep. And sad."

"And stupid. Don't encourage Gilroy, or he'll never stop talking," Dave-two said, pushing the salad cart toward the swinging door. "Have you worked in a restaurant before?"

"This is my first," she said. "I graduated from culinary school last month."

"Oh, boy," Gilroy said. "That means we get a front-row seat to your growing disillusionment and ultimate breakdown."

"Ignore him," Hudson said. "Working in restaurants can be very satisfying." The kitchen crew let out a collective groan.

"Compared to prison, maybe," Gilroy said.

"Come on, Anzi, let me set you up to make muffins," Hudson said.

After Anzi assembled the ingredients and began measuring and stirring, Hudson moved to his station to make a batch of Hungarian mushroom soup. Probably the five-hundredth batch he had made in this place, he thought.

As LuRon clocked in for the night shift, Hudson introduced Anzi.

"Oh, a pleasure to meet you," LuRon said with mock seriousness, then shot a glare at Hudson. "You know I'm the head chef, right? I interviewed her and hired her."

"Sorry," Hudson said.

"I take off two weeks to be with my new baby and you forget I'm the damn boss?" LuRon grumbled.

Hudson shook his head, embarrassed, and returned to stirring the soup, watching little heat bubbles swell and pop like the mud pots he had seen at Yellowstone as a kid.

"Are you thinking about joining me behind the line anytime soon?" LuRon asked, interrupting his gloomy, soup-based reveries.

"Sorry, yeah," Hudson said, turning the heat down. "Anzi, are you doing okay?"

"Better than you, it seems," she said. She had flour in her hair and a swipe of batter on her cheeks, and she was plopping ice cream scoops of muffin batter into tins.

"You're gonna fit right in," LuRon said.

She slid the muffin tins into the oven. "What's his malfunction?"

LuRon smiled as he cut an onion into impossibly thin slices. "Our boy Hudson here is having girl problems. Specifically, the girl is Roz. She works here too and we all like her a lot better than him because it turns out Hudson got her sister locked up."

"Whoa. Is that true?" Anzi asked.

"No, it's not true," Hudson said. "I haven't said anything out of respect, but if Roz is talking about it, I'd like to set the record straight."

"We don't trust you like we do Roz, but we'll at least pretend to listen," Gilroy said.

"I met Roz's sister when I was tree-sitting. Over on the coast, a big Doug fir. Roz's sister Camille—or Moon, as I knew her then—was supposed to take over for me so I could get a break. Instead, she snuck out and joined an action in Eugene, burning some SUVs. A kid got hurt. People went to prison."

"That Eugene arson a few years back, I remember reading about that," Anzi said.

Hudson nodded. "Yeah, exactly. Anyway, I had nothing to do with it. I was up in my tree doing my thing, hungry and cold, and wondering what happened to my support team. One night, the FBI came in all guns a-blazing, dragged me out of the tree and threw me in jail. Said someone testified I was the ringleader of all that shit that went down in Eugene. They kept the name concealed because, apparently, that's how confidential informants work. It's bullshit, but I had no control over that and got thrown in prison."

"How did you get out? Did you escape?" Dave-two asked. "Are you on the lam?"

"That would be cool. Cool Hand Luke did that, that's how he got out of Alcatraz," Gilroy said.

"There's so much wrong with that sentence," LuRon said.

"That movie was based on true events," Dave-two countered. "He was a scientist, too."

"You're mixing up Cool Hand Luke and the Birdman of Alcatraz. Can we get back to our own convict's story?" Anzi asked.

LuRon laughed. "Like I said, she's gonna fit right in. Go on, Hudson."

"I contacted a nonprofit that helps people wrongly imprisoned. When my lawyer hunted down the security guard at the tree, he swore I was there that night. And that the only person who visited me before that was Moon, who it turns out is Roz's sister, a fact that was revealed to me only last week. She left that night and went to Eugene, and the rest is history."

"You had no idea Camille was Roz's sister the whole time you were … you know, dating Roz?" Anzi asked. She was leaning on the counter, listening intently.

"No," Hudson said, glad to have a sympathetic audience.

"This is like a soap opera," LuRon said.

"Did you sleep with Moon too?" Rob asked, coming into the kitchen after clocking in. "That would be some serious Shakespearean shit."

"Again, no," Hudson said.

"I guess that's why Ione called you mopey," Anzi said. "You're all broken-hearted."

Hudson paused. LuRon, Gilroy and Rob looked over at him.

"I am," Hudson said. "I'm not ashamed to admit it."

"So, who identified you?" Anzi asked.

"All signs point to Moon. Camille," Hudson said.

"What a mess," Anzi said. "No wonder Roz is so bent."

"That is some fucked up head-scratching shit," Rob said.

Just then, Ione came in through the swinging doors and stopped at the sight of everyone leaning around. "I see they've already ruined you," she said to Anzi. "Is that smoke coming out of the pastry oven?"

Anzi swore and jerked open the oven door. Smoke billowed out.

"You must have missed 'timer-day' in culinary school," Ione said. "Great first impression." She turned to Hudson. "Someone out here says they need to talk to you. Make it fast. It's on you now to be sure we have muffins for tomorrow's breakfast since you were distracting the new hire."

Hudson walked out front, hoping it was Roz, but unsurprised when it wasn't. Instead, it was a friend from the old days. Petey, or Crunchie as he was known in activist circles. He was tall and tanned, with long blonde hair hanging over his eyes.

"Hey, Alpine," he said.

"I don't go by that anymore," Hudson said.

"Yeah, man, I heard what happened. Sorry."

"It's in the past."

"I also heard you were working here. I wanted to stop by and say hi. See if you were going to the May Day protest at Fleet Motors."

Hudson tilted his head toward a table near the back of the restaurant, far from customers. They sat down there.

"I wasn't planning on it," Hudson said. "It's too risky for me now. The only way I'm ever going to change the world is by living my life."

"Good, man," Crunchie said. "Glad to hear that. I was thinking about you and came here to warn you off. I think something bad is going down."

Hudson felt a cold ball of dread forming in the pit of his stomach. That awful night they broke up, he remembered Roz saying she would be at the protest. "What are they planning?"

Crunchie looked around before answering. Hudson felt prickles of anxiety in his palms and shoulders.

"I don't know exactly, but I saw the fax." He handed Hudson a balled-up sheet of shiny paper. Hudson straightened it out and laid it on the table. There were only a few words in the message. *Fleet Motors. May Day. Buy three SUVs.*"

"That's pretty clear," Hudson said.

"I wouldn't go anywhere near Fleet Motors on May Day if you want to stay out of the shit. Given your situation, especially."

"I appreciate this, Crunchie," Hudson said. "Let's get together soon. After all this is over."

After he left, Hudson sat alone in the booth, watching

the Portland traffic slide by. The protest was in five days. Roz was in danger, and he was in no position to warn her.

He stared some more at the traffic. A new drizzle was falling. No, he thought, history would not repeat itself. He owed Roz that much.

28

May 1, 1996—May Day protest

Across the street from Fleet Motors

Roz stood motionless in the chaos, rooted to the spot as the police clashed with the protestors and smoke and gas roiled around them. Hudson was still talking, begging her to leave, but his voice sounded muffled and distant, as if coming from another planet.

She took a chance and removed the snorkel mask long enough to wipe away the condensation inside. In just those few seconds, her eyes began to sting and water.

As the fire spread, there were more muffled explosions. At least two SUVs, maybe more, were burning now, the flames sending up black clouds of acrid smoke. Sirens wailed, and reinforcements continued to arrive. People were yelling, screaming, crying and cursing.

A police helicopter hovered overhead like some dark dragonfly, its downdraft sending smoke and tear gas swirling through the streets. A news chopper buzzed around the edges, filming the drama for the evening broadcast. Traffic was stopped, and horns were blaring as angry rush-hour drivers faced the prospect of gridlock getting home.

Roz looked around, trying to process the madness. It had all gone to hell so fast.

The police set up a containment of metal barricades, using their batons and shields on the protestors trapped inside, driving them to the ground where they were handcuffed and shunted to vans idling nearby.

A woman was struggling against the zip ties around her wrists, a line of blood streaked down her face from a nasty abrasion on her forehead. Near her, two cops were carrying an older man propped up between them, one of the aging hippie protesters; he was unresponsive, head lolling to the side, eyes closed. Another cop, wearing a facemask for protection, was casually pepper spraying the face of an agitated protestor held by another officer.

Thanks to Hudson, Roz was on the safe side of the barricades. She was in the clear, and this made her both grateful and angry.

"This doesn't change anything," Roz said.

Yet, it was almost impossible not to laugh, or at least smile, at him standing there in the street wearing a snorkel mask, a bandana wrapped around his mouth, hair going every which way, with milk spilling from his arms as he juggled a half-dozen open cartons.

"Just because you were right about this, just because you saved me from getting arrested, it doesn't change anything."

"I understand," he said, "Can we please start walking? It's time to go."

She took a few steps, then stopped, hands on her hips. "How did you know?"

"We can't stay here," he said, looking behind her nervously.

"Then tell me quickly."

"I'll tell you everything. But not here."

"There's a coffee place three blocks from here, that way." She tilted her head toward the right. "Is that far enough away?"

"Yes."

After a block, he peeled off the snorkel mask and tossed it into a trash bin. She did the same. A block later, he pulled off the bandana and stuffed it into his backpack. He held it open while she crumpled in hers as well—it still reeked of smoke and chemical irritants—and then tossed the whole thing into a dumpster next to a construction site.

As they approached the coffee shop, Hudson scanned the street behind them.

"You really are nervous, aren't you?" Roz asked.

"We both have something to lose here. If you get busted, it will only be worse for your sister. They'll turn you into a media circus, a family of eco-terrorists, or some shit. And I don't want to go back to prison."

"Then why did you risk it?" Roz asked.

He looked at her as if amazed by the question. "You have to know why," he said. "I would risk anything to protect you, to help you."

The simple certainty of his words filled her and somehow amplified her feelings of anger. He made her feel so loved, only to drop her down so far.

"I appreciate the fact that I didn't get tear-gassed or beaten or arrested but hear me loud and clear. I don't want or need your help. That's not your job anymore. Because we're not *us* anymore."

"That's painfully clear," he said. "Let's get a cup of coffee and lay low for a few minutes. I'll never bother you again after this."

"What's going on down the street?" the woman behind the counter asked. She had a nose ring and purple hair. "I heard there was a riot or something?"

"No idea," Hudson said. "Can I please get a soy latte?"

The girl nodded, an almost imperceptible flash of

irritation in her eyes.

"Just so you know, soy lattes are a pain in the ass to make," Roz said. "Just a coffee for me." She turned to Hudson. "I'm going to wash my face."

In the bathroom, she studied her reflection in the mirror above the sink and shook her head at the dismal sight. Her long hair was disheveled. She used her fingers to comb it into some semblance of order. Smudges of dirt and grease were on her face, and her eyes were pink from the chemicals and smoke, ringed by an imprint on her skin where the tight snorkel mask had been.

She ran the water until it was warm and tried to scrub off the grime and soothe her skin and eyes. She had blue eye shadow, mascara and Vaseline in her fanny pack and gave herself a quick refresh. Then she stopped. After all this, why did it matter to her that he thought she was pretty? Idiotic. She shoved her hair into a ponytail and pulled the rubber scrunchie tight until her scalp stung.

Hudson was sitting at a booth in the back, far from the window.

"I added light sugar and half-and-half," he said, pointing at her coffee.

"I don't take it that way anymore," she said. She was aware of how petulant she sounded.

"Should I get you another?"

"No," she said. "This is fine for our last coffee together. Fitting actually. Tell me how you knew about what was going to happen today."

"Pure chance," Hudson said. "A guy I used to run with back in the day, Crunchie, came into the Rose and Thorn. Said he heard I was out and wanted to warn me off the protest. Said some assholes were gonna crash it. I tried to leave a message, but your answering machine was turned off. And you didn't answer your door."

"I wasn't home," Roz said. "I've been staying at Meredith's. She and Rob are being really sweet. Outside of the kinky stuff."

"I was desperate," Hudson said. "I decided to wait and see if you showed up at the protest. You did, and I did what I did."

"Handcuffed us together against my will," she said, sipping the coffee. It tasted good. He really knew how she liked it. Hudson didn't say anything. He was probably exhausted.

"The fact that you knew what was going to happen today doesn't help your claim that you weren't involved back in 1991," Roz said. "In fact, it makes it seem more likely that you were involved."

"I'm going to say this once more, and then we can be done. I had nothing to do with that. I was young and idealistic, but I knew better than to build fire-bombs. I love nature, and I was—still am—willing to die to protect it, but I wasn't willing to kill. Or risk injuring someone. I believe in my heart that I am part of nature, not above it. I never met your sister before those nights in the tree and never saw her again after she left. I never once talked about her to the authorities, although I did mention Moon to my lawyer, but that was after I was already in prison."

"Why did you mention Camille to your lawyer?"

"Because she is the person who lied about me, the reason I got pulled out of the tree."

"Don't call my sister a liar," she said quietly. "My sister didn't lie about you."

"Camille was young, and prison is fucking hard," Hudson said. "I don't begrudge her for trying to shorten her sentence."

Roz shook her head. "She wouldn't do that."

"Trust me, you have no idea what it's like to be locked

up. The fear of disappearing forever turns people all kinds of sideways, I know."

Roz took another sip of coffee. "If prison can turn a person inside out, it can also make a man able to pretend to be someone he's not."

She watched Hudson close his eyes and put his head in his hands. When he lifted his face to her, his eyes were wet. "I understand. She's family, and you haven't known me all that long. But what we have, what we had, you have to know. It was really good. And I'm not a liar."

"You're right, we haven't known each other that long," she said, holding her breath to keep back the sorrow lurking just below the surface of her indignation.

He stood. "I get it. You shouldn't have to choose. She's your sister. I'm sorry about how all this worked out." He sighed. "I wish you nothing but the best. I hope you keep writing. Your poetry is amazing. Just like you." He turned and walked away without looking back.

"Goodbye, Hudson," she said to herself as the café door closed behind him.

After he was gone, she sat at the table, thinking. She pulled out her notebook, but the blank pages were constraining, the jumble of emotions too daunting to capture in words. Instead, she stared at the door. Police cars and fire trucks were still going by, but fewer now.

When she left, it was dusk. The young woman behind the counter smiled. "Soy lattes really *are* a pain in the ass to make. You must work in food service."

"Yeah. I do. At the Rose and Thorn."

"I've heard that place is awesome," the girl said. "Do you love it?"

"It's fine," Roz said with a wistful half-smile. "But it can be a little rough on your heart."

29

May 2, 1996—One day after the May Day protest

The Rose and Thorn restaurant

Hudson stood with his back to the line, preparing a sheet tray of chicken breasts for roasting. First, he brushed them with olive oil, then sprinkled on salt, pepper and fresh rosemary.

Roasted rosemary chicken was a Rose and Thorn signature dish, second only in popularity to the Hungarian mushroom soup. The rosemary chicken showed up in everything from omelets to hot sandwiches to alfredo pasta.

Tonight, more than usual, the feel of the heavy, slippery chicken meat bothered him. Most of the time, he could ignore it, but tonight he felt a little nauseous knowing these used to be living things. Probably, he thought, that was because of what happened yesterday.

After walking out of the coffee shop, he repeatedly fought the urge to go back to Roz—stopping and starting a dozen times—to beg her to change her mind, but ultimately knew he had to honor her clear wishes. No matter the truth, Camille was blood, and he was basically a stranger. Even though they had a connection like nothing he had ever felt, and he knew she also felt it, family outlasted lovers. Family endured. Romantic love was less reliable, in most cases, at least.

Hudson still believed keeping Roz out of harm's way at the protest had been the right thing to do. Mission accomplished. The way to love her now was to move on.

So far, avoidance logistics had been straightforward. Ione had formally moved her shifts so there was no overlap with Hudson. The breakup was mostly old news now, and the kitchen crew seemed to no longer care one way or the other as long as he got his work done. The servers were still steering clear of him, though. Meredith and Kristoph, especially.

The black-and-white TV above the line was airing the local five o'clock news. LuRon and Rob half-watched while they topped off the plastic storage containers on the prep counter. One side was devoted to sandwiches—sliced cheeses, leaves of lettuce, tomato slices, condiments—the other to items needed on the sauté line for pasta dishes—spices and the like.

The news coverage turned to the protest. Hudson didn't watch, but it was impossible not to hear the breathless reporter—he had already forgotten her name—talking about the fire-bombing and the arrests as if the world had temporarily ended, all over a few gas-guzzling SUVs.

"So, H-bomb, tell me why again you were at that protest yesterday?" LuRon asked. "I thought you were supposed to be all innocent and whatnot, but you went to a fire-bombing."

"Not the best look," Gilroy said.

Hudson peeled off his plastic gloves and tossed them. "A risk I had to take." He moved the tray of chickens into the oven and set the timer.

The reporter cut to footage from early in the protest. Rob moved closer to the screen. "Hey, shithead. That's you and Roz."

"Let me see," LuRon said.

"Right there," Rob said, tapping the screen. "They're handcuffed together." He leaned under the window to look at Hudson. "Why are you handcuffed to Roz in public?" He turned back to LuRon. "I knew it. The kink is strong in this one."

A cold wave of instinctive panic washed over Hudson. The video footage meant he was instantly recognizable to the law. But the fear was a reflex—a knee jerk. A remnant of being a felon and worrying it could all come crashing down at any minute. And until this morning, it could have.

As of 9:38 a.m. today, Hudson's slate was officially wiped clean. Innocent. Falsely accused and wrongly imprisoned. His record was expunged. He met with Alison to sign the documents, and then she gave him some more good news. His legal team negotiated a settlement payment from the state of $200,000 to make up for the lost wages and pain and suffering for the years taken from him. He readily agreed to sign the accompanying document in which he gave up his right to sue Oregon.

"Maybe you can make a fresh start," Alison said.

It was overwhelming and, with everything that happened at the protest and after, all his grief and disappointment welled up—the loss of Roz, the imprisonment, the loss of Sophie, the loss of his mother. Alison comforted him, arm around his shoulder, and the authentic moment they shared felt unexpectedly restorative. He was grateful.

Now, he was at work and semi-rich. Maybe he would use the money to travel and see some of the world. Strike out on his own. Get his head back on straight.

As he prepped a second tray of rosemary chicken, he let the kitchen chatter wash over him and then couldn't help himself—he slipped into memories of being in bed with Roz, her red hair fanned out on the pillow like gentle flames, the sheets pulled haphazardly across her beautiful, pale skin and the swell of her breasts.

He imagined them laughing as they dreamed of all the places they would go with the money. A backpacking trip in Canada. The Trevi Fountain in Rome. Someplace tropical. Buy a house together. He could practically hear her joyful giggle.

Though it sounded a little shrill, and Roz was now saying "dude" and her voice sounded a lot like Rob's.

"Dude, seriously, the timer is going off," Rob said, snapping him back to reality.

"Shit," Hudson said, lunging for the oven and pulling out the chicken.

"You burn those birds, Molly is gonna drop the hammer on you. Send you back to the big house," LuRon said.

"She might fire me," Hudson said, "but that's as bad as it can get. I'm a free man now. Got word this morning. My record has been expunged."

"Oh shit, man, that's fantastic," LuRon said. "Congratulations." He threw up a high-five.

"Does that mean you're gonna get some kind of settlement from the state?" Rob asked.

Hudson nodded. "Seems so."

"Are you gonna be a millionaire? Retire to Tahiti?" Rob asked.

"Nothing like that," Hudson said, using a spatula to dislodge the chicken breasts and slide them into a stainless-steel quarter pan. "But I wouldn't mind cooking less meat."

"You thinking of opening your own vegan place?" LuRon asked.

"Too much work," Hudson said.

"Not to mention a quick way to go broke," Rob said. "Rabbit food, no offense, will never take off."

"I don't know," Hudson said, carting the roasting sheet to the dishpit and handing it off to Jon. "We're going to do some real damage to the environment if we keep sleepwalking. Meat production plays a role in that."

"This is true," Jon said. "Climate scientists are convinced the planet is warming."

"How does eating broccoli help?" LuRon asked.

Hudson had read up a lot on this and was ready with an answer.

"First, it takes less fuel and waste to grow plants and grains and turn them into food than to feed the plants and grains to livestock and then turn them into food," he said.

He picked up a knife and began to cut carrots.

"Second, trees that are cut down for livestock grazing release a shit-ton of carbon into the atmosphere. Third, fewer, or even no, livestock keeps gross animal waste out of our water. Fourth, cutting back on red meat is healthy."

He was in the groove and had already sliced through a dozen or more carrots.

"Last, embracing compassion for all living creatures is a good way to live. It's a revolutionary way to live. Being a vegan is an act of revolution."

"That was quite a lecture," LuRon said. "You been practicing?"

"A little too much practicing," Rob said, putting his hand over his mouth, pretending to cover a yawn.

"Cows also give off methane," Jon added.

"So now cow farts are bad for the environment?" LuRon asked. "No matter what, I like my steaks."

"And cheese," Rob said. "Preferably on triple-meat pizzas."

Hudson laughed. "Wait until you try my cashew cheese

pizza with seitan."

"I never will," LuRon said.

"That's gross," Rob said. "I'm gonna go have a smoke and try to forget what you just said."

"Maybe Molly would let me put a vegan item or two on the menu. I mean, the whole vibe here is supposed to be healthy," Hudson said. "The salad bar, the veggie burger."

"Not a bad idea," LuRon said. "A few more veg-friendly options on the menu might bring in a new type of customer, align with our plan."

"Vegan stuff would make the restaurant stand out. Like the Hungarian mushroom soup," Hudson said.

"I don't think you could turn that vegan," LuRon said.

"I'm sure I could," Hudson said, genuinely excited.

"Care to make it interesting?" LuRon asked. "If you can make a vegan version that doesn't make me barf, we'll put it on the menu. If you can't, you take closing shifts for a month."

"You're on," Hudson said. "Okay to break for dinner?"

LuRon looked at the clock. "Take your time."

Hudson took off his apron and walked out front to make a salad. Dave-two was topping off the containers.

"Hey man," he said. "I heard you talking about vegan stuff. It's a rad idea. Like we already have tofu for the salads, we need a dressing. I make this killer tahini dressing at home. It's got like, you know, tahini and a bunch of other stuff. Like green goddess. And all goddesses should be green, in my opinion. But the cheese, man. The vegan cheese is plastic shit, you know? I still eat it, though. I make this tempeh sandwich. It's rad, too. And I bet that would taste so good with green goddess…"

Hudson interrupted. "How stoned are you right now, Dave-two?"

Dave-two laughed. "So fucking stoned. Because that

kind of shit is vegan, brother. That's my number one green goddess." Still laughing, Dave-two rolled the cart back into the kitchen.

Hudson lifted the lid on the tureen of Hungarian mushroom soup warming on the salad bar and stirred the ladle through it, enjoying the savory smell. "I'm going to figure out how to veganize the shit out of you, old friend," he whispered.

He loaded up a plate with salad, topping it with marinated cubes of tofu, garbanzos and veggies. A cup of African groundnut stew and a cornbread roll made dinner complete.

He carried his plate and bowl into the back dining room and sat down with the latest copy of *Willamette Week* to read through the personals. He saw an ad for a poetry reading at Powell's Books, thought about Roz, and then pushed the paper away, staring out the window as he finished his dinner.

At least until he got the money from the state and could take off on a trek around the world, coming up with some new vegan recipes for the restaurant might help take his mind off Roz. Hudson turned back to his salad. After a few minutes, Kristoph came in to set up the back dining room for dinner. He winked at Hudson and then went to work.

30

May 10, 1996—Nine days after the protest

The Rose and Thorn restaurant

"Roz, order up!" LuRon yelled.

"I know, goddammit. You've been buzzing my ass for five minutes," Roz said, loading up her tray with six orders of the nightly special—a burrito stuffed with chicken or grilled tofu, roasted red peppers, sweet potatoes and slow-cooked black beans, all drenched in a mole sauce topped with a dollop of fresco, and served with a side of guacamole and fried plantains.

Customers were going crazy for the burrito special. The dining room was packed, and the kitchen was churning them out by the truckload. There had been a line outside for the last twenty minutes. It was one of the busiest dinners the Rose and Thorn had seen in a while, Roz thought, licking a splash of mole sauce from her wrist.

Molly made the right choice by putting LuRon in charge of the kitchen, Roz thought. Word was spreading about his fresh twists on the menu.

Roz felt a vibration at her waist.

Not all of the changes at the restaurant had been as successful as LuRon's flair for fusion food. Tonight was the second night Ione required servers to wear new buzzers.

The theory was that instead of listening for the bell rings or, eventually, the shouts from the cooks to the servers, the buzzing devices would be more efficient at signaling it was time to pick up orders. So far, the theory was wrong. It turns out that having a device buzz your ribs was distracting and didn't always mean orders were ready.

It's not like people necessarily came to the Rose and Thorn for efficiency, Roz thought. They came to get lost, to waste time, to eat decent food and people watch, to be unbothered. A visit to the Rose and Thorn was for more than just efficient service. It was for belonging and acceptance.

But Ione was insistent. "We are moving into the modern age," she said. "I'm hiring a kid from Portland State to build us a real website next."

"Why does she bother?" Kristoph asked earlier when Roz wired him up. "Have you tried to find a website? It's impossible. AskJeeves is the only one that even marginally works." He giggled when Ione tested his buzzer. "That tickles. I like it. Do it again."

The buzzers looked like a cross between a physician's pager and a miniature telephone clipped to their apron. They were also functionally irritating because they weighed down her apron on whatever side it was clipped, so she was constantly off-balance. Roz felt the wretched little thing buzz at her waist for the hundredth time tonight.

"I'm right in fucking front of you," she said. "Why do you keep shocking me like a misbehaving dog?" She wished Hudson was here. He would laugh. And then make it better somehow.

"Sorry, I haven't quite got the kinks worked out myself," Gilroy shouted over the din of pots and pans and order-calling. He was staring at the new terminal and pressing buttons frantically. "I'm working on it!"

"Maybe someone else should be training to be our resident expert since you're shipping out to Haiti next week," LuRon said.

"I'll show Hudson how it works tomorrow," Gilroy said. "He's young, he'll pick it up."

"Come on, Roz, get a move on," Ione yelled. Roz turned to say something snarky to Ione, but as she did, she caught a glimpse of Ione unconsciously cradling her belly. Despite all the chaos, she looked radiant and was already in protective mama mode. The world stood still for an instant.

"You look so beautiful," Roz whispered.

Meredith stopped and looked at Ione. "You really do. Is anyone throwing you a baby shower?"

"Us!" Roz said, "We have to throw you a baby shower."

"Dara and I have a bunch of stuff we can give you," LuRon said, peeking under the line.

"Does this seem like a great time to plan a fucking baby shower?" Ione asked. "Roz, you've got a four-top that's been waiting almost ten minutes for you to take their order. Meredith, your two-top finished eating fifteen minutes ago and still don't have their check. Turn that table!"

Roz felt the buzz again. "If this stupid thing would stop shocking me when my food is, in fact, not ready, making me waste a half-dozen trips into the kitchen, that four-top would have already been served."

"This is the way of the future," Ione said. "We'll work out the bugs. All of you, stop complaining and do your jobs."

"I'll grab the order from your four-top," Kristoph said, passing by with a tray of dirty dishes into the dishpit. "Miguel is swamped out there. He needs help."

"Jon, take a run around the dining room and pull the full bus tubs!" Ione shouted.

Jon peeked around the corner. "In the dining room?" he asked. "With the people?"

"Do it," LuRon yelled.

Roz bumped against the dining room door with her hip, a full tray hoisted on her shoulder. "For fuck's sake," she said, distracted as the buzzer went off again.

She stumbled, and the overloaded tray tilted. Everyone froze, waiting for the crash and the inevitable echoes of "job opening" and "just set it anywhere" from customers in the dining room. But Roz steadied the tray and slid into the dining room, all smiles and confidence, a round of applause from the kitchen in her wake. She headed to the booth in the far corner and gracefully placed the tray on Miguel's folding stand.

"Is there anything else I can get you?" Roz asked, striving to strike the right balance between personal and hurried as she delivered the food.

They were a cute couple: Walter and Suzanne. Walter was a really nice rich guy who liked to leave obscenely big tips. A few months back, Walter proposed to Suzanne at the Rose and Thorn. It was the whole deal: kneeling on the floor with a ring, a prepared speech, and champagne waiting in the wings. He gave Hudson a twenty to capture photos of the happy moment on his camera.

She remembered Hudson whispering, "Man, I hope she says yes," to Roz.

Suzanne did say yes, and Hudson's photos proved it. Walter brought their favorite image back to the restaurant and pinned it to the overflowing community bulletin board. The wedding was in a park in the Columbia River Gorge later in the summer. Everyone at the Rose and Thorn was invited. Hudson and Roz had planned on going together and then spending a couple of days wind-surfing at Hood River. That was before. She pushed the thought from her mind.

Roz took the empty tray back to the kitchen and tried not to let her simmering depression overtake her, but it was too late. The best she could hope for now was to finish her shift on auto-pilot. She was startled yet again when her waist vibrated. "There better be food ready," she said with a snarl as she entered the kitchen and moved toward the order window.

"There is," Rob shouted, "I got four more orders behind this that I can't even fit inside the window. It's piling up here. Get a move on and take the two orders for Kristoph's table."

"Will this night ever end?" LuRon said, pulling two more burritos from the oven.

"It's about to because we need to 86 the burritos. Onions and peppers are gone, and we only have one skin left," Gilroy yelled. "Spread the word, 86 the burritos."

"Who was in charge of ordering this week?" Ione asked.

"Oh, you want to go there?" LuRon asked. "After you specifically told me to stop over-ordering."

Kristoph rushed in and hung a ticket. He shouted out her order. "One burrito special, one medallion, hold the mushrooms …"

"I said 86 the burritos!" Rob yelled.

"I didn't hear it," Kristoph said. "Because I wasn't in the kitchen!"

"Well, we can't make it. We're out of the ingredients," Rob said.

"A little less panic, children," Ione said. "Meredith, go now, make sure all servers know we're 86-ing special burritos. LuRon, pull Kristoph's order, open the burritos up, add some extra beans, and spread the tofu and peppers out into one more."

He was already doing it.

"What are they drinking?" she asked.

"A bottle of wine," Kristoph said. "Mid-shelf."

"Comp it. Their order will be a bit late. Go tell them."

He nodded and returned to the dining room.

Roz was startled when the buzzer at her waist went off yet again. She snatched it off and tossed it next to the espresso machine. "That's enough for one night."

"Put it back on," Ione said.

"No. It's too much. I promise I'll happily keep working on it and perfect the process, but enough for tonight. Please?"

Ione's expression soured, but she relented. "Fine."

Three hours later, the restaurant was mostly empty. Roz was at the bar, counting her tips. Kristoph walked by as he headed into the dining room to wipe down the tables and chairs.

"Crazy night, huh?" Roz asked.

"Totally. But we cleaned up. I've got enough to splurge on my new sweetie tonight. He's waiting outside."

"You go on. I can clean up."

"Thanks, but no. You already clocked out and I don't approve of working for free."

Kristoph busied himself on the far side of the dining room. Roz stood and walked behind the small bar. She pulled out the fountain hose and tapped it for 7-Up. As the soda streamed into her glass, she looked down at the liquor bottles and mixers lined up like little sobriety-bombing soldiers in the wooden rack.

She looked around the dining room. Kristoph was busy cleaning. Meredith was already gone. Tess was counting up credit card receipts at a table up front by the door. It would be so easy. Mix some vodka with the soda. No one would see. No one would know.

She drank the glass of 7-Up in a long gulp and put her

hand on the vodka bottle. She picked it up, poured the glass a quarter full, then quickly put it back and topped it off with 7-Up.

Roz looked up and Tess was on the other side of the bar watching. How had she moved across the dining room so quickly and quietly?

Roz felt a flush of shame. "It's been a long week," she said. A long life was more like it, she thought.

"I know, sweetie," Tess said. "A hard week, too. But life is going to throw you curve balls from time to time. That's the one thing you can count on. Is this how you want to handle them?"

Inside, Roz screamed. She put her head down and tried to control the boiling knot of emotions swirling inside her. A part of her wanted to tell Tess to fuck off, to save her lecturing for someone whose life hadn't just totally fallen apart.

But Tess was right, of course. Roz poured out the drink.

"It will get better," Tess said.

"Maybe I should quit."

"Quit if you want, your choice, but don't let a man drive you away from your job, your home, your family. We love you here."

Roz sighed. All she wanted to do was hide until the hurt stopped. Like a winter bear, she wanted to hibernate and come out later with everything changed, emerge from months of slumber to a new life full of light, a new Roz.

"I'm heading home now," Roz said. "Thanks for caring."

"You want company?" Tess asked.

Roz came out from behind the bar and hugged Tess. "I'll be fine, really." She grabbed her apron and purse and left the restaurant.

Outside, streetlamps illuminated the sidewalk. Someone

was asleep near the trashcans, but Roz didn't feel nervous. This part of Portland was safe, even at night. In the flower bed alongside the restaurant, daffodils were blooming. Roz bent and clipped a single bloom and stuck it behind her ear.

She walked in the direction of the Hideout. Since she started going there last summer with Clay and then later, with him and Kassi, it had become her favorite spot. Typically, she sat at the bar, had a bowl of chili and a Coke, and talked with Mel. She liked Mel. Mel kept assholes away from her. But tonight, Roz was hoping Mel was off because she would undoubtedly give her the "are you sure you want to do this?" treatment, too.

Why did so many people feel like they had a say over her life? So what if she wanted to have a drink? It was her fucking life, and if she wanted to ruin it, she had every right to do so. It was just one night. She could start the doomsday clock over again in the morning.

Roz rounded the corner and waited at Sandy Boulevard for the light to change. She thought about what kind of drink she might order. Double gin and tonic. Beer with a whiskey chaser. Or maybe start with a dry vodka martini, a double, with olives.

She needed to forget about Hudson and let all that confusion go, just for one night. A night of forgetting would put some distance between her and the hurt, space to clear her mind.

She stepped into the street. A car sped by and honked. Roz jumped back. Shit. That was close. She clutched her purse against her chest, waiting for her heart to settle. After another half-minute, the "walk" light came on. She crossed over to the other side and turned left up Sandy Boulevard.

Yes, that's definitely what she needed. Clarity. That's what she would get. In the morning. All this confusion, this muddle in her head, she just needed one night of not thinking about it. Her unconscious could sort it all out. That's it; she could rely on her unconscious mind if she could stop her brain for one night and give it some room. She would have clarity in the morning. She would know what to do next.

She pulled open the door. *Hotel California* by the Eagles was blasting. A few people were scattered about at the dozen or so tables. Two at the bar. Plenty of room to sit alone. Roz pulled herself onto a stool at the far end of the bar by the window. Rodney nodded as he put a cocktail napkin in front of her. Mel was off. That was good. Rodney was relatively new and didn't know about her. She could drink in peace, free from judgment.

"What's your pleasure?" he asked.

"Double Jack and coke."

"Coming right up."

She watched him grab a tumbler, listened to the tinkling sound as he scooped the ice, stared as he pulled the Jack Daniels bottle from the shelf above his head, smiled when he poured out two shots and then another for good measure—she liked a generous bartender—and felt a tingling joy of anticipation as he added the Coke from the fountain jack.

He set the drink in front of her. "Thanks. Should I start a tab?" she asked.

"Sure thing, beautiful."

In any other circumstance, his remark would irritate her. Now, she wanted him to leave quickly so she could enjoy this drink. She lifted the glass. Cheers to clarity!

An unwanted image sprang into Roz's mind. Waking in the morning. Not knowing where she was. Not knowing who was next to her but knowing what she had done because she was always half-naked. Feeling ashamed.

Hating herself. Hiding that shame with humor. Or offers of more sex. Maybe tomorrow it would be Rodney. She looked up at him. He was handsome enough. Dark hair. A tattoo on his forearm. From this distance, she couldn't make out what it was. As if he knew she was watching, he turned and smiled. Then winked. Sure, he was cute, but not Hudson cute.

Hudson. Always back to Hudson. She raised the glass to take a sip, but the clarity Roz sought arrived before it touched her lips.

All those mornings waking up early together in each other's arms, in love, ready to take on the world. Never hungover or filled with regret. She liked the version of herself she became with Hudson. It was closer to her true, authentic self.

Across the room, a man in a cowboy hat threw a drunken punch at a tall man wearing a backward baseball cap. The cowboy stumbled and knocked over a beer. Three friends of the baseball cap-wearing man stood up, shouting, puffing out their chests. Rodney hustled over, telling them to quiet the fuck down or take it outside.

She put the glass down and leaned her head into her hands. The daffodil behind her ear fell out and landed next to the drink. It was wilting, the delicate petals already fading. She stuck the flower into her water glass.

Roz knew there would be no morning clarity after drinking. She would never stop once she took that first sip, not until it killed her. For the first time in her life, she wanted to wake in the morning proud of who she was and unashamed more than she wanted to hide inside the cocoon of her addiction. She wanted to be the person she saw reflected in Hudson's eyes.

With or without Hudson. That was the only clarity she needed. She was that person now. No turning back.

She slapped a twenty on the bar. It was time to go home, maybe write some poetry, and sit with, not hide from, the hurt.

31

May 19, 1996—18 days after the protest

The Rose and Thorn restaurant

This was it. The first shift they worked together since the protest, almost three weeks ago. The first time Hudson had even seen Roz since then and he was feeling nervous.

He wasn't supposed to be at the restaurant. LuRon was scheduled, but Dara tripped over a toy on the steps and fell. She was in the emergency room getting X-rays to see if anything was broken, and LuRon was there with the kids.

Ione called Hudson and begged.

Ione was waiting like a hawk on a telephone pole when he walked through the back door. She swooped down immediately. "Thanks for covering. Now come with me."

He always thought motherhood was supposed to soften people, but somehow pregnant Ione was even more terrifying. She caught Hudson by the elbow, pulled him into the office and closed the door behind them.

"Look, I know this isn't optimal. But we need you to step up here," she said.

"I'm here, aren't I?" Hudson said. "Seriously. I've made my peace with it. No problem." He moved toward the door, ready to leave.

"Wait," she said, looking at him suspiciously. She leaned against the edge of the desk. "That seems unlikely. You're a man. How did you manage to pull off something most of the world can't even seem to fathom—a virtuous breakup? Don't you remember how bad it was when Clay and Kassi split up? I thought we were going to have to bring in a grief counselor for the rest of the staff."

Hudson smiled and shrugged. "I don't have a great answer for you. Maybe spending so much time alone—as a kid, in trees, in prison—helped me understand a few things about life and how happiness fits into it. I want Roz to be happy. I wanted that when I was with her, and that hasn't changed. I wish she could be happy with me but that's not in the cards." He shrugged again. "It's fine though. When you make your peace with that, it's liberating."

Ione sighed and swiped at her eyes.

"Are you … are you crying?" Hudson asked.

Her moment of vulnerability quickly evaporated. "If you tell anyone, I'll fire you. It's the fucking hormones. I wish the fathers of my baby could be more like you."

"The, uh, fathers, as in plural?"

She pulled a crumpled wad of tissue from her pocket and dabbed her eyes. "It's complicated. We don't know exactly who the father is yet. One of them is okay with that. One of them is not. The third split months ago when he found out I was pregnant."

"I'm not sure what to say here," Hudson said. "Isn't there a test or something?"

"It's not supposed to matter. That's the whole deal with our lifestyle." She absently straightened a stack of menus on the desk. "But apparently, it does."

"People are weird. Love makes us weirder. If you start keeping score, it will warp your mind."

"That's true," she said. "I thought David and David were different."

"They're both named David?"

She sighed. "Just go. Clock in and do your job. And thanks again."

Hudson paused at the office door. "Ione, if there's ever anything I can do, let me know, okay? You took a chance on me. I'm invested in this place and everyone here. You're like my second family. My sometimes terrifying second family."

"You're a good guy, Hudson," she said with a fleeting smile. "Now get out before the hormones surge again, and I murder you."

He opened the door and then turned, hand on the knob. "One quick thing. Does she know I'm working tonight? Roz, I mean. I would hate for her to be blindsided."

"I called her first."

He nodded, closed the door, then walked into the kitchen.

It was Sunday, which meant it was likely they were on the back end of brunch. He was glad his first shift as lead cook wasn't on a Saturday, their always-busiest night, but Sundays were wildcards. Could be dead, could be a madhouse.

Gilroy was working the sandwich line and grill and nodded at Hudson. Russell was plating. Jon was in the dishpit.

Hudson shouldered into his chef's coat and tied an apron around his waist, then moved behind the window to the sauté station, checking the specials board. Fortunately, LuRon had the menu already mapped out.

As he pulled down some pans, he heard the door swing open and felt the air around him change. Gilroy was pretending not to notice that anything was different. Russell made a half-laugh and half-snort sound and reached for a mini-vodka under the line.

He turned and looked at Roz through the order window. He steadied himself on the edge of the stove. Her hair was down and curled so that it bounced and gleamed in the harsh light of the kitchen like delicate flames. She wore a short black skirt and a tight white blouse with black suspenders that emphasized the swell of her breasts. Her blouse was unbuttoned far enough to show a little cleavage.

He felt his heart crash into a retaining wall of memories at a million miles an hour as his body condensed and relived all the moments of pleasure they'd shared during the past few months. The sight of her, the impact, compressed it all into a single lightning strike of sensory overload—remembering the feel of her soft skin against his, the taste of her lips, her delicate fingers wrapped around his ...

He struggled to regain control. He saw her recognize the effort it took, and she smiled in response—not cruelly, just victoriously.

"Hey, Roz," he said.

She held his eye a little too long, but whatever was swimming under the surface was inscrutable.

"Nice of you to cover tonight," she said. "We're filling up fast. It's going to be busy."

"Thanks for the warning," Hudson said.

She nodded and turned to leave, and he couldn't tear his eyes away from the view until the door swung closed behind her.

"You ready?" he asked Gilroy, his voice cracking.

"Not even remotely. After last night, I was hoping for a slow shift."

The orders started coming in fast, but the crew quickly found its rhythm. The special pasta was creamy artichoke hearts and fresh tarragon over penne pasta. The special protein was the same sauce over a chicken breast, baked under a generous portion of parmesan and mozzarella served with roasted potatoes and a side of broccoli and cauliflower.

The specials were selling well—a little too well. It was only 6:45, and if the pace kept up, they would have to 86 the chicken soon.

Ione burst in, dragging Roz behind her. "We've got a problem," she said. "Tell him."

Roz looked chagrined. "I was cleaning booth three when I heard the couple at booth four talking. I'm pretty sure one of them is the food critic for that monthly paper, what's it's called? *Little Town. Our Place*?"

"It's *Our Town*, and he's a hack and hates everything," Ione said. "That little fucker. Why would he even come here? We're not one of those swanky gourmet places."

"What's the problem?" Hudson asked. "We'll cook a nice meal, he'll enjoy it, and he'll write about it. Even if he says he hates it, what's the worst that could happen?"

Ione drummed her fingers against the counter. "Hmm, what's the worst that could happen? The worst that could happen is that he writes a hit piece about how shitty your food is because our head chef is at the fucking ER and enough people read it and it damages our reputation and then customers stop coming here, and the little revival LuRon and I have been working so hard on loses steam, and we have to close and we all end up unemployed and I have to raise my baby under the overpass with David and David begging for handouts by the highway. That's the worst that could happen, and it's pretty fucking awful."

"Damn, girl," Russell said. "You went so dark so fast. Do you need a drink?" he asked, waving a mini.

"I'm pregnant, you lush," Ione said.

"That's not a no," Russell said, cracking his little bottle and draining it into his soda.

Roz put her hand on Ione's shoulder. "Ione, I promise you, you won't have to raise your baby under the overpass because of a food critic," she said. "We got this. You go back to the office, maybe have a nice cold glass of water, and put your feet up. I'll give him excellent service, Meredith will watch my other tables, and Hudson will make a great meal."

Ione nodded. "That's probably a good idea."

Roz nodded her head. "Good, now let me go see what his deal is."

Hudson marveled at how cool-headed Roz was, and how kind she was being to Ione.

When she returned to the kitchen, Ione was gone, and Roz looked distressed. "We may have a little problem after all. His companion can't eat dairy, and she doesn't want the tofu special. They're talking about only him ordering, but it's clearly going to piss him off."

"Not a problem. I can make something off-menu for her. Chef's special, dairy-free. First, though, see if she has any other allergies."

"I'll check," Roz said, hustling back out front.

"Kind of risky," Gilroy said. "What if she hates it? He'll rip us a new asshole, which is where Molly will stand to rip us an even bigger new asshole. Like, inside the new one. It will be like double asshole ripping."

"I got it," Hudson said. "You don't need to worry about any of that. You'll be in Haiti. Or wherever."

Roz bustled back in. "She has no other allergies. Up for anything. He'll have the special pasta and she'll have whatever you whip up."

"I don't know, man, this is flying by the seat of your pants," Russell said.

"Hudson can do it," Roz said. "Dave-two, I need you to clean up the salad bar. I'm going to hard-sell a single trip, but everything needs to be clean and perfect. I'll get them some wine first, so you have time to make it sparkle."

Dave-two nodded, grabbed the salad cart and dashed into the breach.

Hudson closed his eyes and thought. And then he opened them, ready to go. "Gilroy, make some fresh pesto. We've got basil, toast some pine nuts in a pan. No parmesan cheese, though."

Gilroy nodded and ran toward the walk-in to get the fresh basil.

"Russell, make a little batch of couscous with sun-dried tomatoes and peas, no dairy."

Russell drained another mini and grabbed a small saucepan.

Hudson considered his options. He needed something creamy but without dairy. He turned to the counter, pulled down a sauté pan, and added a handful of blanched cauliflower florets, a ladle of veggie stock, fresh garlic, salt and pepper, and a splash of soy milk from the coffee bar. He turned the flame up. When it was hot, he tossed it all into the food processor and ground it into a paste, adding a bit more stock.

Satisfied with the outcome, he funneled it into a squeeze bottle and turned his attention back to the order.

A few minutes later, he dished up a pasta special topped with cheese for the food critic and then a chicken breast sautéed in non-dairy pesto with mushrooms and leeks and served over couscous for his non-dairy-eating friend. He wasn't finished. He carefully drizzled cauliflower cream over the chicken in a cross-hatch pattern and added a side of blanched broccoli.

"Holy shit, that's beautiful," Gilroy said. "You learned that in prison?"

"I learned how to improvise with limited ingredients,"

he said. "And also, how good cooks get protection from asshole inmates. I got good fast."

Hudson buzzed in Roz. She responded immediately and—once inside the kitchen—looked at the food and then up at him. "Wow. Amazing. They're going to love it."

She cleaned a smudge off the edge of the plate and motioned for Russell to replace the wilted parsley in the orange garnish, then carried it into the dining room.

After the rush, they tried to regulate their energy levels as they waited to hear how the dish had gone over.

When Roz entered the kitchen about fifteen minutes later, they looked at her expectantly, Hudson more so than any of the others.

She looked disappointed, but her frown quickly gave way to a grin.

"She loved it," Roz said with a hint of her trademark giggle. "Like, really loved it. She couldn't believe you made something non-dairy on the fly. They had a great time. I mean, we won't know until we read the review, but I think you did it."

"I think *we* did it," Hudson said. "Turns out we make a pretty good team." He caught himself. "Even when we're not together."

Roz half-smiled and nodded. "I'd better go do my side work," she said.

He watched her leave again and thought about how it felt to sit alone in a tree and listen to the silence.

32

June 1, 1996—One month after the protest

Correctional Facility for Women

Roz studied the drab visiting room as she waited for Camille, possibly—hopefully—for the last time.

The shabby tables, the uncomfortable chairs, the faded carpet. She noticed that someone had put some motivational posters up since the last time she was here. The posters seemed from another era, another place—like a Kinko's or a health club in the 80s.

Never give up on yourself—under a picture of someone standing on a mountain peak looking across a sea of clouds below. This one bothered Roz. It seemed like prison might be the ultimate reason to give up on yourself.

Teamwork matters—under a picture of a rowing crew. Another odd choice. The carceral system did not seem to really incent teamwork. More like "self-reflection matters," she thought. Or "atonement matters."

Success will come and go, but integrity is forever—under a picture of a sunset. Okay, that one made a little more sense. Integrity was a great concept, but the whole success coming and going seemed a little like salt in the wound given the circumstances.

The far door opened, and she watched Camille walk toward her, led by a guard. It was Lucinda, Roz's favorite, though the field was limited.

Lucinda nodded at Roz. "I hear we may not be seeing you around much anymore," she said.

Roz smiled. "I hope that's true. I mean, don't take that the wrong way."

"Honey, nothing would please me more than to never see either of you again. And I mean that."

"That's the plan," Camille said.

Lucinda nodded. "Well, you know the rules. There can be no touching, but I'll probably look the other way if there's just one hug."

Roz stood and hugged her sister hard. The stress and emotional anxiety of the last few weeks had taken a toll and she held on longer than expected.

"Are you okay?" Camille asked.

"Yes," Roz whispered, still not willing to let go.

"All right, break it up," Lucinda said.

Camille sat down and looked at Roz worriedly. "What's going on?"

"It's been a long few weeks."

"Is it the new guy you've been seeing?"

Roz winced. "I don't want to talk about that. Let's talk about you. Are things on track? Do you think this will really be the last time I visit you here?"

Camille nodded. "They're reviewing the terms of my release this month." She kept her eyes downcast.

"That's a formality, right?" Roz asked.

Camille took a deep breath but said nothing.

Roz shot a quick look across the room at Lucinda, who was stirring creamer into a paper cup filled with vending machine coffee. She took a chance and reached across the table to touch her sister, laying her hand on top of Camille's wrist with a light squeeze. "What's going on?"

Camille pulled away just as Lucinda stood and yelled,

"No touching! One more time and you're out."

Roz knew Lucinda didn't care if they touched, but there was an entire room of inmates and visitors, and she couldn't break the rules just for them.

"I'm not feeling great," Camille said.

"Have you gone to the prison clinic?" Roz asked, worried.

"It's not that kind of thing. It's a brain thing, a soul thing, really. An integrity thing, I guess," she said, looking over at the motivational poster.

Roz followed Camille's gaze to the image of the sunset. "I don't understand."

Camille hid her face in her hands. "I did something terrible, a long time ago," she said. "Something that has been eating at me. I did it because I was selfish and stupid, and now that everything is moving along, I don't know if I can live with myself."

Roz leaned in with her hands on Camille's knees under the table. "You've paid your dues," she said. "You made a mistake, but it's over now."

"Hands where I can see them," Lucinda called across the room. "I won't say it again."

Roz nodded and put her hands, palms down, on the grimy tabletop.

"That's just it, I haven't done my time. I…" She shook her head. "I lied."

"What do you mean?"

"I cut a deal," Camille said. "I was tired and scared, Roz. They wouldn't let me sleep. They kept yelling at me, telling me I was going to prison forever. I didn't have a lawyer. They said I'd get out early. I mean, I am getting out early."

Roz felt her vision flicker like someone was jiggling the lights on and off in the room. It was so pronounced she actually looked at the light switch and then at the other people before she realized it was happening inside of her, behind her eyes.

"Maybe you shouldn't say anything else," Roz whispered. "Maybe it's best I don't know. Please, don't tell me."

Camille barreled ahead as if she hadn't heard Roz.

"I picked that random guy, the one I told you about, that hippie I tree-sat with and said he was behind it all. I said he was the mastermind. I just made it up. I don't even know his real name."

"Alpine," Roz said, her voice cracking. "His name was Alpine."

"That's right," Camille said. "Alpine. That was his cover name. Anyway, the cops said if I told them who did it, if I became a confidential informant, they'd reduce my sentence. I panicked. I said he did it, that he was the one who showed us how to make the fire-bombs, and he lit them. That's why I'm up for release now, that and good behavior. That was the deal." She drummed her fingers on the table nervously. "Alpine. I don't even know what happened to him."

The room tilted slightly as if caught in a sudden gentle earthquake, and Roz felt her stomach lurch. She held the edges of the table. "He went to prison."

"Oh, no, I wonder for how long," Camille said. She was crying and then stopped, suddenly, confused. She looked at Roz with tears dripping down her splotchy red cheeks. "Wait, how do you know his name was Alpine?"

Roz tried to breathe carefully, in through her nose, out through her mouth, repeat. Finally, she spoke. "We were seeing each other. He was my new guy. Until I found out he was the one who sent you to prison. Or so I thought. His real name is Hudson, and he's a good, decent man who went to prison because of what you said."

"Roz, I'm so sorry," Camille said. "I'll fix it, I'll make it right. I promise."

Roz stood, suddenly. "I'm sorry. I have to go. I have to think."

"Please, Roz, I'm sorry," Camille said, reaching out for her. "Don't leave. Don't go. I'll tell the truth. I'll admit everything."

Roz was already stumbling toward the door, bumping into other people and tables.

"Honey, are you okay?" Lucinda asked, genuine concern in her voice.

Roz shook her head, unable to form even the most basic of words, like "no," or "never again."

Lucinda held the door open, and Roz took one quick look back, freezing at the sight of her sister slumped head down on the table, sobbing loudly, and the stupid integrity poster on the wall behind her. Then, she rushed toward the exit.

The drive back to Portland was a blur. She remembered starting the car, remembered pulling onto the interstate and the next solid memory was that she was parked in front of her apartment. It was like the old days of blackout drinking, only she was sober.

She moved inside her apartment and tried to think about where she might have alcohol hidden. Hudson had been thorough in disposing of her stash. That's okay, there was a market down the street, and she'd bought plenty of tallboys there in the past.

She dug through her purse for cash and Tess's number fell out.

It was like her hands were possessed by the ghost of better decisions. Even as her primal brain, the part that was addicted, was screaming at them to stop, she picked up the phone and called Tess.

"Hello?"

Roz held her breath.

"Who is this?" Tess asked.

"It's me," Roz squeaked at last. "Roz."

"Oh, hey," Tess said. "What's up?" There was a long silence. "Roz, are you okay?"

"Yes," she managed to choke out.

"Roz, listen to me. No matter what's going on, it's not worth blowing up your life."

"Okay," she said, tears in her eyes and voice quavering.

"I'm coming over," Tess said.

"No, no," Roz said, feeling her strength coming back because of Tess's concern and kindness. "I'm fine. I appreciate you, and the offer, but I just needed to hear a voice that wasn't in my head. One that wouldn't tell me to do stupid stuff."

"I'm going to call you in an hour to check in," Tess said. "Don't give up on yourself."

Roz thought about the prison posters and stifled a bitter laugh. "Thanks, Tess."

She hung up and dabbed her eyes. She dropped a cassette into the player. Her favorite sad album, *Yes*, by Morphine. She sat back on her futon couch and tried to figure out what to do next, how to fix this, or what she was trying—or supposed—to fix.

She still wanted a drink fiercely, but she had gotten past this moment before, just last month when she went to the Hideout bar. Remember, she thought, be the person you want to be, the person you are in his eyes.

33

June 3, 1996—One month and two days after the protest

Hudson's apartment

Hudson didn't notice the envelope under his door at first because he was taking a bath in the old clawfoot tub that someone had the foresight to install in his rental years ago. He was grateful for that long-ago bath aficionado and sometimes wondered who went to the trouble of hauling such a heavy tub into his basement studio.

It was odd, he had been told before, for a man to so enjoy baths. But he did. Especially this one because the clawfoot tub could almost accommodate his long body. After years of cold, low-pressure prison showers, a private bath was a luxury.

Leaning back, he remembered how his mother loved water. There weren't many opportunities to swim in their high desert town, although they hiked to a mountain lake in the warm summer months. He could recall the memory vividly, shivering now thinking about how the shock of the glacier-fed water kept him from doing much more than jumping in and immediately jumping out with a screech. His mother laughed and swam happily in the frigid water, gently trying to coax him back into the lake but rarely succeeding.

Tonight, his skin was wrinkling like a raisin. He was reading *Les Misérables* and had just taken the last sip of tea from his mug. He rose up, water dripping down his body—slippery with scented oils—grabbed a towel to wrap around his waist and headed for the kitchen to remedy the empty tea situation.

That's when he saw the envelope.

He bent down, tightening the towel with his free hand as gravity pulled it toward the floor, and grabbed the envelope. He struggled to open it with one wet hand, making a mess of it, then gave up and let the towel drop completely.

It was a poem from Roz.

He stood naked by the door, reading and rereading the poem. It was short and heartfelt, packed with anguish and remorse inside four perfectly rhymed stanzas. His heart was thudding erratically, and he was holding his breath. She knew. She knew everything. And she was sorry. And confused. But mostly sorry.

Then he heard a faint noise outside, a scratching, as if from a lost cat. He opened the door without thinking.

Roz was standing there on the stoop, eyes downcast. She looked up and seeing the surprise in her expression, he remembered he was naked.

"Shit," he said, bending down to grab the towel, mortified that he was already getting hard at the sight of her.

"Hello to you, too," Roz said, watching him wrap the towel around his waist. Her voice was strained, and he could tell she was trying to sound light-hearted.

"I was in the bath, sorry ..."

"It's okay, you weren't expecting me."

"Or anyone," he said. "Will you come in? I'll get dressed, I swear."

"I'm not sure that's a good idea," Roz said. "Coming in, I mean. The getting dressed part is fine. I just wanted you to hear from me in person."

Looking more closely, he could see her eyes were red and swollen. She'd been crying.

"You were protecting your sister."

"I didn't believe you. I called you a liar. I said so many things, mean things.

"Please come in," Hudson said. "We can talk. Or not. We can be quiet together."

Roz hesitated, her head tilted to the side

He looked down at the poem in his hand, drops of water dripping from his wet hair onto the page. "Thank you for this," he said. "It's beautiful."

She didn't answer, and he sensed she was poised to turn around to leave. He had to get her to stay. Hudson pictured his mother swimming, gliding through the frigid mountain water unencumbered; all it took was the certainty of taking one breath after another and before you knew it, you were across the entire lake. That's what she always told him. Please, just give me your hand, she would say.

Hudson set the poem down on the table by the door and reached out his hand. His towel slipped precipitously, but he managed to keep himself covered.

He was rewarded by a faint smile. A faint, tiny, barely perceptible smile.

"Tea," he said, and she looked at him curiously.

"I have loose tea samples from a vendor who wants the restaurant as a new client. Try them with me. Molly wants a report back tomorrow."

She bit her upper lip and wiped away a rogue tear.

"Fresh honey, too. Your favorite from Bunny Farm." Hudson's hand was still outstretched. One step at a time, he thought. Keep breathing.

She let out a sigh so big he feared it would blow her away, but she took his hand and stepped inside. "Tea sounds nice." She paused. "I don't know why you are so good to me," Roz whispered. "You are so patient."

He pulled her in close for a one-armed hug. She rested her head just beneath his chin. He felt as if the piece of him that had been pulled from his body, the gaping hole, was filled, there with her in his arms, and he was whole. Her shoulders trembled as she breathed raggedly. They stayed that way for a while until he worried his body would give him away again. This was not a moment for sex. Even though he wanted her more than ever.

"I don't have another setting when it comes to you, Roz," he said. She nodded, her head still tucked under his chin. "Have a seat. I'm going to put on clothes," he said, gently unwinding her arms, even as he longed to pick her up and carry her to his bed.

In the bedroom alcove, he quickly pulled on a pair of worn-out Levi's and a faded Jefferson Airplane sweatshirt, then spun around, eager to get back to her.

She was sitting on the couch, legs crossed, a pillow on her lap like a shield, looking as if she was trying to take up as little space as possible. It was the exact opposite of how she usually moved through the world.

"Are you hungry? Can I fix you something to eat? I have homemade chocolate chip cookies."

She shook her head. "Just tea for now."

He pulled a small, delicate ceramic teapot from the cupboard. He'd bought it at the Japanese Garden, an extravagance on a cook's salary. He measured out the chamomile, poured in boiling water and then put the pot, two cups, a small bowl of honey, a strainer and four cookies on a matching tray.

He walked back to the couch and placed the tray

between them. Carefully, he poured the steaming liquid through the strainer into the cups and then added a small spoonful of honey to both, stirring until it dissolved completely. She watched his motions, silent.

One thing he learned during the months of not-drinking with Roz was that adding a bit of ceremony and seriousness to the creation of non-alcoholic beverages helped make them seem special, like they weren't merely a bland replacement for booze. That was the theory, at least.

Roz took the offered cup and warmed her hands.

"How did you find out?" he asked.

"It was an accident. I was visiting Camille yesterday to make plans for her release. She was super agitated and kept saying she had done something wrong."

Hudson sipped the tea, silent.

"She admitted she lied to cut a deal, pinned the whole thing on some guy she—"

Roz put the cup down and leaned back into the couch. "—some guy she tree-sat with named Alpine. Said she didn't know what happened to him after she told the police he was behind it all."

He watched as she pressed her fingers against her eyes as if the light in the room was too much to bear. She looked beautiful and vulnerable. She wore a white tank top, a colorful tie-dyed skirt, and simple leather sandals, but uncharacteristically, she wore no makeup—just silver hoop earrings and a pained expression.

"Did you tell her you knew me?" he asked.

"Yes. I told her about you and me, about you going to prison, about how we broke up. She was horrified, distraught. She thinks she ruined your life. And my life."

"Cookie?" He lifted a plate with the homemade chocolate chip cookies.

She took one, nibbled around the edges and then put it

back on the tray.

"Don't you like the cookie?" he asked.

"Didn't you hear me? My sister sent you to prison."

"Roz, this is not a revelation. I knew it had to be her. I've known for a while. I'm sorry for you. It must have been hard to hear."

"I'm so sorry," Roz said. Tears were streaming down her face. "Sorry she did it, sorrier I didn't believe you."

Hudson reached for her and took both hands in his, waiting until she looked up to meet his eyes. "Truthfully, it would have been weird if you didn't believe her," he said.

"You are a strange and wonderful person," she said. "How can I make it up to you?"

"You wrote me that beautiful poem."

"You forgive me?" she asked.

"Completely and without reservation."

She wiped her eyes. He handed her a box of tissues and she used one to blow her nose.

"What does this mean for us?" she whispered.

He leaned closer. "Let's not worry about that now. We have something else to think about."

She looked at him incredulously through tear-blurred eyes. "What could be more important?"

"Camille," he said. "What will she do?"

Roz shrugged. "She can't live with the guilt."

"If she recants her testimony now, she won't get out of prison. She'll serve her full sentence, probably more, for lying."

"I didn't think about that. Oh, what a fucking mess," Roz said. "If she tells the judge, she'll have to stay in prison? I don't think she'll make it. But she has to tell the truth. She can't let an innocent person suffer."

Hudson took a sip of tea and reached for a cookie. He took a bite, then another. "Do I look like I'm suffering?"

"I don't understand," she said.

"She made a dumb mistake," Hudson said. "Telling the truth now won't get me those years back; worse, it won't get her out of prison."

"But she lied. Won't they know that?"

He shrugged. "This stuff, the process, takes on a life of its own. She cooperated. She held up her end of the deal. They won't care that I was innocent. In fact, they won't want anyone to know she was pressured into identifying me. If she recants, it all comes to light, and then they have to act, they have to punish her."

"What should she do?" Roz asked.

"Has she admitted anything on the record yet?"

"I don't know," Roz said. "I was upset. I left abruptly."

"We have to stop her from saying anything."

"I don't understand. Don't you want the truth to come out?"

Hudson placed his cup on the tray, along with his half-eaten cookie. "I'm fine. My lawyer expunged my record. They were able to prove my alibi. I'm innocent. And I have a cash settlement coming."

Roz looked at him curiously.

"Look, it was a terrible experience, but it's over. My life is pretty good. It would have been better if we stayed together, but I care for you and I know you'll be happier if your sister is not in prison."

"Her release will be based on a lie."

"We'll deal with that in a different way. I'm almost sure her rights were violated to get her to talk. My lawyer can probably help with that, but first, we have to get her out. Can you get a message to her to tell her not to confess?"

"Usually, we communicate by mail in between visits."

"That won't be soon enough," Hudson said. "Shit." He stood and paced. "There must be another way to get word to her."

"Today is Monday, right?" Roz asked.

"Yeah, why?"

"Camille calls Mom every Monday."

"Call your mother. Tell her to tell Camille not to say anything and to put us on the list to visit her tomorrow. But please remind your mom that prison calls are recorded. So, be discreet about how she conveys that message. Don't want to raise any suspicion."

"Us?" Roz asked.

"Us, what?"

"You said put 'us' on the list to visit."

"Yes. Us. I think I should be there."

She stood and went to the kitchen wall phone. He watched as Roz punched in the number.

"It's long-distance. Should I reverse the charges?"

"No, it's okay. In-state long-distance calls are included in my plan."

He heard the phone on the other side ring, and ring, and ring again. Finally, someone picked up.

"Mom?" Roz said. "Please tell me you haven't talked to Camille yet today."

34

June 4, 1996—One month and three days after the protest

Correctional Facility for Women

Warm air streamed in the open windows of her beat-up Corolla. The scent of the wild roses lining the median strip mixed with an early morning rain shower flowed into the car. Hudson was next to her in the passenger's seat. He had his elbow propped on the open window's edge, smiling. And, as if the universe was intentionally toying with her mind, Whitney Houston's *I Will Always Love You* started playing on the radio. Roz mouthed the words, Hudson too.

She knew they weren't back together as a couple but at least they were together in the same car, and it felt right. It also felt good to have someone else interested in her sister's well-being; a heavy load was lightened.

After she reached her mom last night, everything fell into place. She hadn't gotten the call from Camille yet, and when Camille did call, Susan was ready. She told her in a don't-talk-back-to-mom-voice that Roz and Camille knew all too well not to share any news prematurely—the language they agreed on—and to approve visitor passes for Roz and Hudson for the next morning.

Roz wasn't crystal-clear on Hudson's plan for after Camille got out of prison, but she agreed the best way forward was to get her out on her already approved early release plan. If Camille wanted to make a full confession—and knowing her sister, they wouldn't be able to stop her—she could do it when she was free and under the protection and advice of an attorney.

The thought of her sister out of prison filled Roz with joy. But she worried that Hudson's insistence on this deception might come at the expense of his emotional scars, that he was subverting his ethics in a way that would cause permanent damage. And, if she was being honest, that it might create a wound between them too deep to ever heal.

"Bigger things are at stake here. Integrity. Honesty. Honor," Roz argued the night before. "And us. We are at stake here."

"All very important stuff, no question. But in this situation, your sister's confession serves nobody's interest. Camille stays in prison. You stay miserable. The damage between us doesn't go away. In this equation, her freedom is the best outcome for all of us, it gives everyone hope where there was none."

After finishing another cup of tea and the cookies, he made up the couch for him and gave her his bed. She would have been fine, more than fine, sleeping with him, even making love—she was desperate for his touch—but he made clear he wasn't ready.

As she tossed and turned last night, she began to see a world where, after Camille was free, maybe they could start over.

And I will always love you …

Whitney was hitting the high point of the love song now. Roz glanced over at Hudson. His eyes were closed, as the air whooshed into the car as if he was letting the world surround him like he was one with the breeze.

"She still has to apologize to you," Roz said. "I will insist on it."

He opened his eyes and turned to her. His expression was calm, and he smiled. "If that's important to you, fine, but let's not get hung up on that now."

"One step at a time."

"One step at a time," he repeated. "This first step is the most important."

She turned left into the prison parking lot. "We're here."

Hudson sat up straight, pulled his arm into the car and rolled up the window. "Wow, it just kind of springs up on you out of nowhere."

"Yeah, it's practically on the Interstate."

"I didn't know it was so close. Or so big."

He pushed his door lock down and then reached over and did the same on her door, even though she was still circling the parking lot looking for an open space.

Roz followed his eyes as his head turned in the direction of the guard towers visible from where they were. Even from this distance, Roz could see men holding shotguns, something she hadn't noticed before. For the first time, she also noticed that the parking lot fencing was topped with barbed wire and that there was only one way in and one way out of the parking lot, even for visitors.

"You okay?" she asked.

He nodded, his face grim. "I'll be fine. Just, my heart is sort of beating fast."

Roz pulled into a parking space and turned off the engine. She turned to face Hudson more fully in the front car seat, unbuckling her seatbelt. "Seriously, Hudson, are you okay?"

"I am, yes," he said, breathing carefully, eyes down. "Sorry." He clicked out of his seatbelt, and they both unlocked their doors. "I'm okay now. Let's go."

"Follow me," Roz said. "Sadly, I'm familiar with this routine."

She wanted to hold his hand as they crossed the parking lot to reassure him, but for some reason, it felt awkward; she sensed he might not be ready for that. She led him to the administrative building, where visitors were processed, searched and once approved, escorted by guards into the waiting room where prisoners waited for loved ones.

"Good, no line," she said. "I guess because we're so early. It won't take long for us to get through verification and search. We might even get there before they bring Camille out."

She opened the door and turned to pass it off to Hudson. He was frozen. Sweat was beading up on his forehead, and his breath was coming in short, hyperventilating bursts. Roz looked around to see if anyone had noticed; not yet, as far as she could tell.

"Come on," she whispered. This time, she didn't hesitate to take his hand. His palm was clammy. He held on to her hand, squeezing hard as they walked back down the ramp. "Tell me what's happening. How can I help?" she asked.

He leaned against a stone wall. Behind him, a small dogwood tree bloomed. He took several deep breaths. Roz pulled a water bottle from her purse and handed it to him. Hudson took a long draw and then splashed some onto his face.

"This is bringing up some things," he said. "Give me a minute. I'll be all right."

"Do you have these often?"

"Have what?"

"Panic attacks."

"I'm not … having a … panic attack."

"You are. It will pass quicker if you acknowledge what's happening and try to steady your breathing." She put one hand on his chest, then placed his palm on hers. "Just follow my lead, breathe, in and out, feel my heart. Bring your heart rate back down to mine. Focus on my voice," she said, trying to sound soothing and comforting.

"What if they find out I'm an ex-con?" he asked.

"Ex-cons are allowed to visit," Roz said. "And you're not an ex-con anymore. Remember? You're innocent."

"I was innocent before," Hudson said.

She could hear the faint edge of hysteria seeping into his voice.

"You don't know what it's like. What if they take me again? What if I get left behind somehow?"

"Hudson, breathe. I'm not leaving you. I fucked up once. I will not fuck up again. I'll tear this prison down with my bare hands to find you if I have to. Now, breathe. In, out, in out …"

He smiled weakly, then closed his eyes and focused on his breathing. She felt his hand on her chest relax. After a few minutes, he looked at his watch. "Thank you," he said. "I'm better now. Let's go, we don't want to be late." He stood, but Roz saw the wobble in his posture. She fished through her purse and handed him the car keys.

"There's a McDonald's two blocks down, turn right out of the parking lot. Sit there, have a soda and some fries, relax. I'll talk to Camille. I'll tell her everything you said. You don't need to go inside a prison ever again."

"How do you know about panic attacks?"

"Camille gets them."

"All the more reason to get her out of prison."

She put her hand on his shoulder. "You've done enough. I can take it from here."

"Will she believe you, that I don't want her to confess?"

"I was the lead in the middle school spring play. I played Stella in *A Streetcar Named Desire.* I can be persuasive." She squeezed his hand. "I'll see you at McDonald's in about thirty minutes. Order me a diet coke, light ice."

He nodded, and she turned, wishing she could stay with him, but they did not tolerate late check-ins. She'd seen guards turn people back for being five minutes late.

She made it through the verification process quickly. Lucinda wasn't on shift today. Someone she hadn't seen before patted her down, and she turned out her purse and pockets. Her pockets were empty except for a lint-flecked spearmint lifesaver and a dusty tampon, and her purse contained only her wallet and a roll of quarters to use at the vending machine inside the visitors' room.

She walked behind the prison guard, her body stiffening when the bars clanged shut behind her, echoing, as they always did. Roz could see how Hudson might be triggered by being here. She hoped he was okay.

She waved to Camille from across the room and slid into the seat at the small table to face her sister. The visitors' room wasn't full, only a dozen or so people. A woman in a red scarf was holding a baby for an older woman to see. Probably the baby's grandmother. The older woman was openly crying, but they looked like happy tears.

Roz looked at her sister. Camille looked tired; she always looked tired. She had been picking at an acne breakout on her left cheek and chin, and the sores were inflamed.

"What is going on?" Camille whispered.

"Don't say anything about anything, okay?"

"I don't understand what you are doing here, and why did you tell Mom—"

Roz interrupted. "When I was here the other day, you told me about what you did."

"Yeah, I told the truth about what I did to Alpine, your boyfriend. Where is he?"

"He decided not to come."

"Was he ever really going to come?"

"Yes, he was outside, but the whole prison thing got a little too real for him. Listen to me. He doesn't care. He wants you out of here, he wants that for me and for you. He was very explicit. Don't admit anything to anyone that will make you have to stay here a day longer."

"I can't promise that," Camille said.

"You have to promise," Roz said, her voice rising. A guard motioned to her to keep her voice down. "You owe it to me. I can't take another day of you being here."

"*You* can't take another day?" Camille said.

Roz stood and pulled four quarters from her purse. She walked to the bank of vending machines, inserted the quarters, pulled a knob, and a Milky Way tumbled down. She pushed open the tray, grabbed the candy bar, walked back to the table and set it in front of Camille.

Camille unwrapped the bar, broke it in two and handed half back to Roz. They sat in silence for a while and chewed.

"It will break all of our hearts if you stay in here," Roz whispered. "I know she hasn't said anything because she doesn't want to worry you, but Mom is dealing with some health stuff. Having you at home, maybe helping out a little, would mean the world to her. And me."

"What's wrong with her?"

"She had a high blood pressure scare. Medication is helping, plus, you know, her depression."

"I don't know how to be out in the world anymore," Camille said. "I would make her life more stressful."

"That's not true," Roz said. "I'll help you get adjusted."

"You'd do that for me?" Camille asked.

"I would do anything for you," Roz said.

"Why?" Camille asked. "How can I live with myself after what I've done? Doesn't it break your heart to know your sister is a liar? I ruined your relationship." She finished her part of the candy and then put her finger inside the wrapper, poking around for any extra chocolate crumbles.

Roz gave Camille the rest of her portion of the Milky Way bar. Camille ate greedily, then licked her lips as she finished. "I love the way caramel sticks to my back molars. It will be a sweet taste for hours if I leave it there."

"Somewhere, three out of four dentists just groaned. Please, Camille. Everyone wants you out. Even the one person your lies hurt the worst."

"How do I know what you are saying about Alpine is true? You'd say anything to get me out of here. He might not have even said that."

"I wouldn't lie," she said, wishing as the words came out of her mouth she had said something, anything else.

"But I would lie, I did lie," Camille said. "I can't have that hanging over my head. What if I see him again? How could I ever look him in the eyes?"

There was a commotion at the door, and Hudson entered. The door was behind Camille, so she didn't see him. Roz nodded at him, and he walked over.

"Brace yourself," Roz said. "You're about to."

"About to what?"

"Look him in the eyes."

Camille swiveled around in her chair and then flinched.

"Hey, Moon," Hudson said.

"Alpine," she whispered.

"I go by Hudson now. My real name."

"Mine's Camille," she said.

"How did you check in late?" Roz asked.

"I was in a middle school play too," he said.

Three loud bells sounded.

"Five more minutes, prisoners. Start saying your goodbyes," a voice called out over the loudspeaker.

Hudson sat next to Roz. He kept his hands next to his side, his posture erect. He was sweating on his forehead, but his breathing was steady.

"I'm sorry …" Camille said.

"We have only five minutes, so I need to talk fast. Please listen," Hudson interrupted. "I don't care. I mean, I do care, it was a shitty thing to do, and you fucked up my life for a while. But you were young and stupid. My life is good now. I want you to have that chance. There is nothing to be gained, not one damn thing, for you to admit the truth now, then have the deal revoked, and stay in prison. Please don't stay behind bars out of some misguided penance or the idea that you need to atone. Prison is hell, and the only thing it will do is break you. The thing that matters to me is that you get out of this hellhole and get on with your life and help your family heal."

"Atonement is a worthy concept," Camille said.

"Maybe," Hudson said. "But atonement can take many forms. Staying inside this prison means you can't do the work of actual atonement, of making things right for the people who suffered alongside you. Your family."

"Seriously, Cammy, we can work on that together when you're out," Roz said. "You can volunteer, go to church with Dad, join the Peace Corps, work on behalf of newly released prisoners, work at a fucking soup kitchen. There's a million things you can do to atone."

"But how can I make this up to you?" Camille asked Hudson.

"Doing this will make Roz happy. That's enough for me. I forgive you. I know that means more when a religious person says it, but seriously, what kind of person would I be if—knowing firsthand how traumatic prison can be—I wanted you to suffer longer for something stupid you did years ago, something you've already suffered too much for?"

Three guards circled the room, asking everyone to wind things up.

"Well? What are you going to do?" Roz asked.

"I don't know. I was ready to tell the truth, to confess. I've made my peace with it. This is the kind of person I want to be."

"Please don't throw your life away," Roz begged.

"You are the kind of person the world needs in it, not locked away from it," Hudson said. "If you want to tell the truth after you get out, I know lawyers who can help you in a safe, controlled way."

Camille stood. "It's good to see you again, Alpine. I hope you enjoyed that beer I left behind."

Hudson smiled. "It was the last good memory of my time with Sophie."

They watched Camille pass through the prisoner doors in line with other inmates; each woman was searched before they re-entered the cellblock abyss.

"What do you think she'll do?" Hudson asked.

"Knowing her, knowing our family history, she'll do exactly the wrong thing," Roz said.

35

June 28, 1996—Two months after the protest

The Rose and Thorn restaurant

More than three weeks had passed since Hudson and Roz spoke to Camille at the prison. They hadn't made any decisions about their next steps as a couple, but Roz was back in Hudson's life, and he was grateful, even though it was only as friends. A semblance of peace had returned to the Rose and Thorn kitchen now that they were no longer at odds.

But the kitchen was facing a new disruption. After ten years working at the restaurant, Gilroy gave notice. The Peace Corps finally identified an assignment for him and Angel—teaching English in Armenia. It wasn't Haiti, as he wanted, but they were going anyway. No more waiting, he told Ione, it was time to start a new chapter.

Gilroy and Angel had already booked their flight and sold all their earthly belongings—which didn't amount to much—at a yard sale, and today was his last day. His leaving left an opening for a new sous chef, and so far, no one had said a word about who might fill it. Hudson figured it would be Rob, assuming LuRon planned to hire from within.

To celebrate and say goodbye properly, Molly was closing the restaurant early and holding a fundraiser with proceeds going to the school where Gilroy and Angel would teach.

LuRon created a mostly Armenian-themed menu and Ione ordered Armenian cognac and mulberry vodka for specialty cocktails. Anzi was making an Armenian dessert. Games and toasts were planned, with one mystery wild card event.

Also for the party, Hudson was fulfilling his promise to LuRon to make a vegan Hungarian mushroom soup. If LuRon liked it, he would add it to the menu to test the market. If he didn't, Hudson had to take the closing shift—including cleaning the grill station—for a month.

He had thought about how to make this soup without dairy for weeks and had done three small-batch trial runs at home. The first two were terrible, but the last one was spot on. Now, the task was to make a larger batch. He was excited for LuRon and others to taste it and he was paying close attention today.

He was also using the soup-making as a distraction. Today was the day Roz would find out what Camille had done. They still didn't know if she decided to confess or would stay quiet about her lie. Camille refused to tell Roz or their mom what she would do, saying she wasn't even sure herself. Roz was at the prison, and she was supposed to call him at the restaurant either way, but so far, nothing. He was getting worried.

In theory, if she kept quiet, Camille would be released today. If her conscience got the better of her, she would remain in prison for who knew how long, months, years even, before an attorney at the Portland Justice Project could help, and that was assuming they even took up her case. Hudson had told Alison about the situation, and she thought they could help, but she was graduating in a week and already had a job with the ACLU. She promised to share the information with the next law student intern at the center when the time was appropriate.

Hudson hoped Camille could accept that she had messed up and get on with her life, but he knew ignoring an unjust debt was a tall order, whether she admitted it today or not. If handled poorly, the feelings of guilt might fester and slowly poison any good in her life.

He stirred the soup in the steam kettle.

He also worried about how Camille's decision would affect his future with Roz. He felt they had a better chance at reconciliation if Camille was out of prison, but he wasn't sure. These past few weeks, a new tentativeness had emerged between them, and last week, he begged her to stop saying she was sorry. It seemed like this imbalance, the fact Hudson would forever be the one who suffered because of her sister's lie, might be too much to overcome, for either of them. The thought was depressing.

"You know it's never gonna work, right?" LuRon said.

"What?" Hudson asked, baffled that LuRon could read his mind.

"This fucked-up soup you're making," LuRon said. "It's never going to work. Why don't you let me taste it here in the kitchen, so you're not embarrassed in front of everybody?"

Hudson smiled. "Have a little faith."

"I will admit that it doesn't smell terrible," LuRon said, looking into the steam kettle and wrinkling up his nose. "But it looks weird."

"It looks exactly like the dairy kind," Hudson said. "Puke-pink and steaming. You think it looks weird because you saw me grinding cashews."

"Nuts do not belong in soup," LuRon said. "That's a scientific fact."

"West African Groundnut stew has peanut butter in it,

and that's a traditional dish," Hudson said.

"Please tell me more about my Black heritage," LuRon said, propping his chin on his fist as if super interested.

"I'm just saying, keep an open mind," Hudson said.

"That would have been easier if I hadn't seen you also putting soy milk in there. I tried a soy latte here, and it tasted like wet dirt. Like a cup of hot mud with an old sock in it."

Hudson laughed. "Kassi made it, right? I tried one of hers before she left. She hated making those things. And it showed. Ask Meredith to make you one. She does a killer soy latte."

"You just worry about the mud soup *you're* making," LuRon said, returning to the line.

Gilroy was leaning on the counter, looking thoughtful.

"Are you going to miss this place?" Hudson asked.

"I won't miss the work dreams."

"They're the worst," LuRon said. "A couple of nights ago, I dreamed we were launching a new chicken dish, and we had to pound them with the mallet first and then bread them, and the orders were flying in, and every time I tried to pound one, they would turn into an undead chicken and fly off into the dishpit. I was yelling at Jon; he came around the corner and had fifteen zombie chickens perched on him. It was wild."

"My dream is always the same," Gilroy said. "I'm chopping onions, and my knife is so dull, it mangles them, and then I realize I'm using a spatula. Ione yells at me. Or Molly. But I never stop chopping. Ever."

He looked down. "I will miss you all, though," he said, a shy tenderness in his voice. "And truthfully, I'm a little nervous about moving overseas."

Hudson grabbed a spoon from the counter, tasted the soup and adjusted the seasonings. "What's got you so rattled?" he asked.

"Strangers in a strange land and all that."

"You'll be great," Hudson said. "Take it from me. Humans can adjust to almost anything."

"I guess," Gilroy said. He was finishing up a traditional Armenian pilaf with vermicelli and rice cooked with raisins, almonds and allspice, carefully checking the recipe again. "It's more than being in a new place. Angel and I have never lived together before, and now we're going to spend two years in a tiny room thousands of miles from friends. Alone. Me and her."

"Oh, I see," Anzi said. She used a grater to curl pieces of chocolate onto two traditional Mikado cakes, thin layers of baked dough held together by a rich buttercream frosting. "It's not so much Armenia you're worried about. It's emotional honesty in your relationship."

"Nobody asked you, new-Dino," Gilroy said.

"Aww, that's cold, Gilroy," LuRon said. "She has a name. It's New-girl."

"Still?" Anzi said with a good-natured sigh. "I've been here two months. And 'girl?' Isn't that a tad patronizing?"

"They had me as New-guy on the schedule literally until you got hired," Hudson said.

'Yeah, but they didn't call you New-'boy,' right?"

"Point taken," LuRon said. "It's New-gal from now on." Anzi rolled her eyes.

"I was called New-guy for months, until after they hired that bald man with the twisted mustache," Gilroy said.

"The dude with the missing finger?" LuRon asked. "Man, that was a dumb hire. I knew the first day he wasn't going to make it. I don't remember his name anymore."

"I hope you don't forget me that easily," Gilroy said. "We've worked together a long time now."

"I could never forget you, Rob," LuRon said.

"That's hurtful," Gilroy said.

"Hurry up in there," Ione said, poking her head in the door. "The last customer left. We're good to go. Also, Angel is here."

"First time I've met her," Hudson said. He tipped the steam kettle to pour the soup into a stainless-steel container.

He followed Gilroy out, carrying the soup like a chalice in a religious ceremony.

Ione was talking to a slender woman with black hair and an easy smile. They paused as Gilroy approached.

"Angel, this is Hudson," Gilroy said.

Hudson balanced the soup against his hip so he could shake her hand.

"He's told me all about you," Angel said, taking his hand. "It's nice to meet you."

"The pleasure is all mine," Hudson said. "I'm sorry it took so long."

"Don't be," she said. "But remember, in two years, we'll be looking for friends' couches to crash on."

"Maybe sooner," Gilroy said. "If it doesn't work out."

"That's precisely the wrong attitude, Gil," she said. "Is this the vegan soup? I can't wait to try it."

"You might be the only one," Hudson said.

The front door to the restaurant opened, and Roz walked in with Camille. Roz caught his eye and smiled. Hudson felt a wave of relief wash over him. "It's nice meeting you, Angel, but please excuse me for a second."

Still carrying the soup, he made his way over. "You're out. I'm glad."

Hudson set the soup by the cash register. He took a step toward Camille, trying to sense what she was feeling or whether he should hug her, but Camille moved back, just a little, but enough that it was perceptible. He understood.

The first few days out of prison were disorienting.

He looked at Roz. "I was getting worried."

"I'm sorry. The pay phone at the prison was broken, and then we got in a traffic jam and decided to head straight for the Rose and Thorn rather than stop to find a phone. I want to get one of the mobile phones everybody is talking about. It would have been so great to call from the car."

"Thank you again, Alpine. I mean Hudson," Camille said. "I'm sorry, and honestly, I don't know what else to say, at least not yet. This day has been overwhelming, and I feel weird being around you."

"It's a big adjustment to have your freedom back," Hudson said. "People expect you to be happy and put everything behind you just like that." He snapped his fingers. "Doesn't work that way. And don't worry about me. It will get easier, I swear."

He wasn't sure about that last point, but what else could he say? He couldn't control how Camile was going to feel. He watched as Roz stroked Camille's back, comforting her, her attention fully on her sister. Hudson picked up the soup. "I need to put this in the warmer. Will you stay for Gilroy's party?"

Roz looked at Camille. "What do you think?" she asked.

"It's a long drive to Coos Bay," Camille said.

"We'll stay for a few minutes," Roz said.

Roz led her to a booth as LuRon and Gilroy started bringing food out. Employees not on shift began showing up, grabbing plates from the buffet, ordering drinks, and buying raffle tickets for a bottle of cognac or one of the Mikado cakes Anzi made.

Molly came in from her office and made her way to the center of the dining room. "Ahem," she said. "Ahem."

"Pipe down, everyone," Ione shouted. "Be quiet. Molly

has the floor."

Molly waved Gilroy to her side. "Gilroy, I will admit, I didn't think you would last here. It's been what, five years?"

"Ten," he said, looking hurt.

"Really? I don't think so. Anyway, you've been an important part of our family for some undefined amount of time, and we'll miss you. But you and Angela …"

"Angel," Angel said. "We've met like five times."

"Angel, okay, sure, whatever," Molly said. "May I continue?"

The employees collectively nodded, along with Gilroy.

"I'm glad the next chapter of your lives together will focus on making a difference for those who need extra support. The energy that motivates you to join the Peace Corps is the same energy that makes this place special. All of you have it, and while I am proud of you and your work here, it makes me even prouder when you're ready to take that energy into the broader world, like caterpillars becoming butterflies. Gilroy, you are ready to fly. When you get to Armenia, I hope you'll think of us occasionally and make a few of our signature dishes for the locals."

"I will not be making Hungarian mushroom soup," Gilroy said. Everyone laughed at that, and Gilroy beamed, happy people thought he was funny.

"Speaking of the best soup in the world, I understand that Harrison made a vegan version for us to try tonight, and there's a lot riding on it."

"Hudson," Roz said, with a smile, from the booth where she sat with Camille. Nobody heard her except Hudson.

"LuRon, would you do the honors?" Molly pointed at the soup.

LuRon made a big show of ladling a serving into a bowl, then swirling and sniffing it like a glass of wine. "I don't know," he said, dipping a spoon in. He took a taste, grimaced, and reached for a glass of water, emptying it slowly while tension and silence built.

When the glass was empty, he clanked it down on the table. He looked around, enjoying the tension. Finally, he spoke. "Well, like I expected … it's not terrible."

Ragged cheers broke out, and Hudson smiled.

"It's not as good as the regular kind, but it's not completely awful. I mean, I don't think anyone will ever knowingly choose to eat this, but I guess we could add it to the menu, like for a joke."

"That's faint praise indeed," Molly said, dishing up her own bowl. She took a bite and rolled her eyes. "LuRon, you fibbed. This is delicious."

Ione made her way to the soup bar. She tasted a small spoonful, nodded, and then ladled a good-sized portion into a bowl. "This is delicious." She affectionately rubbed her tummy. "The baby is moving! The baby likes it. You'll need to keep this on hand."

She moved closer to Molly, who put her hand on Ione's belly and smiled at the strong kick.

"Not bad, H-train," LuRon said, holding up his fist for a bump. "You did good."

As the Armenian liquor began to flow, Hudson and Roz snuck away for a private conversation in the back dining room.

"Your soup is great," she said.

Hudson smiled. They were drinking club sodas with blueberry syrup, the no-alcohol version of the special Armenian cocktail.

"Good enough to send Gilroy packing to a whole other country?"

"I guess it pays to always have your passport current," she said. "Just in case you're faced with vegan soup."

"I'm not sure mine is current," he said. "I should check."

"Mine is," Roz said. "There was a time I thought maybe I should just up and leave. Start over. I still think that sometimes."

"Like a caterpillar becoming a butterfly," he said. "That was a surprising metaphor Molly used." Roz giggled, and the sound made his heart sing. There was simply no other way to describe how happy Hudson was in her presence.

Then, abruptly, she stopped giggling, and her face got serious. "I'm not coming back," she blurted as if trying to get the words out before she could stop herself.

"What do you mean?" he asked.

"This thing between us," she said, her words coming quickly, "it's a huge, good thing. And also a huge, bad thing. The bad thing is partly my fault, partly my sister's fault. And I …" She looked at him helplessly. "I don't know how to process it. I don't know how to be with you or how to be without you. I am so confused and can't see another path except to put some distance between us while I try to get my head on straight."

He nodded slowly. "What will you do?"

"Get Camille situated. Maybe help her find a job. Help my parents get back on their feet. They need me now."

"You're moving back to Coos Bay?"

"It won't be forever." She stopped, eyes downcast. "I mean, it might be, I guess. I don't know. Things are so complicated."

"Are they?" Hudson asked.

"Aren't they?" Roz asked. "The love of my life went to prison because of my sister, who lied to cover up her crime and now regrets it. And even though I treated a decent man like an asshole, he risked everything to keep me safe, and how did I reward him? By calling him a liar and a whole lot worse than that."

"Okay, it's a *little* complicated," he said. "Sure, there's some shit between us, stuff we'll have to work through, but I never stopped loving you. Even when you thought I was a lying asshole."

"I know," she said, touching his cheek. "Can't you see how, I don't know, how unbalanced this will make us?"

Hudson sighed. "I see that possibility, yeah, and was worried it would keep you from being with me. You must know, though, I would never make you feel beholden, ever. Not Camille, either. If anything, I'm beholden to you for all the good things you brought to me, for showing me how wonderful life can be, for loving me."

"That's exactly what I mean," she said, standing on tiptoe to kiss him quickly. "Don't forget me. But don't wait for me either. More than anyone, you deserve a happy life."

"I don't understand why it has to be this way," Hudson said, pulling her in tight.

They stayed that way for more than a minute, and then she gently pulled away.

"Don't go," he said. "Please, don't go."

"I have to," she said.

"You don't have to. We can try."

"I'll write."

She held his hand for another few seconds and then walked away. Hudson felt utterly blindsided. He watched her leave, standing in the doorway of the back dining room, as she hugged people, giving Gilroy the biggest hug of all, smiling and saying she'd keep in touch, that she would write to everyone. She finally ended what would have been another round of hugs, saying she and Camille needed to make it to Coos Bay before dark.

And then she was gone.

Hudson swiped at the tears collecting in the corners of

his eyes, put his hands in his pockets, and left the Rose and Thorn by the back door. The weather was pleasant. The sun would set in another couple of hours. Hudson started to walk. He didn't know where he was going, but that didn't matter. Today, he would walk until he couldn't walk anymore. Decisions about what to do next could wait.

36

September 1, 1996—Four months after the protest

Coos Bay, Oregon

Families are resilient. That thought rattled around in Roz's head as she watched her mom bring food to the table. It was Tuesday, and that meant tacos.

Susan placed a steaming bowl of seasoned ground beef simmered in canned enchilada sauce and another of refried beans on the table. She went back into the kitchen to bring out all the sides: shredded iceberg lettuce, grated American cheese, sour cream and salsa. Last, Susan poured out four glasses of fresh lemonade.

"Oh, forgot the rice, back in a flash," she said.

Her stepdad, Stan, was smiling across the table at Camille. His anger and hurt had subsided, replaced by gratitude that his baby girl was home. It was already changing his behavior. He no longer felt ashamed by the judgment of timber neighbors and spent more time at home and less at church. He was working part-time at the hardware store. Most important, he wasn't drinking.

Camille had long ago forgiven him for his part in it all. Turns out Stan had mailed Camille a letter every week for the duration of her stay in prison. Half news, half penance; she saved every letter and showed them to Roz and their mom like treasure.

Roz reached for the beans. Stan coughed, stopping her.

"I'd like to say grace first, please," he said.

Susan joined them at the table, setting down the rice, a bowl of chips and a smaller bowl of guacamole, and they joined hands.

"Dear Lord," Stan said, eyes closed and head bowed. "I thank you again for bringing my girl home safely, both my girls. We are forever in your debt. Amen."

"Amen," she said.

Roz started building a pair of tacos, skipping the meat.

"I was talking to Mrs. Gault at the library today," her mom said. "She said you've been spending a lot of time there working on something."

Roz nodded, caught in the middle of a bite of taco. The crispy shell broke, and she struggled to contain the damage as strips of lettuce, bits of cheese and drops of salsa rained down onto her plate.

"Geez, new mouth?" Camille asked.

Everyone laughed.

"I'm so happy we're a family again," Stan said, beaming. "The Lord works in mysterious ways."

"Seems like the Lord could have picked something easier than sending Camille to prison," Roz said.

"Dear, don't be sharp," her mom said. "What have you been spending your time on at the library?"

"A little poetry thing," Roz said. "I'm using a computer there."

But it was more than a little thing. Old Growth Publications, a small press in Eugene focused on environmental writing, was publishing a collection of her poetry. She wasn't quite ready to talk about it with her parents, worried it would open old wounds, and why risk that? They'd find out soon enough. "That's wonderful, honey," her mom said, spooning out Spanish rice. "Mrs.

Gault is so fond of you."

Roz nodded. She owed Mrs. Gault for kindling her interest in poetry years ago and then for continuing to fan the flames. She'd been helping Roz edit the poems and format the manuscript ever since she got back. To help repay the debt, she'd been volunteering part-time at the library. It was Mrs. Gault who put her in contact with Old Growth Publications.

The poetry collection, *Seeking Redemption Through Small Acts of Contrition*, was about more than environmental topics. It was also about love and loss, grief and joy, and the nature of forgiveness. If she was honest, it was about Hudson and her. She was still trying to process what happened, to make sense of it; poetry was helping. Her advance copies were supposed to arrive any day.

She was developing a new perspective on her activism, starting to believe that protecting the planet was important but it required more than protests and direct actions. It also required taking steps to improve and grow yourself, to make sure you were worthy of the planet. Part of that required forgiving yourself, truly and completely, for past mistakes, and finding new ways to live. She wasn't there yet, but she could tell something in her was changing.

Camille was adjusting reasonably well to life on the outside. She had a job at the video store. Mostly, it meant rewinding VHS tapes while watching '80s horror movies and flirting with her co-worker. At first, she had panic attacks almost every day, and Roz would have to drop everything and hang out in the store to help keep her calm. But that was starting to ease up, as were the nightmares. Walking near the Pacific Ocean seemed to help, too.

To Roz's surprise, Camille confided in her father about her lie, and his response surprised her even more. He took it upon himself to help Camille find peace. They read relevant Bible passages and volunteered at the community homeless shelter together. Stan was encouraging Camille to get counseling, and they were waiting for their insurance to approve the expense. In the meantime, Stan and Camille had long philosophical discussions about the nature of atonement and forgiveness.

Having both girls home fussing over her, Susan's mental health was improving. During the dark years, she took up beekeeping to distract herself. Now, she had a little side business selling honey—to locals and tourists—and a well-pollinated garden. She was branching out to selling beeswax candles now. Roz promised to help her build a website, although first, she'd have to teach herself how.

The one time Roz talked about moving back to Portland, Susan begged her to stay, suggesting instead that she pick up her old diner job downtown. Roz was thinking about it. The disability payments her dad got and the honey money weren't enough to cover the bills.

After dinner, the girls cleaned up while Stan and Susan made tea and settled down in the living room to watch their new favorite show, *Seventh Heaven.* Roz wasn't feeling quite full and rummaged around in the pantry for something sweet. She found a box of 'Nilla wafers. She checked the expiration date, then the calendar on the wall, and shrugged. "Close enough."

"You doing okay?" Camille asked as she folded the dish towel, watching her sister pull out a handful of stale cookies.

"What makes you think I'm not?" she asked, crumbs falling from her mouth. "Because I am eating crappy expired cookies?"

"That's one reason," Camille said. "Have you talked to him yet?"

For the past couple of weeks, Camille had been urging

Roz to call Hudson, even if just to check in and see how he was doing. She kept telling Roz she didn't need to solve everything with the first phone call.

Roz shook her head. "No. Not yet. I don't know what I'd say."

Camille grabbed a cookie from Roz's hand, popped it in her mouth, and then grimaced. "How about 'How's the weather?' Roz, come on. It doesn't matter what you say. Just call. It's been more than two months."

"He could call me."

"You left him," Camille said. "There are rules."

Roz shook the now-empty box, made a fake pouty face because there were no cookies left, and tossed it in the trash. "I think he may be part of my past. A good part. But a memory."

"I know that's not true," Camille said.

"Let's not talk about it."

Roz did want to hear his voice. She wanted to know how he was. She had written him multiple heartfelt letters with lyrical, aching words about how much she missed him and how she was trying to find a path back. Needed to find a path back. But each letter ended up in a crumpled ball tossed first on the floor and then, when enough built up to remind her of her embarrassing lack of follow through, dumped into the firepit and turned to ash.

"I'm going downstairs and work on a new poem I've been thinking about," she said, heading into the basement.

"And maybe call him? Really, what do you have to lose?" Camille asked.

Only everything, Roz thought. What if he's moved on?

Down in the partially finished basement, Roz had a change of heart. Why not? He'd probably be working tonight, so she could leave a message. A message couldn't hurt. It was the best way. Test the waters. Ease into it.

The basement was Roz's favorite place to talk on the phone, a habit formed in childhood when she spent hours talking to her best friend, Rose. She would crawl under Stan's big old library desk, stretching the phone to the very limits of the spiraled cord, and then lay on her back with her feet propped up on the desk chair, hidden.

She hesitantly took the wall phone out of the cradle.

"Sorry I missed you. I wanted to say hi and see how you were doing," she whispered, practicing her message.

She dialed Hudson's number from memory, crawled under the heavy desk, and assumed the familiar position as it began to ring. She was transported back to being a little girl in a blanket fort, her back pressed against the thick ratty shag carpet, hidden from the rest of the world.

Over the years, she'd doodled a rich tapestry of drawings, snippets of poetry and other scribbling on the light composite wood under the desk. She studied it while waiting for his machine to pick up. The latest doodle was a heart with Hudson's initials and hers inside and an arrow piercing it. She drew that when she came home for the holidays months before everything went to hell.

"Sorry I missed you. I wanted to say hi and see how you were doing," she practiced again, waiting for the beep.

She was looking at his initials and thinking about how love slips away under the steady grind of time when Hudson answered—the actual Hudson, not his machine.

"Hello?"

She froze.

"Roz?" he said, his voice hopeful. "Is that you?"

She stayed silent for a long beat. How could he possibly know it was her?

"Roz?"

"Sorry I missed you. I wanted to say hi and see how you were doing," she squeaked.

"Uh, okay. It's good to hear your voice," he said. He sounded almost solemn.

"Hi," she said, heart hammering.

"Are you all right?" Hudson asked.

She nodded.

"Are you nodding?" Hudson asked. "I hope you're nodding. But you know I can't see you, right?"

She laughed. "Yes, I'm nodding. Sorry. It's weird to hear you. Good weird. I'm okay. How are you?"

"I'm okay."

"Are you still, you know, at the Rose and Thorn?"

He laughed. "Because why am I not at work? Clearly, you didn't expect me to answer."

"Well," she said. "Kind of."

"You want to keep talking?"

She propped her legs on the chair and pulled it closer to the opening of the desk. It felt good talking to him.

"Yeah, I do. Tell me why you're not at work."

"I'm taking some time off. It's been super busy. LuRon had jury duty, and I had to cover for him for a month."

"You must be exhausted," Roz said.

"Ione has been off this past month, she had the baby, a little boy."

"The baby! What did she name it?"

"David."

"So now it's David, David and little David?" she asked.

He laughed, and hearing it felt like how honey tastes.

"Here's the nutty part. Molly is filling in for her."

"That is nutty. And probably terrifying."

"For sure. Ione is back next week. I was glad I could help, but I need a break. How are things in Coos Bay?" he asked.

"Things are going well enough. Camille has a job."

"Oh, that's great," he said. "The first job can be hard."

"I still remember your first day at the Rose and Thorn," she said. She was rocking the desk chair slightly back and forth with her bare foot.

"I do, too," he said. "I'll never forget seeing you the first time. Took my breath away. Just thinking about it still does." He paused. "Your parents? How are they?"

She reached for a pencil and began nervously doodling on the underside of the drawer while they talked. "My mom is doing better. And my dad is making progress. But you know, it's up and down."

"I'm sure they're glad to have you there," Hudson said. "How are you in all this?"

That was such an open-ended question. Lonely. Confused. Horny. Sad. Hopeful. "I'm okay," she said.

"Have you been writing?"

She nodded, emotions close to the surface.

"I hope you're nodding again," he said.

She tried to laugh, but it came out choked. "I have been writing—a lot. I have a little project I'm working on. It's pretty cool."

"That's awesome," he said. "Will I get a chance to see it?"

"At some point," Roz said.

"Good. I hope so. I miss you," Hudson said.

She closed her eyes and tried to think of what to say. She hadn't given up but felt unable, or maybe it was unworthy, of putting the pieces back together.

"I know you told me not to wait for you," Hudson said. "And I haven't, but I want you to know that there will always be a place for you in my heart and my life. No matter where life takes us now."

She shook her head. "You deserve someone better than me," she whispered. "Someone who isn't so broken. Someone who treats you better."

"You're not broken, Roz," he said. "You just see yourself in a broken mirror. I've told you this before, but it bears repeating. If you could see yourself through my eyes, you'd never feel doubt again. Never feel bad again. You'd know." His voice was thick with emotion and reinforced with certainty.

"You're a good person," Roz said. "So committed to saving the planet, so kind. You're a special person, Hudson."

"You are, too, Roz."

"I'm not, but I'm learning to live with it."

"With what?" Hudson asked.

"With disappointment. In myself. I made some bad choices along the way. And what I did to you was the worst. I don't know how to come back from it."

There was a long silence.

"Roz, listen to me," Hudson said. "We're human. We're going to make mistakes, we're going to disappoint ourselves and others. It doesn't mean you quit. It's the same when you try to save the planet. It comes from the same place as saving yourself. It will never be perfect, and sometimes it will seem hopeless, but you keep trying. You can't give up. You have to forgive the shortcomings in yourself and in others. It takes patience and a little faith."

"I think my faith is busted," she said.

"Sometimes, it's okay to lean on someone else until you get it back," Hudson said. "Until you find your strength."

The pencil tip snapped off as she traced the heart with their initials again. "I'd better go," she whispered. "Can I call you again sometime?"

She heard a sigh through the phone and Roz realized that his tone had been all off this phone call. Kind, but distant. Neutral. Suddenly, she dreaded the words that were about to come.

"You won't be able to reach me for a while. I'm making a change. I'm going to see Sophie for a few days, back where all this started, and then I'll be leaving this area."

"You quit the Rose and Thorn?" she asked.

"Yeah, it's time. I'm using some of my settlement money to start over."

"Where are you going?"

"Costa Rica."

Roz felt something shift inside, as a future in which she might never see Hudson again came into view.

"Why Costa Rica?" she asked softly.

"That's a story for another time. Give me your address, and I'll write once I get settled," he said.

He took down the address and then was quiet. Roz couldn't stand it, and decided it was best to end this miserable goodbye. Why torture herself?

"Take care of yourself, Hudson," she said, then disconnected. She lay there in the dark, listening to the buzz of the dial tone.

Eventually, Camille brought her a ginger ale. "How did it go?" she asked.

"How did you know I called?"

"Sister's intuition."

"It did not go great," Roz said. "He quit the restaurant. He's leaving the country. If I hadn't called tonight I wouldn't have been able to reach him, maybe ever again."

"Good thing you called then." Camille took Roz's hands. "I can take care of Mom and Dad. You've done more than your share. It's my turn to support you. Please don't give up on yourself, or him. Don't give up on love."

Roz sniffled and hugged her sister. "I don't know," she said. "But can you show me on a map where the tree you were in with Hudson is located?"

37

September 3, 1996—One day before Costa Rica

Former old-growth forest near Veneta, Oregon

Hudson was laying on the ground next to the stump of Sophie, his head resting on the edge of weathered wood, watching the clouds moving past. He was using the stump like a pillow. A single green twig of a sprout was growing from the center of her faded rings, with two delicate, bright green leaves unfurled in the sun.

She was felled when he was in jail. The whole valley was clearcut. His best efforts had been for naught.

He had a campsite set up nearby and was saying goodbye. He'd found a job as a vegan chef at an eco-hotel in Costa Rica and was leaving tomorrow.

"I won't be around again for a while," Hudson said. "Going to see if I can do a better job protecting the forests in Costa Rica." He closed his eyes. "I'm sorry, Sophie. I let you down."

The wind was moving through the replanted trees, thin and gangly like teenagers. The sun and emotions were making him drowsy. In something like a waking dream, he finally heard her speak again.

"You didn't fail me," Sophie said. "You tried your best, and trying is always believing in a better future."

"But you're gone. And the planet is in trouble."

"You still believe," Sophie said. "After everything, you still hope. And where there is hope, there is potential."

"I couldn't save you," he said.

"You had to save yourself first," Sophie whispered. "Remember, accepting love is the truly revolutionary act."

He woke with a start. What the hell was that?

Why are talking trees in dreams so obtuse, he wondered, stifling a yawn, the dream already fading away. His mind turned to the future.

Costa Rica would be nice. Eco-tourism seemed like a great way to help protect the wilderness. He would be living in a tree house next to a new national park, so it was like he was still tree-sitting, only getting paid for it. It was a luxurious tree house with an outdoor shower and a composting toilet. It was big enough for two, so there was plenty of room compared to his old slab of plywood lashed to Sophie.

"Hey, are you supposed to be here?" a voice called out. He leaped to his feet. He wasn't supposed to be there—this was private land now—and he wasn't eager to be tackled by any FBI agents again.

Only it was Roz.

She looked beautiful, her long red hair gleaming like a waterfall of rubies. She was wearing denim shorts with hiking boots, and a tank top. She shouldered out of a large backpack and dumped it onto the dusty ground.

"Hey, stranger," she said.

"Roz, you're here," he said.

"Is that okay?" she asked.

"More than okay," he said. "What are you doing here?"

"Thought I'd get a little camping in. Know any good sites?"

"Well, yes," he said, gesturing over his shoulder. "I'm

camped about a mile from here."

"Think maybe I could share your campsite?" she asked.

He nodded, a joyous smile spreading across his face.

"One thing, though, I don't have a tent," she said.

"You can have mine. I'll sleep outside."

"What if it rains?" she asked. Hudson looked up at the clear cloudless blue sky.

"We can double up in mine if it rains."

"It won't be too crowded?"

He shook his head, grinning. She was flirting. He felt a crack in his gloomy heart where, for the first time in months, a ray of light shone through. "Definitely not."

"So, is this Sophie?" she asked, pointing at the stump.

Hudson nodded. "She's a lot different now than when I first met her."

"Is it okay if I sit on her?" Roz asked. "My legs are tired."

"I think she'd like that," Hudson said. "I know I would."

She sat down and took a long drink of water from her canteen, then began rummaging in her pack. "I have something for you." She pulled out a small paperback book and handed it to him.

"*Seeking Redemption Through Small Acts of Contrition,*" he said, reading the title. "A collection of poetry by Roz Anders." He looked at her, smiling. "This is fantastic."

"Check out the dedication," she said.

"To Hudson," he read. "For always reminding me that it's the mirror that's broken, not the person reflected in it." His voice was choked with emotion. He sat down beside her, and she leaned into him. "Thanks," he said. "I can't wait to read it."

"I've been thinking," she said.

"Oh, yeah?" he said.

"It may be too late, I get that, but I want you to know I believe in us. I believe what we had was special and eternal. And I know I fucked up. But do you think there is any way we can start over?"

"Your timing isn't great," he said.

It was not the answer she expected, and her eyes reflected momentary hurt and hopelessness.

"I'm going to Costa Rica. Tomorrow night. I have a job at an eco-tourism lodge, cooking vegan food."

"You're leaving that soon?" Roz asked. "Can you postpone it, even for a few days?"

"I can't. The lodge expects me. They're sending a jeep to pick me up in San Jose and drive me south to the new national park. There's no public transportation to the site."

"I see," Roz said. "I guess it would be hard to get a hold of them to change the date."

"Come with me," he said.

"Come with you where?"

He reached into his pack, pulled out an envelope and handed it to her.

"What is this?"

"A plane ticket for you to Costa Rica," he said. "Turns out my tree house is big enough for two."

"You bought me a ticket? But you didn't even know I'd be here."

"I had hope. And where there is hope, there is potential. A wise tree once told me that."

She opened the envelope and pulled out the ticket. "Costa Rica. It's hard to imagine."

"You said you wanted to start over. Why not in a new country? We'd be leaving everything behind. All the angst and mistakes, all the bad memories. And it doesn't have to be forever. My contract is only one year."

"My family …" she said quietly. "They would be so …"

He tensed.

"…happy for me," she said.

"You mean that?" he asked.

"I want a life with you," she said, kissing him. "Starting it in a tree house sounds perfect."

He closed his eyes and felt the warmth and heat of her lips on his, her hands slipping around his waist. He felt a sense of happiness emanating all around him, amplified by the rings in Sophie's trunk and vibrating out into the newly planted scraggly trees. The birds picked up on it, singing with extra passion, and a butterfly fluttered past. At least, that's how he imagined it.

When he finally pulled away from the kiss, they were both breathless.

"Let's go back to my camp," he said. "I have a thermos of vegan Hungarian mushroom soup."

"Aww, one last memory of the Rose and Thorn," she said. He helped her put her backpack on and then she took his hand. "Maybe we shouldn't eat right away," she said, looking pensively into the clear blue sky. "Looks like rain. Maybe we should crawl into your tent and wait it out."

"I like how you're thinking," he said. He kissed her again, then took one last look over her shoulder at Sophie, at the tiny sprout of a twig waving gently, hopefully in the breeze.

THE END

ABOUT THE AUTHORS

Poetic Justice: A Restaurantland Romance is the twelfth book by Clark Hays and Kathleen McFall. They live and work in the Pacific Northwest region of the United States. Please visit the Pumpjack Press website for more information and to sign up for their newsletter.